The Call that Changed my Life

The Call that Changed My Life

Robert Peprah-Gyamfi

Thank You Jesus Books

The Call that Changed My Life
Revised Edition

All Rights Reserved. Copyright © 2010 Robert Peprah-Gyamfi
First Published by iUniverse in 2004.

No part of this book may be reproduced or transmitted in any form or by any means, graphic, electronic, or mechanical, including photocopying, recording, taping or by any information storage or retrieval system, without the permission in writing from the publisher.

Published by THANK YOU JESUS BOOKS

For information, please contact:
THANK YOU JESUS BOOKS
P.O. Box 8505
LOUGHBOROUGH
LE11 9BZ
UK

www.thankyoujesusbooks.com

ISBN: 978-0-9564734-1-7

To Rita, my wife, who took care of the kids and maintained order in the home whilst I was locked up hours on end in my study trying to put my thoughts together; and to the kids themselves, Karen, David and Jonathan for bearing with my frequent absence.

Contents

Foreword... x
Introduction: Decision to Write 1
Chapter 1   The Last Minute Rescue 5
Chapter 2   Fighting my own member 9
Chapter 3   Mother's close call........................25
Chapter 4   The village boy in town....................30
Chapter 5   In the company of the affluent.............34
Chapter 6   An unexpected evangelist...................39
Chapter 7   New convert 47
Chapter 8   Shattered hopes............................50
Chapter 9   'At long last we have met in Europe!'......55
Chapter 10 The revelation of my Muslim Neighbour 60
Chapter 11 Struggling to make it to the Land of Lenin 64
Chapter 12 One step forward...........................73
Chapter 13 Agege, here we come 85
Chapter 14 Plans almost hijacked......................100
Chapter 15 See you later, Africa......................106
Chapter 16 Finding my way in a divided city...........111
Chapter 17 Surviving in a crazy world 120

Chapter 18	The Asylum procedure	124
Chapter 19	A back yard of flowers	126
Chapter 20	'Africaman' in Europe	129
Chapter 21	German for Beginners	138
Chapter 22	American Lutheran Church in Berlin	142
Chapter 23	The three-way friendship	145
Chapter 24	At the mercy of the 'gods' in white	152
Chapter 25	My difficult neighbour	160
Chapter 26	On the verge of success	162
Chapter 27	Face to face with West Berlin's Governor	166
Chapter 28	I wished I were a privileged foreigner	172
Chapter 29	Passport Number Two	176
Chapter 30	Come down, Berlin Wall!	183
Chapter 31	Facing Deportation	186
Chapter 32	Attempt at U.S. Visa	197
Chapter 33	The Countdown Begins	199
Chapter 34	D-Day	209
Chapter 35	Hannover Medical School	223
Chapter 36	The Lord providing for my needs	229
Chapter 37	All's well that ends well	234

FOREWORD TO THE REVISED EDITION

Since it was first published in June 2004, *THE CALL THAT CHANGED MY LIFE*, an account of how the Lord called me from my little village Mpintimpi in rural Ghana and led me all the way to the Hanover Medical School in Germany, has been favourably received by the majority of readers who have contacted me about it.

The Revised Edition, apart from correcting a few typographical errors in the original version and also depicting a new cover design, is completely unchanged from the original version.

It is my hope that this amazing account of determination and perseverance in the face of seemingly insurmountable odds will inspire the reader to strive, with the help of Almighty God, to overcome any hurdle that comes his/her way in life.

Robert Peprah-Gyamfi

Loughborough, UK
May 2010

Foreword

This inspiring story tells of the courage of a young Ghanaian boy who, having failed to achieve his aim to become a medical doctor by attending a university in Ghana or by virtue of a scholarship to the USSR, raised funds by working on a building site in Nigeria to pay for a daring one-way flight to East Berlin to become an asylum seeker in West Berlin—a route by which he realised his dreams and became a medical doctor in Germany.

The Call that Changed my Life is a Christian autobiographical book and goes right back to the time when the young Ghaneain schoolboy had to face a catalogue of difficulties and challenges, surviving illnesses and horrendous treatments by traditional witch-doctors, and attending school in spite of having to traverse remote bush paths. Today he is a medical doctor in Duesseldorf, a city about three hundred kilometres to the south-west of Hannover. The story of how he achieved this goal is an inspiring testimony of how God called him to be a doctor and led him to work in Europe. It is an uplifting and encouraging book, showing how faith in God and a firm goal together with perseverance will lead to success. It was early on, when he was still a struggling student in Ghana, that Robert Peprah-Gyamfi received a powerful visual manifestation of his goal—a vision of himself and a friend meeting in a street in Europe—and it is this visual goal that spurred him on in overcoming countless hurdles, first as a construction worker in Nigeria, then as an asylum seeker in Berlin, and later as a medical student in Germany threatened with deportation. It is a powerful, heart-warming testimony written with a sincerity that flows from the author's total commitment to his calling.

Further information about the book and the author's Christian mission may be found at www.diadembooks.com/robert.htm

Charles Muller
MA (Wales) PhD (Lond) DLitt (OFS) DEd (SA)
Diadem Books
www.diadembooks.com

Acknowledgements

My thanks go to the Lord of Heaven and Earth for the good health I enjoyed throughout the time I worked on this book and for the good health I continue to enjoy.

My thanks are also due to the Servant of the Living Lord Dr. Charles Muller, proprietor of Diadem Books, for the wonderful editorial work he carried out on the manuscript, helping to give it a final beautiful finish.

Thanks are also due to the International Bible Society, Colorado Springs, for pointing out the guidelines for quoting from the New International Verison (NIV) of the Bible. Scripture texts from the King James Version are included by kind permission of the National Bible Society of Scotland.

I am indebted, too, to Keith Underdahl of AGES Software for permission to quote the passage by H. Smith. The quotation in question forms part of the CD called *Charles Spurgeons Collection,* Version 2.

Robert Peprah-Gyamfi

Introduction

❖

Decision to Write

I have decided to write this testimony for the simple reason that I can no longer keep quiet about it. It is like when one begins to pour water into a cup or when rainwater begins to fill a container exposed to it. Should the filling continue, a time comes when the water level reaches the brink of the vessel; should the pouring continue the water overflows in accordance with the laws of physics.

I find myself in a similar situation. Over the years I have been privileged to continuously taste the goodness of the Lord. For a while I decided to keep quiet.

'Don't write, otherwise people will begin to think you just want to blow your own trumpet—just to be heard by men!' So I reasoned with myself. So I kept quiet.

God's kindness towards me did not cease, however. On the contrary, the Almighty Father continued to glorify Himself in my life. Still, I was reluctant to open my mouth—at least not boldly enough.

Like a stream, God's kindness had flowed continuously to fill the pond of my life. Now the point has come when my cup is overflowing.

As I sat down recently to recall all that God has done in my life a still small voice whispered to me: 'No, friend, you cannot keep quiet any longer!'

At that moment something pretty obvious occurred to me: Christianity has survived because of the witnesses of others! For, unlike other religious leaders, our Lord Himself is not credited with having written anything Himself.

The small voice in me continued: 'What would have happened if people like Apostle Dr. Luke, Apostle Matthew the Tax collector, Apostle Peter, Apostle Paul—the list is endless!—had adopted your attitude and failed to write down their witnesses for posterity?'

At that stage I realised the need to bear witness to others to the glory of the Lord. So, in line with the clarion call: 'Go ye into all the world, and preach the gospel to every creature!' (Mark 16:16—KJV), I have decided to write down my testimony.

For the sake of the young convert to the faith whose untrained legs might waver in the storms of life, I am writing.

For the sake of the battle-torn Christian about to be overwhelmed by the ferocious attacks of the evil one, I am sitting down to write.

For the sake of the sceptic who partly as a result of the evil and injustices of the world around us doubts the existence of a loving Father, I have decided to write.

I am also writing for at least one other reason: though Christianity is founded on the Rock of Ages which never stumbles and does not need any advertisement to survive, if only to satisfy my own conscience, I want to make this book a sort of platform to counter some of the arguments the atheists are spreading in our world.

In recent years, a phenomenon that began in the US is gradually spreading to several places in the whole world. I'm referring here to the live TV - debates among candidates for the high political offices of their countries—the office of President, the office of Prime Minister, the office of Chancellor etc.—which happens a few weeks prior to election day.

One thing strikes me often when I view them on television—there is the tendency for each candidate to refute whatever arguments the other puts up, be it good or bad.

As I mentioned earlier, Christianity does not survive on argument. I beg to ask, though, if only to appease my conscience, how others dare to spread fallacies. How dare they pollute the minds of others with claims that there is no God when I have walked so close with Him, like a personal friend?

'You must be crazy,' someone will tell me. 'How could you know He was close beside you?'

I shall answer that question with a question: Do you switch on your radio every morning because you see the waves around with your naked eyes, or do you do so because you believe they exist?

My walk with God began one afternoon in September 1978. That was when the Lord sent His servant to call me under mysterious circumstances, in a small apartment room in Accra, Ghana.

Barely three months later, the Almighty God revealed to me in a dream His intention to lead me to Europe. At that time I had passed my High School and was desirous of studying medicine.

This book is an account of my experience — the struggles, the trials, the disappointments, that preceded the fulfilment of God's promise.

I knew all along God would bring to pass what he had promised to. There were several instances, though, when the clouds gathered around me to darken my path—when all the doors seemed to close around me.

But as the saying goes, when God closes a door, He opens a window! You can be sure of that! Just as there seemed to be no hope, God raised His hand and saw me through. I can assure fellow Christians that our God, whom we serve, will surely make a way when there seems to be no way.

To God be the glory.

1

The Last Minute Rescue

I was born into a tiny village with the big name of Mpintimpi. The small settlement is situated about 150 kilometres to the north of Accra, Ghana's capital city. Strangers to our village had such difficulty pronouncing the word *Mpintimpi* that for a while the residents seriously considered renaming the village. That is yet to happen!

According to my mother I was born in the small rectangular wooden structure that served as the family bathroom. It measured about one metre in length and eighty centimetres in width. The wooden wall rose to about a metre and half above ground level. At the top the structure was open to the free tropical skies. The floor was not cemented but covered with fine gravel.

When I compare the surroundings and the circumstances of my birth to the first delivery I was privileged to witness myself, I can only be amazed! The delivery I witnessed happened during my early years in medical school.

The district hospital at Neustadt am Ruebenberge, a small town a few kilometres away from the northern German city Hannover, where I was doing my elective, was equipped with the latest equipments in the field of Gynaecology and Obstetrics.

Immediately the eyes of the baby girl, christened Ina by her mother, saw the light of day, the midwife and the obstetrician on duty took pains to check meticulously whether all was well with the new arrival to our troubled planet. And as if that wasn't enough, a few minutes later they invited the paediatrician on the adjacent ward to check her as well!

I could only dream of the privilege Ina enjoyed at birth! There was no specialist around to attend to mother as she went into labour. She had to bear all the pain with no medication available to minimise her suffering.

When I finally arrived in the world, I took my first breath and screamed in protest for having been forced to leave the comfortable conditions prevailing in mother's womb for the prevailing tropical heat of Africa! No specialist was around to examine me to determine whether all was well with me—whether my heart was sound; whether my nervous system was in order; whether the channel through which air passed from outside to my lungs was completely open; whether the tube through which food and fluid passed on their way to my stomach was not blocked along the way! No one checked me for any deformity. In line with the Twi proverb 'God drives away the disturbing flies from the beast deprived of a tail', my parents looked to Providence to take care of their tiny new arrival to the world.

That is not to say that mother wasn't attended to by anyone.

Papa Osei, the village 'doctor', diligently directed affairs. Papa Osei—what a person he was! He never received any formal education. He had neither an idea of human anatomy nor of pathology. Terms like physiology, biochemistry, pharmacology sounded like Latin in his ears.

Yet he dutifully and meticulously went about practising his art of healing—from the common cold to severe malaria; from ordinary headache to migraine; from menstrual pain to the inability of a woman to bear children, Papa Osei was the first person residents of the village contacted for help. In time his name spread far beyond the boundaries of our small village as the sick travelled many kilometres to consult him.

The villagers who consulted him hoped and prayed that he would find solutions to their problems. They hoped to be spared the need to travel to Nkawkaw, a town located about thirty kilometres away. That was where the next hospital was located.

Others chose to bypass Nkawkaw and travel about twenty kilometres further, to Atibie. The reason they gave for this was that the latter generally charged lower fees as compared to the former.

Taking the sick to hospital was something the villagers did as a last resort, not only on financial grounds. Even if one were financially in a position to do so, the means of transportation could bring further difficulties. The village happened to be located on a road linking two district capitals. Every morning about half a dozen vehicles travelling in both directions passed by. Often there were no seats or only a couple of seats left by the time they got to the village.

After the 'morning rush-hour' hardly any more vehicles passed by until late in the evening. That was the time when the vehicles that passed in the morning were returning from their destinations.

Even in this the people at Mpintimpi were somewhat fortunate, for elsewhere there were villages that had no roads linking them. Those villagers had to carry their sick on makeshift stretchers to the next available road to catch the next vehicle which may or may not arrive that day!

There was a third factor in the calculation. The villagers were small-scale farmers. They grew what they ate and ate what they grew. Accompanying the sick to hospital could cost them a whole day's work on their farms. They could not boast of any government agency that would compensate for the loss.

My arrival on this planet did not affect any existing statistics. Why not? The answer is simple. My birth, like many others that occur in rural areas of Ghana (the same could be said about many parts of the developing world) was not registered.

Needless to say, no one issued my parents with any birth certificate. Without any official document at hand, my date and place of birth went through several alterations, depending on who was filling a form on my behalf at a particular time.

The fact that I did not possess a birth certificate was not an issue until I arrived in Germany. All of a sudden, issues like date of birth, birthday celebrations, birth certificates and so forth assumed a different level of importance! I had no choice but to instruct my brothers to help get me a birth certificate.

Even before I had the time to familiarize myself with the planet I had elected to visit, something happened to threaten to cut short my stay here. I was barely eight months old at the time. As any child born into the harsh environment I have described will tell you, right from the word go we were exposed to all kinds bacteria, viruses, parasites—too numerous and too varied to list here. They could be found in abundance in the water our parents gave us to drink; there were hordes of them in the atmosphere waiting for their chance to attack through any openings in the skin, minute or large or both; and then there were the innumerable specimens that sought entry into our bodies by means of the very air we breathed!

As if these enemies were not enough, the ubiquitous mosquitoes also introduced deadly plasmodium parasites en mass into our bloodstream.

I did quite well in the initial stages warding off one onslaught of germ attack after the other—but on one occasion the microscopic soldiers defending me succumbed to a horde made of millions of bacteria which attacked me from the left side of my neck! This initially resulted in a small boil. In time the swelling increased in size. Ultimately, not only did it threaten to choke me, it also threatened to poison my whole body system as it kept on pouring trillions upon trillions of bacteria into my bloodstream.

There is a common belief that persists to this day in my culture to the effect that handling boils is not the speciality of conventional medicine! Mother and father decided therefore to resort to traditional medicine. Nevertheless, this showed no sign of being capable of managing the situation, for the boil continued to grow and grow in size. The little me was dying!

'Why didn't your parents use a razor blade, for example, to cut the boil open to allow the pus to empty?' someone might ask.

Good advise, friend! Don't afford blame to them, though, for not having had the courage to do so. Indeed, one can only applaud them—considering what those two simple farmers could achieve in life with the scant resources at their disposal! Hats off to them!

This time round, however, Papa Osei was at his wit's end in his attempts to help me.

Just before all involved in the fight were close to throwing in the towel, someone directed my parents to a traditional healer at Afosu, a comparatively larger settlement about six kilometres to the south of Mpintimpi. My parents hurried to the traditional healer, mother bearing me tenderly in her arms.

'Very serious, very serious!' the healer shook his head as soon as he saw me. 'The next few hours will decide whether your little child will survive or not.' Imagine the effect of his words on my despairing parents! A few minutes later he left for the woods. He returned after a while with some herbs in a small bag. He pounded these into a paste and applied it to the boil.

In the meantime I could hardly breathe and the battle was going terribly against me. The three adults watching my struggle with death could hardly suppress their tears.

Then came the turning point! All of a sudden, as if an invisible hand had used an invisible instrument to cut it open, the boil literally exploded!

During mother's lifetime she always had difficulty holding back her tears whenever she came to this point in the narration. According to her, so much pus issued from the boil that for a while it looked as I would drown in it!

And so—praise the Lord!—I was soon on the way to recovery.

2

Fighting my own member

Neither mother nor father attended school. As father used to tell us, he had a burning desire to go to school but his parents did not have the means to enable him to fulfil his childhood dreams. Father did not completely succumb to his fate, however. In the course of time a playmate whose parents had managed to send him to school taught him how to write the basic alphabet as well as arithmetical figures.

In one respect, I was more fortunate than my parents. About the time of my birth the then Gold Coast gained independence from the British colonial administration. It was renamed Ghana. The person who led Ghana into independence, the legendary Dr. Kwame Nkrumah, introduced free and compulsory education to every child of school going age—male and female. Woe unto anyone who refused to take a child of school-going age to school!

◆ ◆ ◆

For the sake of understanding later events I need to provide readers with a brief explanation of the school system existing at that time. It consisted basically of three cycles. The first cycle took a minimum of six years and a maximum of ten years to complete. From there one could move on to the second cycle or secondary school.

In contrast to the first cycle where schools were spread throughout the country, the second cycle depended on schools that were located mainly in districts and regional capitals as well as the national capital Accra itself.

To make this second cycle of education accessible for as many as possible the majority of schools were run as boarding schools. The academic year consisted of three terms, each lasting about twelve weeks. Tuition was generally free, but students had to pay for their boarding and lodging.

After five years in secondary school students had to sit for the GCE 'O'-Level (General Certificate of Education, Ordinary Level) examinations. Those who performed well could proceed to a further two year course at the end of which they sat for the GCE 'A'-Level (Advanced Level) examinations.

Three passes at the 'A'-Level could open the way for one to study in one of the three universities existing in the country at that time. Not only was tuition free at the universities at that time, students did not have to pay for boarding and lodging.

◆ ◆ ◆

When I was about six years old I was sent to school. Mpintimpi, being a very small village, could not boast of enough children to justify the setting up of a primary school.

Its neighbour Adadekrom, also about the size of Mpintimpi, shared the same fate. The children from both villages were therefore required to attend school at Nyafoman, a larger village about three times the size of Mpintimpi. Our companions at Adadekrom were better off than ourselves—situated about halfway between Mpintimpi and Nyafoman, they needed to traverse about half the distance we did to get to school.

Elsewhere one had the benefit of school buses that would drive from village to village to pick up the children to bus them to school. We couldn't boast of such a facility. Together with about ten other young children we walked to school every day—a total of about six kilometres daily.

I started going to school at the same time as my older brother who was two years my senior. It was customary in those days for children, particularly when they were of school-going age, to take what we termed 'Christian Names'. Since my parents did not attend school themselves they were not versed in these European first names.

Ransford, our senior brother who at that time was in the ninth class in the first cycle school, took it upon himself to look out for Christian Names for his two brothers about to embark on their journey into the academic world.

His method was not without ingenuity. First he wrote down several European first names familiar to him. Next he instructed us to listen attentively as he read them out. The rule was for us to shout 'STOP!' should he call out a name that appealed to us.

We don't quite remember any longer as to which of the two of us first asked Ransford to stop at a name. In any case, Kwame was so excited by the sound of the name 'Edmund' that he responded at once. For my part I plumbed for Robert—and that name has since accompanied me through life!

On some occasions some of my African friends, desirous of promoting African culture, have advised me to drop it—but partly because of the circumstances that led me to it and partly because I have the tendency to hold on tenaciously to things the moment they come my way, I've decided to keep it to the end!

At the time we began to go to school my brother and myself were short in stature for our age .This fact would soon lead us to gain the nickname Mpintimpi—Dwarfs.

I was different from Kwame in one respect: in addition to being short in stature, I also carried a disproportionately big head. As a result I was mocked, not only by my peers, but also by some adults. Some used terms like 'coconut head' to describe me! I was so infuriated by such mockery! How could they mock me on something I was not responsible for, I wondered. Was there any direct correlations? Or was it only coincidental? I couldn't tell. But the fact remains that it soon became evident that the young dwarf carrying the unusually big head happened to be invested with something that would make him the envy of many a classmate—extraordinary learning capabilities.

Was it exercises in written arithmetic? Was it doing arithmetic calculations mentally? Was it in English reading or grammar? Was it geography or history? Whatever the subject or discipline, hardly any of my classmates could match my performance. Even Edmund was no match and had to content himself struggling with the others for the second best position. Naturally I don't want to dwell further on this issue to avoid being accused of being in fact a veritable 'big head' and blowing my own trumpet! Whoever wishes is free to contact any of my schoolmates for an independent view on the matter. And so my school reports were all full of praises for the promising pupil from Mpintimpi.

When I got to Primary 5, something happened to me to threaten an abrupt end to my educational carrier.

All of a sudden, and for no apparent cause, my left ankle joint began to swell up. Initially the accompanying discomfort was bearable, permitting me to continue to attend school. In time, however, the pain increased in intensity. Despite the increasing discomfort, I refused initially to stay out of school. For obvious reasons, I enjoyed going to school and stayed away from school only when it was absolutely impossible for me to go.

A time eventually came when no choice was left for me other than to stay at home; so unbearable was the pain that I could hardly stand on the affected leg.

Initially my parents considered consulting some family friends in Nyafoman to ask them to permit me to stay with them during the week to enable me attend classes. Later they gave up their plans. The condition of my left ankle deteriorated to the extent of eventually making me bedridden. The least movement, even passive, brought with it severe pain.

At the time—and today, too—superstition is widespread in many areas of Africa. The fact that the best pupil in class had suddenly been stricken by a mysterious disease that resulted in an abrupt end to his education led to a whole lot of speculation. Some pointed accusing fingers to some of the members of my family. It was speculated that, possessed by evil spirits, they had used their supernatural powers to bring about my illness. In a situation where the term 'family' is not restricted to the nuclear but has a broader meaning—including cousins, nieces, half brothers, half sisters, stepmothers, grandparents (both maternal and paternal)—the net of possible culprits responsible for my malaise could be cast very wide indeed.

Others pointed accusing fingers in the direction of my classmates—envious of my learning capabilities, one of them, they argued, had possibly decided to use juju to get rid of me!

In the eyes of others I was but the innocent victim of a spell meant for someone else. The thinking here was that I had accidentally stepped on a spell placed by the roadside but meant for someone else.

Partly because of the cost involved in sending me to hospital and partly because my parents did not entirely disbelieve the theory of the spell, they resorted initially to traditional medicine (it is generally believed that conventional medicine can have little or no influence in healing a spell cast by the forces of evil).

Again my parents contacted Papa Osei for help. As usual, he decided to do what he could to help. There were two aspects to his therapy. He would gather from the forest several natural ingredients—leaves, shrubs, roots and barks of trees, seeds, kernels, etc.

Each herbalist had his or her own peculiar formula. That was a business secret. Some even took the composition formula to their graves. The usual practice, however, was for them to pass the secret on to their close relatives shortly before their deaths.

The ingredients we received from Papa Osei were placed in a wooden mortar and pounded together into a fine mixture. Some water was added if necessary to make the mixture stick together. The mixture was then applied to the joint. With the help of the broad leaves of the plantain or banana tree, a crude bandage was made to tighten the herbal medicine to the joint. The bandage was kept in place for a minimum of three days. At the end of that period the makeshift bandage was removed. The patient could then have a bath. The next stage involved applying a herbal cream, also prepared from a mixture of natural ingredients, to the affected part of the body.

Later, during the course of my illness, I experienced a more painful aspect of the therapy from other healers. Probably to ensure a more intense penetration of the mixture into the body, they used razor blades to inflict several small cuts on the skin of the affected joint before applying their medicine.

One may not have any idea of the burning sensation I experienced, particularly during the first few minutes after the cream, some of which contained sharp ingredients such as pepper and ginger, was applied.

Several weeks passed without any significant improvement in my condition. Though not completely restricted to bed, the only way I could move around for a while was with the help of a long bamboo stick along which I hopped with my right leg!

After I had been in that situation for about four weeks, my parents decided to send me to hospital. To be able to do so, they took a loan from one of the residents of the village. As was usual in the village, father offered his cocoa farm as a guarantee.

They decided to bypass the Roman Catholic Hospital at Nkawkaw and take me instead to the SDA Hospital at Atibie. Not only for the reason mentioned earlier: Atibie was also credited by the villagers as being superior to Nkawkaw regarding the issue of illnesses involving the bone.

Father accompanied me on the first journey. After I had undergone a thorough clinical examination and several tests had been conducted on me including an X-ray examination of the affected leg, we were asked to go home and report the next day.

It was too late for us to return to Mpintimpi. Father consulted a distant acquaintance in Atibie to beg him to allow us to spend the night in his home, and he readily consented.

We consulted the next day as required. The doctors decided to place the affected leg in a cast for three weeks.

One thing they failed to do was to instruct us to report back immediately should the cast turn out to press tightly on my skin. Even as we travelled back home I began to feel the cast gradually squeezing on my muscles. The initial discomfort increased to the level of terrible pain, the intensity of which words can hardly describe.

Up until that time the pains were limited to the area of the left ankle joint. This time the whole area covered by the cast, extending from the toe to the knee, was under severe pain. It felt as if my leg was being squeezed away. Profuse sweat covered my whole body to soak my bed.

The disturbing noises of the ubiquitous mosquitoes (mosquitoes spread malaria, remember) that filled our room every night but hardly registered on normal nights for reason of familiarity, became intensely evident to me, adding salt to my injury. The whole night passed without my eyes closing even for a moment in sleep.

Laymen as my parents were in matters of medicine, the idea did not occur to them to take me back to hospital ahead of schedule. To them the words of the 'gods in white', as Germans sometimes refer to their doctors, was final. We thought even that the tightening through the cast was intentional, a necessary therapeutic strategy!

The ordeal continued over the next several days. Gradually the severity of the pain subsided somewhat, though not to any significant degree.

Finally the three weeks elapsed. Accompanied this time by mother, we returned to Atibie. We informed the 'semi-gods in white' about my ordeal.

'Why didn't you return earlier with your son, mama?' they asked, aghast.

'Your nurses told his father to wait three weeks!'

'But under such pains as you are describing it should have occurred to you not to wait that long!'

'How could we know, sir? We were abiding only by instructions. We know you know best.'

'Mother! We are also human beings, subject to making mistakes.'

Next the doctors instructed a nurse to remove the cast. I could read the anger written on her face after she had cut the cast open. Wearing the tight cast for three weeks had resulted in a significant shrinking in the size of my left leg!

No one talked to us about physiotherapy. Even if they had, it would not have been practicable for me to receive it. Such a facility was not available in the vicinity of Mpintimpi. My parents could not afford to pay for my transportation to allow me to travel to the hospital regularly for treatment.

And so conventional medicine meted out to me at Atibie did not lead to any significant improvement in my condition.

◆   ◆   ◆

The academic year ended without my ability to return to school and my classmates moved on to the next class. The staff unanimously agreed to allow me to join my class should I recover anytime soon.

I went through very trying times, not only as a result of the physical pain, but on account of the much worse emotional pain or frustration. Whenever Edmund returned from school and reported what had happened that day, I could hardly bear it. I wished I had wings that could help me fly to school.

I read whatever suitable book that I could lay hands on. Under the prevailing circumstances the selection was limited. Somehow, I came across R.M. Ballantyne's *The Coral Island*. I do not now remember how often I read through it! Even to this day I can recite some of the opening lines:

> Roving has always been, and still is, my ruling passion, the joy of my heart, the very sunshine of my existence. In childhood, in boyhood and in man's estate, I have always been a rover, not a mere rambler among the woody glens and upon the hilltops of my own native land, but an enthusiastic rover throughout the length and breadth of the wide, wide world.

I even began to write a book! I titled it *The Bitter Struggle*. In it I tried to expose the injustices inherent in the inheritance system peculiar to the Akan ethnic group whereby inheritance is passed on along the matrilineal line, in particular the children of one's sister, leaving one's own children to go empty-handed. Unfortunately, partly due to lack of material to write on I was unable to complete my work.

In their desperation, my parents consulted any traditional healer recommended to them and who offered them some hope. But nothing significant happened.

Just about this time a stranger from the northern part of the country arrived at the village. He was there on a visit to his next of kin who had settled in years before I was born. His host, a good friend of my parents, told his relative, said to be a traditional healer whose fame was well known in the area he lived, about my situation. He offered to help.

Eventually my parents were informed about the willingness of the famous healer from the North. Soon a meeting was arranged. Accompanied by my parents we called on him.

He asked father to narrate the history of my ailment. Father did as requested and the healer listened attentively. From time to time he glanced at my swollen left ankle. When father came to the end of his story, we waited anxiously for the reaction.

We didn't have to wait long:

'I have read the star of your son,' he began, looking intensely at me. 'He is destined for great things. The forces of evil are seeking to prevent that from happening. Don't be afraid, however. The witches and wizards that have stood up against your child will face defeat!'

He asked us to give him a day to develop a healing strategy.

We returned at the appointed time the next day. After he had prepared a concoction of herbs, he placed the mixture in a large black pot made of clay. Then he poured some water on the mixture and placed it on an open fire. Soon the mixture began to boil.

Next he took a small razor blade and inflicted several cuts to the skin over the sick joint. He then called for four strong young men in the neighbourhood. He asked them to hold me firmly.

Next he took hold of my left leg. One hand grasped it firmly at the level of the knee joint whilst the other did so a few centimetres beneath the first. With the ailing leg fixed that way he brought it close to the opening of the boiling pot!

The steam coming from the boiling mixture, he explained, did not only carry healing powers but was capable of neutralising the spell cast on my leg as well!

I screamed on the top of my voice as the steam burnt on my skin.

'You have to bear it, my little boy; that is the only way I can help you!' he consoled me.

Big drops of sweat covered my body as I continued to shout for someone to set me free.

After a few minutes into this extraordinary therapy my mother could no longer stand the scene and hurried out of the room. I could hear her sobs as she left. That didn't influence the traditional healer cutting short the ritual, however. On the contrary, he urged the men holding me not to relax in their duty.

At last, after I had been in the position several minutes, the all relieving words, 'It is enough!' fell from his lips. The helpers carried me to my seat.

After a short silence the traditional healer turned to father: 'The battle has been won; the evil forces have been defeated. In a very short time you will notice a significant improvement in the condition of your son.'

Before we left for home he gave father a small metal container.

'It contains a cream I specially prepared for your son. It should be applied to the affected leg twice daily, morning and evening,' he added.

What a horrible experience that was! Even as I write, the terrible scene is vivid before my eyes.

But contrary to his assurance, my condition remained unchanged.

◆   ◆   ◆

At last my parents decided to consult the fetish priest at Amantia, the small town where mother's eyes first saw the light of day. (That is where she lived until she met father. After they got married mother followed him to Mpintimpi where they engaged in farming. Since then she visited there only on important occasions.)

Amantia in former times was a point of attraction for many from far and near. This was because of the diamonds discovered there. Apparently they did not exist in quantities to merit large-scale commercial mining, but seemed to be enough to merit some small-scale exploration.

In time the population of the town swelled with professional small-scale miners as well as lovers of adventure in search of fortunes. These used simple instruments and crude methods in their search for the precious jewels. As the yields became scanty the makeshift diamond mines were eventually deserted.

One aspect of Amantia continued to attract travellers to the little town long after the diamond mines had ceased to exist. There resided in the town a fetish priest whose worshippers credited him with the possession of extraordinary powers. People came to consult him, not only to seek his protection from evil forces, but also to solicit his help on issues of everyday life, be it medical, social, financial or whatever. From barren women desiring to conceive their own children, to people seeking improvement in their businesses, right down to those afflicted with all kinds of diseases, the fetish priest was the last resort for many who came to consult him.

Once every six weeks the fetish priest put up an open display of his powers. The event took place in a big open arena in the middle of the large fetish compound. To the sound of big African drums, accompanied by rhythmic songs emerging from the throats of dozens of worshippers, the fetish priest danced powerfully. Occasionally he would fall in a trance. Those possessed with witchcrafts, we were told, needed to shiver at a moment like that, for it was in such moments that the fetish priest launched his attacks on them. That was said to take place initially in the spiritual realm. In due time things manifested themselves physically—in the form of various illnesses. Confession in such a situation could lead to pardon, and that could lead the sick to regain health. Confession could still lead to death, depending on the gravity of the offence committed. It was generally believed that no matter what the nature of the offence, whoever failed to confess and repent of the evil committed faced certain death.

Apart from such public displays of power and authority the fetish priest held private consulting hours for those needing his help. These usually took place twice weekly. They began very early in the morning, around 5 a.m., a period of day that is said to favour the work of the spirits. Shortly before the consultation got underway the spirits came to possess the priest. In such a state he was credited with the ability to find solutions to the spiritual, physical and mental needs of his clients.

Clients were not allowed to communicate directly with the priest. Even if they were, it would not be to their advantage. Why not? The answer is not difficult to imagine. The moment the spirits came to take control of him, he began to speak in a strange language—a language that was understood only by special assistants specially trained for that job. Sources had it that they underwent several months training in order to acquire this capability.

We left home very early in the morning for the consultation. That was my first direct confrontation with fetishism. Deep inside me, I did not believe that the gods could make any difference in my situation. I followed mother because I had no choice but to do my parents' bidding. Even if I had the choice not to go, I think I would have gone there all the same so as not to offend them. Indeed I was sorry for my parents, particularly mother, who appeared to be quite devastated as a result of my never-ending agony, for the suffering and inconveniences they had to bear because of me.

A couple of others had preceded us when we got there. After waiting about an hour it was finally our turn. Mother narrated the reason for our consultation. The interpreter translated our message. A short silence followed. At last the priest began to speak. The translator interpreted simultaneously.

'Beware of some people very close to you, my daughter! They know your son has a bright future. They have vowed to prevent that from happening. Don't be scared, though, my daughter! Your son will be well. We shall stand by you. The enemy will face total defeat.'

The priest paused for a while.

For the moment the whole room, about sixteen square metres in size, and filled with several statues made of wood or clay or both, and which depicted the figures of the gods the priest served, was silent. One could have heard a pin drop.

Finally the priest continued.

'There is the need for a blood offering, my daughter. Go and look for a young male cat as well as an adult male fowl. They have to be offered on the alters of our shrine.' Thus he ended his speech.

Through the interpreter, mother expressed her thanks to the gods for the promised help. Apart from the usual consultation fee, she pledged a substantial sum of money should I regain my health.

Without any waste of time, mother went in search of the requested animals. Three days later we returned with them. It followed a ritual ceremony, performed not by the priest himself but by one of his several aides.

As we gathered around one of the many alters erected on the compound, the aide, a man in his mid-forties, began the ritual. First he poured gin from one of the three bottles filled with the strong alcoholic drink mother had been asked to present in addition to the two animals. From a glass filled with the alcoholic drink, libation was poured to solicit the help of the spirits, including in particular those of my parents' dead ancestors, in the fight against the witches and wizards who were purported to be the cause of my suffering. The libation ceremony lasted for a few minutes. Then the aide moved on to the next stage of the ritual—the blood offering.

He urged everyone present to remain quiet as he concentrated on his task.

Without any show of emotion, he took hold of the cat. Murmuring a few words he took hold of a sword and cut through the throat of the poor beast. He sprinkled the blood gushing out from its vessel on the alter. After holding the dying animal firmly for a while he dropped it onto the floor.

The dying animal struggled for a while and finally gave up the fight. It died lying on its back.

Next he cut through the throat of the fowl, sprinkling its blood on the alter as well. After holding it for a while, he threw it also to the ground.

The dying bird, after struggling for a while, finally gave up the fight. It also died lying on its back. The officiating assistant, on noticing the position both animals had assumed in death, shouted in excitement: 'Hurray! That is the victory sign! The evil forces have been conquered!'

Having put the spiritual aspect of the therapy behind us, we were left with the physical aspect. Mixtures made up of herbs, shrubs, roots and barks of trees, etc., were applied to my afflicted leg. This aspect of the therapy differed from what I had already referred to, probably only in the make-up of the ingredients involved.

In all, we spent about three months in Amantia. Our stay there, apart from leading me to win several new friends and offering me the opportunity to get to know mother's place of birth closely, did not bring any remarkable improvement in my condition.

On our return to Mpintimpi we continued with herbal medicine, trying the formula of one traditional healer after the other.

Towards the latter part of the second year of my affliction, I began gradually to notice a significant improvement. The pains reduced in intensity, though not to the extent that they permitted me to do away with my walking aid completely.

In the course of time I tried, gradually, to do away with the walking aid. Sometimes the resulting increase in the intensity of pain forced me to abandon my attempt for a while, but finally, a little over two years after the start of my problems, the condition of my left ankle improved to the extent that I was able to discard my crude walking aid.

Which healer could we singled out for credit for the positive turn on events?

A very difficult question to answer! We tried so many herbal medicines from so many healers that we might as well have given thanks to all of them for their help.

◆   ◆   ◆

That is not to say that the problem was gone for ever. Over the next several years I would experience several recurrences. At one stage, things got so bad we had to return to the SDA hospital at Atibie. The doctors there eventually found themselves at their wit's end and gave us a referral letter to Korle Bu, the highest place of call in the issue of medical care in the country. I stayed with Ransford, who resided at that time in a military barracks in Accra.

After going through several checks, the doctors at the Mecca of Medicine in Ghana decided to place me on a series of injections.

Pardon me, dear reader, if I no longer remember the exact number of injections my two buttocks received altogether. It's no exaggeration, but unquestionably they amounted to no less than fifty. Needless to say, I did not receive them all in a day! Instead, I was required to travel there every day, apart from the Lord's day, to receive them.

I covered a total of about twenty kilometres on the round trip from the military barracks to the teaching hospital to get the medication pumped into my body. No one told me exactly what the solution injected into my body contained. I don't want to apportion blame here. They probably assumed the teenager they were desirous to help could not understand anything. I was inquisitive to know, nevertheless, so one day I took advantage of a favourable moment to look closely at the writing on the syringe. In the end I made it out: injection streptomycin. What on earth could streptomycin stand for, I wondered? Unfortunately I didn't have the nerve to ask the nurses.

◆　　◆　　◆

For the moment, however, the situation improved to the extent of permitting me to resume my elementary education. The prospect of being able to return to school filled my heart with joy. My parents began to make plans towards the resumption of my education at the beginning of the 1968/69 academic year. Accordingly, they began to look for a family at Nyafoman where I could stay during the week and return home at the weekends.

Just about that time something happened to the family that turned out to be very favourable for me. Ransford, who had completed his secondary school education the previous year, was signed on by the Ghana Education Service as a pupil teacher beginning with the 1968/69 academic year. His first posting was to a town about 100 kilometres away. Without hesitation he agreed to take his younger brother along with him.

Thus, in the 1968/69 academic year, after more than two years break, I was privileged to resume my first cycle education. I resumed at the seventh class, known at that time also as Middle Form 1.

The break did not have any negative effect on my performance for I soon emerged as the best pupil in the class.

Barely six months later, at a time when I was becoming used to my new environment, Ransford broke the news to me: 'We will have to leave here at the end of this academic year!'

'You must be joking!' I replied.

'No, I mean it. I received a letter today informing me that my attempt to enter the Ghana Air Force has been successful!'

'Really?!'

'I will be enlisted towards the end of the year. I will resign my present position at the end of the academic year!'

For the moment I was speechless. While sharing in his joy at finding a job he clearly liked, I was disappointed because it meant I would have to leave the school I had in the meantime learnt to cherish; furthermore, I would be leaving behind the many new friends I had made.

'What will happen to me?' I inquired.

'I'll discuss the matter with father and mother,' he said. 'Eventually you may have to return to Nyafoman.'

At the end of the academic year I bade farewell to my mates with a heavy heart and returned to Mpintimpi.

◆   ◆   ◆

At that time one of my uncles, father's half-brother, was teaching at a first cycle school at Afosu which, as I said before, is small town about six kilometres to the south of Mpintimpi. He had a small room at his working place where he stayed during the week, returning home at weekends to see his wife and children.

Father begged him to allow me to stay with him at Afosu to enable me to continue my schooling there. He agreed.

Thus in the 1969/70 academic year I enrolled in the eighth class, also known as Middle Form 2, at the Afosu Local Authority Middle School. There, too, the dwarf from Mpintimpi would surpass his classmates in almost every field of study.

The odyssey of changing schools as well as those I could stay with to enable me to pursue my education seemed to have no end.

After spending one year with my uncle, he was transferred to head the primary school at a neighbouring village. He could not take me along because his new school offered classes only up to the sixth grade.

What was to be done? In Afosu resided a middle-aged man with whom father and mother had very close contact. They informed him about my situation and pleaded with him to allow me to stay with him to enable me go through the remaining two years of the first cycle education. After he had discussed the issue with his wife, they agreed to our request. And so I moved to them at the beginning of the 1970/71 academic year.

Even to this day the wife of my host remains deep in my memory. She was a loving, dutiful and hardworking young woman who did all she could to make me feel at home with them. As it happened they were childless, and he blamed her for this. This unfortunate situation cast a shadow on their marriage and led to considerable tension in the relationship. As I learnt later, he eventually left her for another woman.

To gain admission to a secondary school at that time, one had to pass an assessment test—the Common Entrance Examination. This was organised once in a year in March by the West African Examinations Council. The examining board is a legacy from colonial times. It was set up by the English Colonial administration to cater for the schools in their colonies in West Africa—Sierra Leone, Gambia, The Gold Coast (later Ghana) and Nigeria. The test was written simultaneously by all pupils wishing to enter the second cycle school in all the named countries.

A minimum of six years first cycle education was required of candidates wishing to sit for the test. In Ghana the wealthy and affluent of the society sent their children to so-called preparatory schools. There they were groomed and grilled in such a way as to enable most of them to pass the test at the sixth class level. The situation was different with children attending normal public schools. Most of them attempted the test at the ninth class level.

Sitting for the test was optional. It was one thing passing it; it was another matter whether one's parents could pay for the costs of education at that level, for most of the schools were organised on a boarding school basis. The boarding fees were quite substantial.

At the beginning of the 1970/71 academic year I registered to sit for the Common Entrance Examination. Just as I was looking forward to taking the assessment test, misfortune crossed my path to threaten to disrupt my education one more time. Compared to the surrounding villages, Afosu was relatively blessed. Apart from boasting of a school where one could complete the first cycle education, it had a post office as well as a police station. Many of the surrounding villages, including Mpintimpi, made use of the post office there. Mpintimpi, for example, rented Post Office Box 18.

Sometimes I was given the key when I left for Afosu at the beginning of the week. I carried the letters with me at the weekend and distributed them on to their owners.

One day I accompanied some of my mates to empty the letter box of our school. After we had collected our mail, someone suggested we tried our key at other letter boxes. One of them, probably without an owner, happened to be unlocked. The moment one of my mates inserted the key into it, it opened! Just at that very moment the postmaster, a very stern person in his forties, appeared from nowhere!

He accused us of attempted theft. For reasons best known to himself, he singled me out for blame. He wouldn't let the matter rest. He held me by the collar of my shirt and dragged me to the local police station, a stone's throw away.

Was it because the police did not want to incur the displeasure of one of the influential residents of the town? I cannot tell for sure, but one thing happened for sure—they decided to lock me up in one of their cells! The news of my detention spread like wildfire. Soon it got to Mpintimpi.

Father, on hearing the news, rushed to my rescue, and after spending several hours behind bars I was finally set free late that evening.

Mainly because of that incident father decided to remove me from Afosu. He reasoned that probably as a result of my good performance, I had made secret enemies who could hurt me if they had the chance. Besides, the tensions in the marriage of my hosts, instead of subsiding, were gradually boiling up. And so Father decided to send me back to Nyafoman. This time, at least, the condition of my leg permitted me to walk to school.

So, just as I had begun the first cycle education there, I returned there to end it.

In March 1971 I joined some of my former schoolmates at Afosu to travel to Kade, a large town about 70 kilometres away to sit for the Common Entrance Examintion (examination centres were available only in large towns and cities).

Out of a total of about sixty candidates from Afosu, only two candidates, myself and another pupil from the tenth class, were successful.

3

Mother's close call

At the beginning of the 1971/72 academic year I was admitted to the Oda Secondary School. With my admission to the second cycle school my dream of studying medicine received a big boost.

Why medicine?

Well, since the time I was big enough to reason, long before the problems with my left ankle began, my desire was to become a doctor. The human suffering I witnessed around me played a significant role to influence my decision. The reader might recall what I mentioned at the beginning in regard to the difficulties citizens of my village faced in bringing the sick to hospital. Added to the general situation were several particular incidents that had a lasting impact on me and which contributed to my decision to study medicine. For example, one day as we walked home from school, four people carrying someone on a makeshift stretcher emerged from a bush path that linked some of the surrounding farmlands to the main road. As we learnt from them, the man they were carrying had been bitten by a snake whilst working on his farm about one kilometre away. After tying a rope some distance to the affected site on his left leg, they decided to carry him to the main road in the hope that they would find a vehicle that would transport the injured man to the hospital at Nkawkaw.

Our ways parted, for we were heading in different directions—but during the following several days the scene recurred in my mind. The question that preoccupied my mind for some time was whether they ever make it to the hospital. And if so, were the doctors able to save him?

Then there was the case of Dugiri, the young girl aged about ten years who nearly bled to death from a serious cutlass wound to her right thigh! As blood oozed profusely from her vessels, the alarmed villagers instinctively tied a cord firmly above the wound in a desperate attempt to stop or at least to minimise the loss of blood.

'Dear God, please send a vehicle to transport her to hospital!' we prayed.

We waited and waited. The agony in her eyes reflected the pain she was going through. Oh, what a pitiful sight to behold! Hardly anyone could hold back the tears.

Finally, after waiting more than an hour, a truck came by and was hailed.

Today, as I write, I know it was not the best of vehicles to use to transport a person in that state of health. But away with luxurious fantasies—we were just overjoyed at the opportunity of bringing the much loved young girl to the attention of the doctors at Nkawkaw! And, thankfully, Dugiri survived the near-death encounter and eventually returned, after about two weeks of hospitalisation, to a hero's welcome.

Then came my own personal experience with my left leg. If only to satisfy my own curiosity, I vowed to become a doctor in order to understand the mysterious ailment that nearly brought an end to my own education.

Every indecision in this regard was swept away by an event that occurred in August 1968. It happened at a time when the pains from my leg had subsided just sufficiently to allow me to walk a considerable distance without the need for any walking aid.

Mother, who had not been feeling well for the past days, decided, despite her poor health, to visit one of our farms to harvest food for the family. We did all we could to persuade her to stay at home.

'How can I do that?' she countered. 'You are all aware there is not enough food for the family!'

'We shall manage!' we chorused. 'We will purchase some on the market.'

'Where is the money?'

'But we can buy on credit!'

'We will still have to repay, wouldn't we?' She shook her head. 'Don't be too concerned about me. I will make it.'

Mother was an iron-willed person who, once she had made up her mind, didn't change it easily. It became clear to us that we would not get her to reverse her decision.

Schools were on holiday at that time. One or two healthy members of the family could have accompanied her. For reasons that I can no longer recall everyone found an excuse not to do so.

At that time the trouble with my left ankle had subsided to the extent that I could walk a considerable distance without encountering severe pains. Because no one wanted to do so, I decided to accompany her.

This particular farm was located about five kilometres away from the village. About a quarter of the distance was along a lorry road. We could walk along it without fear of being knocked by traffic. As I mentioned earlier, traffic along it was sparse. Besides that, the nature of the road did not allow vehicles to travel fast. Usually, we heard the sound of an approaching vehicle minutes before it got to where we were—giving us enough time to enable us to 'park' ourselves comfortably and safely on the sides of the road.

The rest of the walk to the farm was by way of a bush path. Towards the end of the walk to the farm I noticed a considerable deterioration in mother's condition. She would increasingly stand still for a while and pant for breath.

'You are not well; we better return home before things become too bad,' I advised her.

'You are right,' she agreed. 'Since we are almost there, however, let's go ahead. When we get there, I will hurry and harvest some foodstuffs. We will then return home without delay.'

Finally we got to our destination. As she had promised, she hurried to harvest some foodstuffs. Just as we were to embark on the return journey, her feet could hardly carry her.

'Sit down and rest for a while,' I urged her. She agreed.

After resting about ten minutes, she turned to me.

'Help me get the load on my head.'

'Let's leave it. The strong one will come pick it up tomorrow.'

'You help me get it on my head.'

'But that must be too much for you!'

'Don't worry. I shall manage it. We have to get some food for the home!'

I only wished I could carry the load myself! But I couldn't. Walking the distance there had brought about an intensification of my own problem. Mother remained adamant, so I had no choice but to help lift the load to her head. We set out to return home.

She could walk only slowly. On more than half a dozen occasions she stood still for a while to gasp for breath. I prayed to God to give her enough strength to make it home. The thought of her collapsing and perhaps even dying before we could reach home caused my whole being to shiver.

Normally the bush path was quite frequented by others who had their farmlands along it. I prayed for some strong men to come by to carry her home. On that particular day, however, the whole world seemed to have deserted us.

On and on we went, iron-willed mother not prepared, for the sake of her children, and despite the severity of her condition, to abandon the load she was carrying. Even to this day I cannot explain how she managed to make it home!

Finally, about two hours after we set out on the walk home, we reached the compound of our home.

'Children, you help me get the load off my head!' mother cried as she began to fall to the ground. All those present rushed to her aid, in time to get the load off her head before she collapsed and fell to the ground. Before long she lost consciousness!

There is a common belief in our culture that just at the moment when a person faints, the indwelling soul emerges from the individual to set out on the journey to the land of the dead. It is commonly believed that the departing soul can at that juncture be persuaded to reconsider the decision to leave the land of the living for the dead—if people ran in all directions and shouted at the top of their voices the name of the dying, saying something that might persuade the soul to reconsider his or her decision to leave.

With that thinking at the back of our minds we set out to do two things simultaneously.

One group attended to her directly by pouring cold water on her (a common practice in the village, applied to anyone who fainted, notwithstanding the underlying causes), whilst the other run hither and thither shouting her name and saying things like: Why do you want to leave us alone? Where are you heading for? For the sake of your children, in particular for the sake of Afia Serwaa (our youngest sister was barely three years old at that time) reconsider your decision to depart for the land of the dead!

Because of her generosity, kind-heartedness, sense of humour and plain talk, mother had grown to become one of the most loved residents of the village. The news of her illness spread like wildfire through the small settlement. Soon almost the entire village was assembled in our home.

Papa Osei, who had a close relationship with our family, hurried to the scene. On seeing the situation he hurried for the woods. A few minutes later he emerged, carrying some herbs in his hands. At his instructions they were ground into a fine mixture. Next, he pressed out some drops of green liquid from it into the eyes and ears of the dying.

We waited anxiously for her condition to improve. To our delight she opened her eyes after a while and began to murmur some words, though inaudible. Despite that sign of life, her condition remained very grave indeed.

Father realised the need to get her to hospital. After consulting a couple of well-to-do citizens of the village, he was able to raise enough of a loan to enable her to be sent to hospital.

As in the case of Dugiri, we were faced with the problem of finding a means of transporting her there. After waiting several minutes, a vehicle heading for Nkawkaw stopped at the village.

Our joy was short-lived, for the vehicle was almost completely filled with passengers. Only a couple of seats were unoccupied whereas a sick person could only be transported in the supine position and needed more space.

Some of the passengers, on hearing about the seriousness of mother's condition, volunteered to interrupt their journey to make room for her!

Finally, about three hours after she first collapsed, the vehicle carrying her was set in motion. Father and one close relative accompanied her.

Hardly any of us could sleep that night. We prayed and hoped for her recovery. Mother was the pillar of the family. How could we make it without her?

Our prayer was heard. After spending nearly two weeks in hospital she was discharged in good health.

By then my mind was completely made up. I would become a doctor—not only to understand all that was behind my own sickness, but also in order to be able to help relieve the suffering around me.

My young mind began to fantasize about a kind of Hospital-on-Wheels that would move from village to village to provide medical care for the inhabitants.

4

The village boy in town

Ransford played a key role in bringing about my admission to the second cycle school. Whereas father was keen to educate all his children to the highest level based on their intellectual capabilities, his meagre resources placed a constraint on him.

A few years before my eyes saw the light of day, he married a second wife. From then on his attention became divided between his two wives. About five months before my birth, my stepmother delivered her first child, Afia Kraah. Five other children would follow her.

By the time I passed the common entrance examination, three of his children, apart from myself—Thomas, who was five years older than me, Edmund, and my half-sister Afia—were potential candidates for further education. For the sake of fairness he decided in favour of Thomas and Afia.

Ransford, who in the meantime had passed out of his initial military training and attained the rank of Lance Corporal, offered to pay for the cost of my education.

Although tuition was free at that time, a substantial amount of money was needed to cover my boarding and lodging. Ransford managed to shoulder the financial burden—which was substantial in the first year of every boarding student. The state of his own private life favoured me—not only was he unmarried but, as far as I knew, he had no commitment to do so in the foreseeable future. Thus he could afford to invest part of his salary in my education.

This condition would not prevail for long. Not long after my admission to Oda he met the woman of his dreams. Shortly afterwards they were married. A few months later Abena, their first child, was born.

Before the changed situation could have any adverse effect on my education, however, the Hands of Heaven were stretched in my favour.

A scholarship scheme existed to cater for students who excelled in their respective classes. Based on my performance in the first and second term examinations,

I became a beneficiary of the scheme. Initially the award covered about eighty percent of my boarding and lodging expenses.

Soon I was granted what was termed a full scholarship, to cover all my boarding and lodging costs.

◆   ◆   ◆

While at Odasco I got to know Kwadwo. We were not only in the same year group, we were housed in the same dormitory as well. Eventually a close friendship developed between us. In due time I got to know more about him. He came from a well-to-do home. His uncle, the brother of his mother, was a wealthy man who owned a substantial amount of property. Among other things he was the sole proprietor of the leading cinema house in the district capital. At that time the cinema house was well patronised.

My friendship with Kwadwo brought me several advantages.

Although a full scholarship-holder, I needed money to acquire additional provisions. The boarding school served not only children of the district but also students from other parts of the country. The school authorities took pains to serve food which was not only familiar to the local residents but which also took into consideration the dishes of students from other parts of the country. The result was that one could sometimes come across a meal that one was not very much at home with. Even if one were confronted by a favourable dish, a paradoxical situation could arise in which the good taste of the food led one to yearn for more. Naturally there was a limit to the quantity of food the school could serve! Thus the need for the student to supplement the meals through his or her own means was ever present.

Usually every student arrived from home with two boxes, one containing clothes and hygienic items, the other filled with provisions—sugar, tins of milk, sardines, mackerel, corned beef, etc. In addition to that was gari—a ready-to-serve meal made from cassava roots.

The cassava is milled and put in a sack. The water is allowed to drain through the sack and then roasted in a shallow pan. This form of cassava can be stored for months because it has been preserved. Many parts of Africa eat this meal. In Ghana it's also known as the student's companion. Most students eat it with a hot sauce called shito. Every student had gari and shito in his/her provision box, commonly called *chop box*.

As a result of financial constraints, my provision box was rarely filled. The situation was different with Kwadwo and another companion, Emmanuel. Their provision boxes rarely went empty.

Kwadwo not only had a wealthy uncle who was generous to him—his home was also only a few kilometres away. He either travelled home at the weekends to refill his box or his uncle instructed his chauffeur to drive to the school with additional supplies.

During the holidays Kwadwo was my supplier of daily newspapers. At Mpintimpi one could at best obtain days old if not weeks old newspapers. Kwadwo, bless him, made sure I received newspapers on a regular bases. He had a good contact with a driver of a passenger truck that travelled every day to Nkawkaw and back to Oda. Through him the dailies arrived regularly; when the driver didn't have to stop, he simply let the papers fall through the window of the passing vehicle. With my name boldly written on them, the newspapers soon found their rightful owner.

The friendship between us developed to the extent that some even took us to be brothers. On several occasions I spent part of my holidays at his home in Oda. In the process I got to know several of his relations.

Kwadwo did not have his roots in Oda but rather in a small town situated about ninety kilometres to the north-east of Oda. On a few occasions I visited him there.

During one of my visits there, he introduced me to Grace (name changed), one of his several cousins. Like Kwadwo and myself, she was also there on a short visit. One thing was conspicuous about her—she boasted outstanding beauty!

Later Kwadwo told me more about his close relative. She was a few years younger than him. After completing her basic education she opted to become a seamstress. She had in the meantime completed her training and was working in a nearby city. He went on to tell me that owing to her good looks she was permanently chased by men, some of whom were wealthy and prominent. They all seemed to have one thing in common—a desire to win her heart and eventually her approval in marriage.

As a result of my visits to Kwadwo's hometown I also got to know Yaw, Kwadwo's long-time playmate and friend. I came to admire him for his extraordinary talent in drawing and painting. He could just look at you for a moment, and in the next moment produce a good replica of your face!

At the beginning of the fifth academic year at Oda we began to make preparations for the G.C.E. 'O'-Level examination. These were to be held shortly before the end of the academic year.

At the same time arrangements were made for the period following that stage of the educational ladder. As was customary in those days, those wishing to continue their education to the GCE 'A'-Level were required to fill forms to select their choices of school. One could choose three schools in order of preference.

Oda Secondary school had an advantage over several other secondary schools in that one could continue one's education there to the sixth form level. My teachers persuaded me to remain there for the sixth-form course. I would disappoint them, however—not that I did not enjoy my time there. The truth is that the desire to explore the unknown overweighed my affection for my school.

As my first choice school, I opted for Mfantsipim School. Built in 1876 by the Methodist Missionaries sent to the Gulf of Guinea to spread the Gospel, it prided itself for being the first secondary school in the country. A large number of famous people had passed through its walls.

It was a bold decision not without risk. The school naturally would give preference to her own 'O'-level candidates desirous to do their further education there. Having become an elite school I expected to face, in addition, competition from the children of the rich and mighty of the society desiring to enter there from elsewhere for the sixth form course. This meant the only way I could 'make it' there was to distinguish myself in the 'O'-Level examination. Bubbling with much self-confidence, I did not allow anything to deter me from selecting the famous school as my first choice.

In May/June 1976 I sat for the West African Examinations Council GCE O-Level. At the end of the series of exams there was no doubt in my mind that I would do well. I was not disappointed, as it turned out, since I emerged as the best student of the year, passing with distinction.

5

In the company of the affluent

My expectations were realised when I was admitted in the 1976/77 academic year to do my sixth-form course at Mfantsipim School. As was usual in those days, I was required to offer three main subjects at that level. I chose Biology, Chemistry and Physics. Each candidate was required to write a test on general knowledge. This was termed General Paper.

Mfantsipim was different from Oda Secondary School in several respects. It was a boys only boarding school. With no students of the opposite sex to distract attention, students could concentrate only on their books.

Although I was used to serious learning at Oda, I was astonished at the extent even first year students went to in their studies there. From my information some of them were even capable of reciting considerable portions of passages from their notes.

As I mentioned earlier, it was a school for the rich and powerful. During my time there the school even boasted of being home to one of the sons of the then head of state of the country.

Oda secondary school, at least from my own perspective, had one important advantage over Mfantsipim. The food supplied at Mfantsipim, while being of good quality, rarely matched that offered at Oda in quantity. At Oda, particularly during the weekends, many female students stayed away from the dining hall—to the delight of the male students.

That the quantity off ood served at Cape Coast was not sufficient to satisfy the average student was no secret. That did not bother the majority of students, however. Needless to say, most of them had the means at their disposal to supplement the meals served. Not so with the poor student from Mpintimpi. Ransford, who had assisted me at Oda, was himself struggling to cater for his wife and their children, the number of which had grown to three. He had little or nothing left to offer me by way of assistance.

In the meantime a bond of friendship had also developed between me and Kwasi, one of Kwadwo's cousins. His father had virtually entrusted him with the running of the whole cinema business. Kwasi gave me money from time to time. On the whole, however, the means at my disposal were not adequate enough to permit me to supplement the meals served to the optimum. As the saying goes, one cannot blow a horn on an empty stomach! Nevertheless, I did my best to make the best of a difficult situation, though the harsh conditions would in the end have an adverse effect on my performance.

As was usually the case in all boarding schools, each dormitory had a captain selected from a student from the most senior class. His duty was to see to it that order prevailed in the hostel. He selected other students to help him in his duties. Every evening a roll call was made to make sure everyone was present. The house captain was accountable to the Housemaster or, in the case of the female dormitory, the Housemistress.

Those wishing to leave the premises of the school could do so only with the help of a so-called *exeats*. Usually those who left the school on normal exeats were expected to return the same day. Those wishing to spend the weekend at home needed special permits to do that.

One Sunday, towards the end of my second and final year at Mfantsipim, rumours began to circulate to the effect that one of the students in the junior classes had gone missing. The news reached me quite early, for the person in question happened to be in my dormitory. Later further details emerged. He had left the previous day to visit his girlfriend at a girls' boarding school at a nearby town. Contrary to his custom, he had failed to return. Since then all contact with him had been lost. The Dormitory Captain reported the matter to the Housemaster.

Just before he could take further action, two young police officers came to the school to find out whether anyone there was missing. They went on to say that the authorities at the main hospital in the city had notified them about the unclaimed body of a young victim from a traffic accident that occurred the previous evening. Eventually the dead boy was identified as the missing student. Still later details emerged regarding the circumstances of his death.

At the end of his visit to his girlfriend he had waited at a bus station to catch a bus to Cape Coast. Just then a saloon car passed by. The driver offered him a lift and they had gone only a few kilometres when the vehicle became involved in a serious accident. Our schoolmate was killed instantly.

Although I knew him only casually, his tragic death at the age of about 15 years sent shock waves through me. All of a sudden the awareness that life could end very suddenly came home to me pretty powerfully and gave me food for thought.

Before the body of our companion was driven to his hometown for burial, a memorial service was held in the large school chapel in his honour. At one stage in the solemn service we were permitted to file past the body to pay our last respect to the dead.

Up to that time I had witnessed a couple of funeral ceremonies at Mpintimpi. As the dead lay in state, various mourners drew near to pay their respect. Children were generally not permitted to go too close.

For the first time, however, I was experiencing a close confrontation with the dead. Our compatriot, who a couple of days before was going about his life like any young person of his age, now lay motionless before us. Where, I wondered, would he spend his eternity?

As I mentioned earlier, Mfantsipim Boys is a school within the Methodist tradition. As in all worship services, we sang on that day from the Methodist Hymn Book. Among the songs we sang on the occasion was Hymn 157:

> Jesus Calls us! Over the tumult
> of our life's wild restless sea,
> Day by day His sweet voice soundeth
> Saying: Christian follow me.
>
> As of old, apostles heard it
> By the Galilean lake,
> Turned from home and toil and kindren
> Leaving all for His dear sake.
>
> Jesus calls us from the worship
> Of the vain world's golden store,
> From each idol that would keep us,
> Saying: Christian love Me more!
>
> In our joys and in our sorrows,
> Days of toil and hours of ease,
> Still He calls, in cares and pleasures,
> That we love Him more than these.

> Jesus calls us! By thy mercies,
> Saviour, make us hear Thy call
> Give our hearts to Thine obedience.
> Serve and Love Thee best of all.

I am not a person easily overtaken by emotion. As we went through that song, however, the words touched my heart to the extent that I could hardly suppress my tears.

I began to reflect on the hymn. Though I believed in the existence of God and attended church regularly I could neither boast of a personal relation nor a full commitment to Christ. The bitter realities of this world had all but made a sceptic of me.

Yes indeed, the issue of universal suffering in the presence of a loving God really troubled me. Whenever something terrible happened around me the question sprang up in my mind: if there were a loving God, why should the world be full of so much evil—war, crime, injustice, confusion here, confusion there, confusion everywhere?

Yet on that day, as we were bidding goodbye to our departed classmate, the new call of Jesus the Lord to me, to follow Him, came home even more powerfully to me.

Even as we sang the song I dipped my hand into my pocket, removed a pen and placed a big mark on the hymn number: 157. That was the only song in the whole book to be singled out that way.

Over the next several days the death of my schoolmate occupied my mind. The thought that I could face a similar fate at any time would not leave me in peace. Should something like that happen to me, where would I spend eternity?

Soon life returned to normal. I continued to attend Sunday evening worship service, as was required of every student, without any conscious commitment to leave this 'world's vain golden store' to follow Jesus, as the hymn invited me to do.

The two-year sixth-form course at Mfantsipim ended in June 1978. Shortly before we wrote the series of examinations aimed at the West African Examination Council GCE 'A'-Level certificate, we filled the university admission forms. I selected medicine as my first choice—at the University in Accra as well as in Kumasi. Only two of the three universities in the country offered medicine.

My feeling, when the examinations were over, was that this time I did not do as well as two years before at the 'O'-Level stage. Few questions were asked in the areas I had concentrated my energies when revising in the few days prior to the test. Thus I was forced to resort to my broad knowledge to deal with several questions. I knew I would be successful, but I did not feel as triumphant as I did two years before.

6

An unexpected evangelist

From Cape Coast, I first travelled to Mpintimpi. After spending a few days there, I left for Accra. My hope was to find vacation employment that would enable me to earn some money prior to beginning my university education in October that year.

I lived in a suburb of Accra known as Asylum Down. I lived in the same apartment building as Ransford and his family. Because their small chamber and hall provided just enough room to house him, his wife and their three children, I couldn't live with them. Instead, I shared a room adjacent to theirs with Rex and Cox.

I got to know the two through Papito, a distant relative of mine. Originally Papito shared the room, barely sixteen square metres in area, with them. He had in the meantime returned to Mpintimpi to engage in a small-scale farming venture.

Cox and Rex, both from a town about 100 kilometres to the north of Accra, had both schooled up to the GCE 'O'-Level. They were both employed as junior clerks in the public sector, though they worked in different departments.

For a while finding a job seemed elusive. Penniless as I was, I managed to survive on what is commonly known as African solidarity. My friends did not require me to contribute towards the cost of rent, water and electricity. Before leaving for work Mondays to Fridays they bought bread at the next kiosk that could go round for all. Lunch was usually skipped.

For dinner, my companions contributed money to enable us to buy some *kenkey*. Kenkey is eaten mostly by the coastal population of Ghana. It is made from maize that is first milled into flour. The flour is then mixed with water and allowed to ferment over a few days. Next, it is formed into balls, wrapped with the dry leaves won from the maize plant and boiled for several minutes. Kenkey is usually eaten with sauce and fried fish. As a result of our meagre means we could hardly afford to add fish to our meal. Whenever we went to buy the kenkey, we did not wait for the vendor to ask whether we wanted some fish in addition, but rather went on the offensive: 'Only kenkey, no fish, please!' we stated categorically.

Usually during the weekends, and sometimes for dinner, I received some additional meals from Ransford's wife.

Even as the prospects of eventually finding employment began to evaporate, I resolved to hang on in Accra come what may. The other option, to return to Mpintimpi to await my results, was not attractive enough.

One day I decided to go on a stroll through the streets of Accra in an area not far from where I lived. While on the street I unexpectedly heard someone call my name. I turned to have a look.

It was Grace, Kwadwo's attractive cousin. It was a pleasant surprise; the last time I saw her was about two years before. At that time I was in their village to celebrate Christmas with Kwadwo.

'What are you doing on the streets of Accra?' I inquired.

'What are *you* doing here?'

'I am here on holiday!'

'How far have you come with your education?'

'I have just passed out of sixth-form. I'm just waiting for the results to be released.'

'Oh, I see.'

'Have you heard about Kwadwo?' I inquired. (After passing out of Oda he went on to do a post secondary course that would qualify him as a teacher. Since then personal contact had been sporadic.)

'We met at the village recently. At that time he was fine.'

'You still haven't told me what *you're* doing here?' I pressed.

'I am now living in Accra!'

'Indeed?'

'Yes.'

'Where?'

'Here—in Asylum Down!'

'You don't mean it!'

'Oh, I do. Do you see the double storey building at the other end of the street?' She pointed to an apartment building about two hundred metres away.

'That's where you live?'

'Right!'

'Then we are almost neighbours!'

'Yes indeed? Where do you live?'

I pointed to our home which was a stone's throw from where we stood. The two buildings were barely three hundred metres apart.

The conversation continued for about five more minutes. Finally she took a look at her watch.

'Well,' she smiled, 'I have to leave you. I need to get one or two things done.'

I was hardly about to let the opportunity of getting to know Kwadwo's delightful cousin slip by. 'What about coming round for a visit?' I ventured. 'That will be a good opportunity to talk further—about the village, Oda, Kwadwo, and so on.'

'No objections—I have plenty of time these days.'

Her answer surprised me. Based on what I knew about her, I thought she wouldn't want to have anything to do with an ordinary student like me. But in the end she promised to visit around midday a few days later.

I could hardly wait for the day to arrive! To say that I didn't harbour my own selfish interests would hardly be truthful. I was at a stage in life when one becomes aware of a need to look out for contacts that could lead to a future partner.

Partly because I was so much preoccupied with my studies, and partly because I didn't have the means to entertain anyone, I had so far not made any headway in that direction. Though I didn't give myself much chance of wining this attractive young lady in view of what I knew about her, I nevertheless didn't entirely wish to rule out the possibility. For the moment the idea of even becoming an ordinary companion to her was soothing!

Grace turned up for her visit as promised. It was around midday on Thursday, September 14, 1978. My roommates were at work so I had the room to myself. Initially our conversation revolved around issues of general interest—our last meeting at the village, my friendship with Kwadwo, about my education and my plans for the future.

Then came the surprising moment! Turning to me, she asked unexpectedly: 'Have you already given your life to Jesus the Lord?'

I was startled by her question and for a moment I was lost for words. 'Well,' I replied thoughtfully, choosing my words carefully, 'I can't say I understand what you mean by that. I'm not an atheist. I do indeed believe in God. I do not attend church regularly, however.'

'My question is,' she said, 'have you made a conscious decision to follow the Lord? It is not enough to go to church from time to time. I also used to attend church from time to time. But I was still living a wild life—until I got to know the Lord. Now I am free, free, free!' She smiled. 'As the scriptures put it, "If the

Son makes you free you will be free indeed!" Another scripture says: "God so loved the world that He sent His only begotten son, that whoever believes in Him will not perish but have eternal life."' She smiled and looked at me expectantly.

I looked at her in bewilderment. For the moment I thought I wasn't hearing her correctly. Though I couldn't call myself an *active* Christian, I had quite a good *knowledge* of scripture. The thought that went through my mind as I sat face to face with her was of the nature: 'Is Saul also among the prophets?' She might have read my thoughts.

'Well,' she went on, 'I know for sure that Kwadwo and the others have told you something about me—in particular in regard to the wild life I used to live!' She smiled, but her words were serious. 'Indeed, in former times I lived to please the flesh. Yes, I allowed my flesh to dictate my actions. I was a wretched sinner, used by the Devil the way he wanted. Not that I really enjoyed all that I did. Often I felt so miserable I sought a way of escape, but escape seemed nowhere near. While feeling miserable within me, I feigned happiness to show the world around me everything was okay. But deep within me was misery—deep misery. Things came to a head recently. I went through a very severe crisis.' She took in my look of surprise. 'Oh yes, my life seemed for ever shattered. Just at that moment God, through mysterious circumstances, came to call me. I obeyed the call and gave my Life to Jesus the Lord. Now I am free, free, free!'

She continued her testimony for a while. She spoke eloquently about her new-found hope, from time to time quoting scripture to stress her point. Her eyes sparkled with joy as she spoke—a joy not feigned. I sensed her genuine happiness that radiated from deep inside her.

For a while I wondered whether the scene was real or whether I was day-dreaming. Was the woman actually sitting face to face with me, the same person I had known before, the woman whose beauty and reputation had so intimidated me?

Finally she turned to look me in the eyes: 'I am inviting you to accept Jesus into your life. I have heard from Kwadwo and others that you are a brilliant scholar. Give your life to the Lord Jesus and He will use you to His glory.' She smiled but again spoke earnestly. 'Oh indeed! You will never regret your decision to follow the Rock of Ages! If the Lord can change someone like me He can do the same with you.' She paused for breath, then continued: 'Please give some thought to what you have heard. The Bible says in Rev. 3:20: "Behold, I stand at the door and knock; if any man hear my voice and open the door, I will come into him, and will sup with him, and he with me". (KJV.) Today may be your last chance! I don't know whether you worship in any church at all. In any case I want to invite you to worship with us on Sunday. I could pass here on my way to church to call on you.'

Once again I was lost for words. Eventually I found my tongue. 'You *really* want me to worship with you?'

'Oh indeed! The congregation will be glad to welcome you.'

'What kind of church is it?'

'It is known as the Open Bible Church.'

'Open Bible Church?'

'You have never heard of the Open Bible Church?'

'No.'

'Well, it is a Pentecostal Church—a truly Bible-based church. You may come and see things for yourself!'

'You'll have to give me time to digest all that you've told me today!'

'Don't harden your heart, my dear! Today is the day of your salvation; tomorrow may be too late.'

'Will you please give me some time to think about it?'

Not long afterwards she begged to leave—but before she left she asked me to join her in a short prayer.

She prayed that the Lord would open my heart and help break the last resistance remaining in me.

I accompanied her to the gate of the house.

As I returned to my room, some of the co-tenants gathered in the big compound of the house looked at me with inquisitive eyes.

'Have you found your partner at last?' one of them joked.

'What led you to that conclusion?'

'Well, it's my own guess!'

'She's only a good acquaintance,' I replied defensively, 'the cousin of my best friend!'

'That's what they usually say!' my inquisitor laughed. 'Next time you meet her she'll tell you she's expecting your offspring to arrive in a matter of days!'

I didn't pass any comment on that but headed for my room.

Grace's testimony would not give me rest. That she of all people would be the one to talk to me about salvation! I had heard and read about the transforming power of scripture. I did not need to search for a living testimony of those assertions—for Grace indeed was an embodiment of that testimony!

Just at that moment my eyes caught sight of my Methodist Hymn Book. It happened to be lying on one corner of the writing desk.

Even to this day I cannot explain why I decided to pick it up. The moment I got hold of it, behold, it opened up at Hymn 157, the only hymn marked in the book, the hymn that had spoken to my heart so powerfully a few months before at the funeral at Mfantsipim.

The lines stared at my face:

> Jesus Calls us! Over the tumult
> of our life's wild restless sea,
> Day by day His sweet voice
> soundeth
> Saying: Christian follow me.
>
> As of old, apostles heard it
> By the Galilean lake,
> Turned from home and toil and
> kindren
> Leaving all for His dear sake.
>
> Jesus calls us from the worship
> Of the vain world's golden store,
> From each idol that would keep us,
> Saying: Christian love Me more!
>
> In our joys and in our sorrows,
> Days of toil and hours of ease,
> Still He calls, in cares and pleasures,
> That we love Him more than these.
>
> Jesus calls us! By thy mercies,
> Saviour, make us hear Thy call
> Give our hearts to Thine obedience.
> Serve and Love Thee best of all.

I read through the whole hymn, verse by verse. I re-read it the second time. Goose-pimples formed all over my body as I went through the lines.

For a while I could hardly control my tears.

Grace's testimony alone might not have been enough to move my stony heart. That sign—the hymn—following so closely on the heels of her touching testimony served as the proverbial last straw that was needed to break the back of the camel.

'The Lord has found you at last,' a still voice within me seemed to say. 'In the past you did not heed the call. This time there is nowhere you can run to.'

An unusual quiet filled the room. Without knowing what I was doing I was on my knees, praying.

When I got up, I looked out for a Bible. There were a couple of them in the room. I got hold of one and began to read from a passage in the New Testament. All of a sudden the words began to speak to my heart in a manner that I had not experienced before.

I contacted Grace the next day to let her know about my willingness to accompany her to church the following Sunday. As expected, she was delighted at the news! We arranged for her to pass by my home on her way to church. Together we would drive on a Tro-Tro to the church which was located about five kilometres away.

I accompanied her to church the following Sunday as planned.

As Grace pointed out, the Open Bible Church is an evangelical church. The mother church is based in the US. As I later learnt, the head Pastor in Ghana was a graduate of the Open Bible College in the US. On his return from his stay in the US, he decided to establish a branch of the church in Ghana.

The church in Ghana had its headquarters in Kumasi, Ghana's second largest city. Apart from the branch in Accra, there were a couple others in other parts of the country.

The church in Accra, located in a suburb of Accra known as Kotobaabi, could not boast of a building in the classical sense. It was housed in a rectangular makeshift wooden building, about fifty metres in length and twenty metres in breadth. The wooden wall extended approximately a metre from ground level. From there it was open to roof level. An aluminium roof shaded it from rain and direct sunshine. Less than fifty metres from the church was a refuse dump. Despite its humble setting, Sunday service was well attended.

The pastor of the Accra Branch, Pastor Ofosu Mensah, like the founder of the Ghana Branch, studied at the Open Bible College in the US. I estimated his age to be about 50.

The church service began around 10:00 a.m. with praise and worship. This was followed by Sunday School which took about forty-five minutes. At last, the sermon was delivered and the session ended around 2 p.m.

Pastor Ofosu-Mensah delivered a very powerful sermon on my first visit. As was his custom, at the end of his sermon, he asked anyone wishing to give his or her life to the Lord to come forward to the altar to be prayed for. Without hesitation I heeded the call. I was joined by another worshipper. After he had congratulated us on our decision he asked the whole church to rise up as he prayed for us.

Amid the cheerful applause and shouts of 'Welcome home! Welcome home!' we returned to our seats.

7

New convert

Those who have gone through the experience Christians refer to as the new birth will bear me out in regard to what I am about to say. The initial experience is usually accompanied by a flood of enthusiasm that can last for several weeks or months.

One literally is on fire—is keen to tell others about his/her experience, is eager to read the Bible, to pray and even fast regularly. Yes indeed, the fire glows in us, we bubble with energy, enthusiasm and fire. My experience was not different.

I rarely missed any activity in church. Apart from the normal morning service, there was also an evening service on Sundays. Wednesday evening was time for Bible study. Friday was set aside as a day of fasting and prayer. Except on medical grounds, our pastor encouraged members to take part in the fast. This was generally broken around 6 p.m. in the evening. Once every four weeks we received Holy Communion. Members were encouraged to dedicate the week leading to the communion service to prayer and fasting. Members needed, in the words of the pastor, to prepare themselves spiritually for the meal with the Lord.

Pastor Ofosu Mensah's teachings were Bible-based, pure and simple. In this regard he did not shun controversy. Nor was he afraid to incur the displeasure of men. He told his congregation not to rely on him for the ultimate truth. He was there only to guide us. In this regard he urged each member to read the Bible regularly so as to become conversant with the simple truths it carried.

His teachings on the issue of marriage, in particular, became an invaluable source of help in the following years. He encouraged the unmarried members to wait patiently on the Lord. Citing his own experience, he taught us how fervent prayer could move the Lord to lead one to the suitable life partner. He also solemnly entreated members to refrain from pre-marital sex.

Pastor Ofosu Mensah! I found him to be a very good shepherd of the flock entrusted by the Lord. Even to this day I am grateful to the Lord for using him to help build a good foundation in my Christian life. Those solid truths he taught contributed in no small way to enable me to weather some of the storms that would soon follow.

◆ ◆ ◆

After I had become a member of the Open Bible Church, Grace and I became very close associates. Several factors contributed to this. First and foremost was our common love for the Lord Jesus Christ; then was the fact just mentioned—membership in the same church. Equally important was the fact that we lived very close to each other. Furthermore, each of us had plenty of time at our disposal.

She was working on her own, earning her living through sewing new clothes and repairing torn ones. Her clients were mainly relatives, members of the church, friends and other acquaintances. Normally there was little pressure on her to finish work on the items brought to her at a specified time. She preferred working at her own pace.

On my side the prospect of finding work before my possible admission to the university dwindled with each passing day.

Our friendship was further boosted by virtue of the fact that each of us was single. Besides that, neither Grace nor I had any commitment to anyone in that direction. Grace on her part, partly because she had gone through several broken relationships, and partly because of the peace her new-found faith had brought her, was not in a hurry to get into any new relationship. She told me she had made it her policy to tell any man who approached her on issues pertaining to marriage that she was already engaged. When they went further to inquire who the person was, she would reply: 'I am engaged to the Lord Jesus Christ!'

We spent much time together—in regular Bible study, in fasting and in prayer. Every Sunday she passed by our home to call me to church. Not only in the area of spiritual things did we co-operate. We united resources also in the issues of everyday life—helping each other financially when necessary and possible, going shopping together, preparing meals together, etc. The close relationship between us led to a whole lot of speculations. How often did we have to explain to others that apart from being 'brother and sister in Christ' there was nothing else between us!

Not that I was not interested in her. Since we were about the same age, and besides, since I had good contacts with her family, I wouldn't have found anything wrong should our relationship have developed beyond the ordinary brother-and-sister stage. As the saying goes, however, it takes two to tango. My beloved sister in Christ took pains to emphasize the fact that we should better leave things as they were. She could not rule out the changing of her mind in the future. At that moment however she was so traumatised by the past that she felt very comfortable in her new life with Christ. I prayed to the Lord to help me play by the rules and save me from doing anything that would jeopardize the cordial relationship between us.

In due course she revealed her plans for the immediate future. Her senior brother was residing in Southern Germany, she told me. He was married to a German citizen. For reasons that she could not explain, her sister-in-law had developed a deep affection for her. Together with her brother, they had decided to help her settle in Germany. Their plans were at an advanced stage; they needed, however, to put one or two things in order before they could finally give her the go ahead to join them. Her planned journey to Germany was thus first on her prayer request list. She was confident the Lord would in His good time help her to settle in Germany.

At that time telephone links between Ghana and Germany were very underdeveloped, to put it mildly. One could only make a call to Germany after one had gone through a wearisome procedure. Owing to that, communication between her and her relatives in Germany was restricted to the exchange of letters.

Grace had a weakness in this regard—she was not keen on writing letters. As she confessed to me, it took her several days to reply to letters that she received from Germany. All that changed after our meeting. Not only did I write swift replies on her behalf to the letters she received from Germany, but I often took the initiative to write to just keep her relations in touch with the latest development regarding their family in particular and the situation in Ghana in general.

8

Shattered hopes

A few days after my decision to follow the Lord, the A-Level results were released. For the first time in my educational career, disappointment was written on my face when I learnt of my results. Although I passed in all the four subjects, scoring good grades in Biology, my performance in Physics and Chemistry fell short of what I was capable of achieving. The fourth subject—General Studies—did not have any bearing on the selection for the university.

It was exactly a situation of this nature that I had worked hard to avoid. As I mentioned earlier, at that time there existed only three universities in the country. Of the three, two had medical faculties. The one in Accra was well-established. Kumasi had opened a medical faculty only a few years before. Together they admitted only a few dozen students. As expected, the competition among students wishing to study medicine was very strong indeed.

In theory, my grades were enough to gain me admission to my well-cherished field of study. Indeed, as I later learnt, some of my classmates with grades similar to mine gained admission to one of the two medical schools. They boasted of something I didn't have—influential parents and/or relatives with good contacts at the top. A very good performance was the only means at the disposal of a poor student from rural Mpintimpi to ensure outright admission!

I was disappointed beyond measure. Still, I did entertain some hope of being invited for interview by one of the two medical schools. (Pre-selection interviews were conducted in medicine and a few other competitive fields of study. The rest did their selection only on the basis of the grades of applicants.)

After several days had passed without any letter of invitation arriving, I began to give up hope for medicine. As was the practice at that time, a few weeks prior to the beginning of the academic year, the names of all students admitted to the three Universities that year were published over a period of days in the two leading national dailies. I went out early every morning to line up for the day's newspaper.

Eventually my name appeared—the University of Legon in Accra had admitted me for a course of study that would lead to a Bachelor of Science degree.

A degree in the sciences! That had never been my dream. During my days at Oda, I was a member of the Debating Club as well as the Drama Society. That had led some to advise me to become a lawyer—a field I was also quite interested in.

Then there was my passion for writing. I used to contribute articles to our school magazine and that made some advise me to consider becoming a journalist—a profession I quite admire. For reasons mentioned earlier, however, I clung adamantly to medicine as my goal.

During my days at Oda a slogan had gained popularity there. It was the *Medico or Suicide* slogan. 'Medico' was short for Medical School. One of my classmates was so obsessed with studying medicine that he went about telling everyone 'Medico or Suicide!' Although I did not say it out loud, my love for the field was just about the same as his.

What was I to do? Theoretically, I could choose to re-sit the examination with the aim of improving my grades. Financially it was almost impossible; apart from paying for the evening classes, I also had to pay for the examination fee.

Even if I had the money to pay for the revision course, there was no guarantee that an improvement in my grades could lead to my being selected. From my information, priority was given to candidates passing out of sixth-form in a particular year. There was surely going to be several hundred school leavers the following year with good passes at 'A' level wishing to enter medical school. Such a turn of events in my academic life I had never imagined.

I turned to my new-found faith for strength and consolation in the confused situation. Passages of scripture like the following were an invaluable source of strength and encouragement:

> 'And we know that all things work together for good to them that love God, to them that are called according to his purpose.' (Romans 8:28.)
>
> 'Now faith is the substance of things hoped for, the evidence of things not seen.' (Heb. 11:1.)
>
> 'But without faith it is impossible to please him; for he that cometh to God must believe that he is, and that he is a rewarder of them that diligently seek him. (Heb 11:6.)

◆ ◆ ◆

Just about that time I accompanied Ransford on a visit to a friend of ours living at Osu, a suburb of Accra. Yaw Asante, our friend, grew up in a little village near Mpintimpi. A few years before Ransford passed out of Oda Secondary School, he was admitted there to begin his second cycle education. Ransford became his mentor.

When I got there in 1971. Yaw Asante was just about to pass out of sixth form. He in turn became my mentor. From Oda he made it to the University of Cape Coast to do a degree in economics. From there he moved to Accra where he gained employment in one of the ministries.

During our visit I told him about my failure to gain admission to study medicine.

'Don't be disappointed—I have an alternative for you!' he said on hearing my story.

'What alternative?'

'The Soviet Union!'

'What do you mean by that?'

'I can help you gain a scholarship to study medicine in the Soviet Union!'

'You must be joking!'

'No, I am serious. All you need to do is to join the Ghana-Soviet Friendship Society.'

'The Ghana-Soviet Friendship Society? How do I become a member?'

'You be patient. I'll give you the details. About twenty metres from where I live is the Soviet Cultural Centre. That is where the Ghana Soviet Friendship Society meet. One day someone invited me to one of their meetings. Well, I decided to go and see things for myself. Eventually I decided to be a member. I have in the meantime been elected General Secretary of the Accra branch.'

'What do you do there?' Ransford came in.

'Blah, blah, blah! The communists blow their horn, claiming to be the best. They give the West the blame for all the evil in the world. As for me, I regard it as a welcome change to my daily routine. Once every month we meet there to talk and debate about issues of general interest.'

'I hope they don't make a communist out of you,' Ransford remarked.

'May God forbid!' our friend exclaimed.

'And you think they will grant me a scholarship?' I asked.

'Sure! Every year a number of scholarships for studies in Universities and other institutions of higher learning in the Soviet Union are placed at the disposal of the organisation. Only members are eligible to apply. The selection is done by the executive of which I am part.'

'That sounds very promising!'

'You are familiar with the Akan proverb: *wo nsa da mu a yenni nya wo* (he who has his hands in a bowl containing a meal has the right to the meal). How can I select others and drop you? Besides that, from my previous experience, your grades would be among the best if not the best we can expect from applicants. As I mentioned earlier, however, you have to be a member of the organisation to be selected.

That was an encouraging piece of news. I was not unaware of the so-called Eastern Scholarships. It was a scheme whereby the countries of the then Eastern Block placed at the disposal of countries of the developing world—from Africa, South America and Asia—hundreds of scholarships to enable their citizens to study in the countries behind the so-called iron curtain..

The scholarships were allegedly offered without any strings attached. At the back of the minds of the donors was of course the hope that the beneficiaries after their long stay in their society would return to propagate the communist ideology in their various countries.

In the case of Ghana, I knew the scholarship was channelled through a government department, the Scholarships Secretariat. I didn't consider that as an option for it was an open secret that only those with contacts at to the top or who could pay substantial amounts could dream of attaining such a scholarship.

What I was not aware of before the meeting with Yaw Asante, however, was the fact that non-governmental left-wing organisations such as the Trade Unions Congress and GSFS also benefited from the scheme.

Before we left him. Yaw urged me to do all I could to attend the next meeting of the Organisation which was a couple of days away. Grace who had shared in the disappointment of the last few weeks was glad to learn about the latest development.

◆ ◆ ◆

I was one of the first to turn up at the Soviet Cultural Centre at the appointed time. Shortly after my arrival, Yaw also arrived. He introduced me to some of the colleagues around. Soon the meeting got underway. The aim of the organisation, I was told, was to help foster friendship between the people of

Ghana on one hand and those of the Union of Soviet Socialist Republics on the other.

Was it not strange for a firebrand Christian to become a member of the GSFS? Indeed, I was not unaware of the atheistic view of the communist ideology. That fact didn't bother me, however—as long as membership did not threaten my Christianity.

'If I could train in the Soviet Union as a doctor without compromising my Christianity—what was wrong with that?' I said to myself. Most important, I trusted in the Lord to preserve my faith should I make it there.

I knew Yaw himself to be a devoted Christian. During his days at Oda he was a staunch member of the Scripture Union. Later he was elected to the executive. If he had become a member, why not me?

At the end of the meeting I formally registered to become a member of the organisation, in the process paying my dues for that month.

From then on I attended the meetings, held regularly once every month. Apart from the monthly meetings, members were encouraged to learn the Russian language. The opportunity to do so existed: the cultural centre provided a free Russian language class for beginners and I didn't hesitate to register for the course. Lessons were held once a week. Not only was the course free—textbooks, workbooks and other relevant material were also supplied free of charge. Those who have had to learn Russian will bear me out that it is quite a hard nut to crack. The hope of being selected to study medicine in the Soviet Union motivated me to make great efforts to learn it. Soon I became conversant with some of the basics of the language

I joined the society at the time when the Cold War showed no sign of abating. Our meetings provided a good forum for various speakers to lash out at the western imperialist and their capitalist allies worldwide who were assigned blame for being the main cause of misery, poverty and instability in many parts of the developing world. Our duty was to resist them wherever they surfaced.

Religious issues, on the other hand, rarely came up for discussion.

9

'At long last we have met in Europe!'

Some are baptised as babies. As grown-ups they either continue on in the faith or they severe all relations with it. Some even become so disillusioned with the Christian faith they wish they could reverse the baptism they went through without their will.

At the time of my birth my parents were not associated with any church. They left the issue of faith in God to their children to decide for themselves.

Thus at the time I joined the Open Bible Church I was not baptised. Naturally my greatest desire after my decision to follow the Lord was to be baptised. I discussed the issue with our pastor.

He made it known to me that he conducted baptisms at regular intervals based on the number of those seeking baptism at a particular time. He asked me to exercise some patience until the appropriate time. An announcement would be made in church to that effect.

At last one Sunday, about two months after I had become a member of the church, the long-awaited announcement was made. Those wishing to be baptised were requested to submit their names to one of the deacons. I did as requested.

About two weeks later a second announcement was made on that issue.

The pastor had decided on December 23 as the day of baptism. The ceremony was to take place in the afternoon at a lagoon at one of the popular beaches in the city.

'Why December 23 of all days!' I said to myself. Keeping the appointment would mean I would be forced to spend Christmas in Accra.

The reason was that it would be almost impossible for me to find the means of transportation on Christmas Eve to join the rest of the family at Mpintimpi.

As might be the case in some other parts of the world, Ghanaians working in the cities and urban areas travel in their tens of thousands to the rural areas at

Christmas for a re-union with other family members. I had looked forward with joy to seeing my parents and other family members at Mpintimpi. The prospect of that not happening because of the impending baptism saddened my heart. Bubbling with much enthusiasm in my new-found faith, my spirit was not dampened for long, however.

About a week prior to Christmas some of my acquaintances began to leave Accra for the countryside. Eventually Cox and Rex, my roommates, also left. Grace, who had already been baptised by Pastor Ofosu Mensah, left shortly before Christmas for the countryside.

Finally the day dawned—December 23, 1978.

At the appointed time, about 2 p.m. local time, I, together with a couple of other baptism candidates, gathered at a small lagoon near the Labadi Beach in Accra.

After a short meditation, our pastor began the solemn ceremony.

We walked a few metres from the shore. When we got to a point where the water reached up to waste-level he began to baptise us—one after the other.

Soon it came to my turn:

Holding me by the shoulder and looking me in the eyes, he began: 'I baptise you in the name of the Father'...*s-p-l-a-s-h*...my body was immersed in the salty waters of the Atlantic Ocean. I gasped for air...up came my head above water once more...'and of the Son'...my head was thrown beneath water once again and then back into the air...'and of the Holy Spirit, Amen!'...for the third and last time my body was buried under water and then brought back to air.

'Congratulations, brother,' our beloved pastor shook my hands. 'You have officially died with Christ to awake with Him in His Kingdom. May His grace accompany you throughout the rest of your days on earth!'

◆ ◆ ◆

Alone in Accra, with few friends around to visit, I decided to dedicate most of the time between Christmas and New Year's Day to fasting and prayer. I avoided food and fluid during the daytime until well after dark.

On one of such days, after a long night of prayer, I retired to bed. Was I really asleep or was I half-awake? One thing I am aware of, I was not fully conscious. Suddenly a scene flashed before my eyes—it was so vivid that even to this day I can very clearly recall it! In the scene I happened to be walking on the streets of a strange city. All of a sudden Grace emerged from one corner of the street. Surprised at seeing me, she exclaimed:

'Peprah! At long last we have met in EUROPE!'

Just then my eyes opened and I came back to myself. I looked around me—all was deep silence. The walls of the room became familiar. It dawned on me that I had been in a dream

'Gracious Lord Jesus!' I said out loud. 'You are not only going to send Grace to Europe—but me too?' I fell to my knees to thank the Lord for His plans for our lives.

The dream would inspire my thinking, direct my steps and shape my plans for the future. Soon those in the environment around me—parents, close relatives, friends—would only wonder at what was leading me to take some of the decisions I took. I would not be deterred by the attitude of the environment, though. I recalled the story of Abraham, the great man of faith, and how God asked him to leave his home for a land he would lead him to and how he obediently left the familiar for the unfamiliar—recounting the numerous difficulties, struggles and trials he would encounter until prophecy was fulfilled.

Without trying to compare myself to that giant of faith I vowed to draw inspiration from his experience and follow God obediently and believe Him to bring to fulfilment what He had promised me in the dream.

Human as I am, I tried to interpret the prophecy the easy way.

As far as Grace was concerned, things were clear: her relations in Germany were still determined to help her settle there.

On my part I had a good chance of gaining a scholarship to the Soviet Union. But how could we meet in Europe when she was in Germany and I was in the Soviet Union? From various sources I knew foreign students studying in the then Soviet Union were permitted to travel to the West during the long summer holidays. I could take the opportunity to visit her in Germany then.

Mortal man with my extremely limited abilities to understand the mind of the Divine! Who was I to set out to think for Him!

On Grace's return from Christmas, I described what had happened to me, including the vision that involved her. Her response was that if it was the will of the Lord it would surely come to pass. Apart from her, I revealed the dream to no one else except our Pastor.

'Oh yes, the Lord still talks,' Pastor Ofosu Mensah remarked on hearing what I had to tell him. 'He has revealed His will for the future to you. He will do what he has said he will do.'

♦   ♦   ♦

The dream strengthened my resolve to concentrate on our planning towards leaving Ghana.

At the beginning of January 1979 an advertisement by the then Post and Telecommunications Corporation (P&T for short) looking for junior clerks appeared in the newspapers. I decided to try my luck at it. I was confident I would leave the country in August that year for the Soviet Union. In the meantime the position could be a source of income, not for me only, but for Grace and possibly my parents as well.

Matriculation at the university was a few days away. What would I do should I be given the job? I did not give serious thought to that, for I did not give the prospect of my being selected a big chance.

To my surprise, however, shortly after I had despatched my application, I was invited for an interview. One of the first questions centred on the issue of reliability. The job was a responsible one, the head of the panel explained. It would require a reliable person. How could I convince them in that regard?

I was so much on fire for the Lord at that time that I viewed the question as an opportunity to bear witness to my newly found Friend.

'On my own I may not be reliable, but with the Lord Jesus by my side you can rely on me.'

I looked around me. The surprise written all over their faces was very evident!

'So you call yourself a Christian?' one of the interviewers responded. 'I know quite a lot of them who are not living in line with their calling.'

'Formerly I also attended church, though not very regularly,' I said. 'A few weeks ago, however, the Lord sent His servant to call me. Since then He directs all my steps. At work, I will take pains not to do anything that will bring His name into disrepute.'

They seemed to be lost for words, for shortly thereafter they asked me to leave.

'Would they offer me the job?' I wondered as I left them.

Yes, they did! Not long after the interview, I received a letter from them offering me the job! I was posted to the P&T External.

As I mentioned earlier, at that time the communication network in Ghana was underdeveloped. The ordinary citizen could not make direct phone calls abroad. Instead one had first to book an appointment at the P&T External. The same was true of telegraphic and telex messages being sent out of the country.

I worked in the book-keeping section. I was at my post for almost two years. At a period of serious economic crisis, my position contributed in no small way in helping to keep my head above water.

10

The revelation of my Muslim Neighbour

In the 1978/79 academic year, I matriculated as a student of the University of Ghana located at Legon, at the outskirts of Accra, the capital of the country. Normally the academic year began in October. As a result of a students' unrest in the middle of 1978 to protest against the military government of the day, the University was closed down for several weeks on the orders of the government. That led to other disruptions in the academic calendar. The academic year subsequently began in January 1979 instead of October 1978.

At the time I responded to the interview at P&T, I was yet to matriculate at the university. As I mentioned earlier, I did not give myself any good chance of being selected. When I was selected, the dilemma was whether to give up the position or whether to matriculate at the University.

I prayed to the Lord for wisdom. In the end I decided in favour of both.

At that time not only was tuition free at all institutions of higher learning in the country, but students also didn't have to pay for boarding and lodging. I was offered accommodation at one of the hostel complexes of the University known as the Legon Hall.

Two students were allocated to a room about twenty square metres large. The bathroom and the toilet facilities shared by all the students in a particular hostel complex were in an extra building. Three meals were served daily at the university canteen.

Was it by accident or by design that I was assigned to a room already occupied by a student who was a Moslem? He was a Nigerian by nationality, though his behaviour and thinking was more Ghanaian than Nigerian. No wonder, for he had lived in Ghana all his life. Years before his birth his parents moved from Nigeria to settle in Ghana. He was a law student. At the time of our meeting he was in his final year.

Despite our differing religious convictions we got on very well. I didn't make any attempt to evangelise directly; instead, my strategy was to make my life bear witness to the changing powers of the Holy Spirit—for the Bible says that 'by their fruits ye shall know them.'

In the end a close relationship bordering on friendship developed between the two of us. He was surprised that I hardly attended lectures. He advised me to change my attitude towards the course of studies I had been offered. After obtaining a first degree in the sciences, he argued, I could move on to an area such as biochemistry which, in his opinion, would offer me a chance for a promising future. On the other hand, if I wasn't interested in the course from the outset, I could contact the Department of Agriculture to see whether they would allow me to switch to that department. He knew a couple of students who had already done so.

I thanked him for his advice, but did not act on it. Naturally I did not want to reveal my dream to him. How could I expect him to believe me? He probably would have taken me to be a fanatic Christian who had lost his mind!

I left the University campus every morning to work at the P&T. When my work schedule permitted it, I went to sit in the lecture hall to listen to some lectures. I found the material being taught so dry that I could never imagine myself graduating in that field! From conversations with some of the students, I got to know that one needed to be present for the practicals. One had to sign one's name at the end of the day. That didn't bother me. I saw myself as a traveller sitting on his packed luggage. I was only waiting for the Lord to give me my marching orders.

On a few occasions, Grace visited me at the University. On one such visit we were walking in the streets of the large campus when we bumped into an old acquaintance of hers. As it turned out he was also matriculated at the university. After we talked for a while I invited him to accompany us to my room. He obliged. Both of them had not seen each other for a while and were desirous to continue the exchange in my room.

Grace took the opportunity to witness to her former close companion about her new-found Friend. Our visitor, who prided himself on being an atheist, engaged us in a protracted argument, citing several reasons which, in his view, disproved the existence of God. My roommate who happened to be present followed with interest the exchange between the two Christians on one side and the avowed atheist on the other. Apart from intervening to clarify one or two points on the issue raised by our debate in regard to the attitude of Christians towards Moslems, he did not take an active part in the discussion.

The meeting ended without our guest budging a millimetre from his standpoint. Our prayers for him were not in vain, however. As I learnt later, months after our meeting, the light of the Good Shepherd penetrated his darkened heart and led him along the path of Righteousness.

◆ ◆ ◆

One day, whilst I was alone with my roommate, he turned to me suddenly and began:

'I want to confess something to you. Believe me, it is not something born out of my own fantasies. I wouldn't narrate it to you if it were not true…'

'Go ahead, I'm listening…'

'As I have told you, my parents reside in a little village a few kilometres away from Jasikan.' (Jasikan is a district capital located in the Volta Region of Ghana, about 250 kilometres to the north-east of Accra.) 'There is no proper road linking our village to the town,' he continued. 'The two places are connected only by a bush-path. The villagers have no choice but to go by foot whenever they wish to visit the town. At the end of one holiday I left home very early to walk to Jasikan to catch a vehicle that would bring me to Accra. It was still quite dark at that hour of day. I was about half way through my journey when all of a sudden a strange object emerged from the woods and took its position on the path a few metres ahead of me. The object had the stature of a human being. What was terrifying was this—flames of fire radiated from all over its body! It was a terrible spectacle to behold. I was so horrified at the sight that for the moment I was frozen with fear.

'The area around Jasikan was talked of as being infested by witches, wizards and all sorts of evil spirits. Accounts of people who claimed to have had confrontations with such beings circulated all over the place. Until that day, however, I had dismissed them as being products of the fantasies of others.

'My fear was aggravated further when the strange being, after standing at the spot for a while, began to move towards me! I was frightened to the point of death.

'"This is the end of me!" I said to myself.

'As a Moslem the first thing that came into my mind was Mohammed. A voice in me urged me to call on MOHAMMED for help.

'"In the name of Mohammed I command you, strange being, to depart from me!" I screamed at the top of my voice.

'But the strange being didn't budge; instead it drew even closer to me!

'For the second and the third time I incited the strange being to depart in the name of Mohammed. Nothing happened.

'From the gestures it made, it seemed even to mock at me! The monstrous being drew closer and closer. I was very desperate.

'At that moment an idea flashed through my mind: "Try the name of Jesus!"

'More out of desperation than conviction, I decided to give the idea a try. With all the strength that remained in me I yelled at the top of my voice: "You evil spirit, I charge you in the Name of JESUS CHRIST, depart from me immediately!"

'You cannot imagine it, friend!

"The moment the Name JESUS CHRIST emerged from my lips, the strange object took to its heels and sped into the surrounding forest. Soon it was out of sight. There I stood, not able to fathom what had just happened.

'I want to reiterate, my friend, that I was born a Moslem. What interest do I have to glorify Christianity at the expense of my own religion? I am just telling you the story the way it happened. As a matter of fact, I should have become a Christian the next day!'

He paused for a while. He seemed to be fighting with his emotions.

'What has prevented you from that decision?' I inquired after a while.

'Well, you may be aware of our culture; all members of my family—my parents, brothers, sisters, uncles, aunts—are all Muslims. They will immediately disown me the moment I convert to Christianity.'

My Muslim neighbour passed out of law school successfully at the end of the academic year. Shortly afterwards he left for Nigeria to practice there. We kept contact for a while thereafter. Unfortunately, somehow along the line our contact was broken.

11

Struggling to make it to the Land of Lenin

During our monthly meeting in January 1979, members wishing to study in the Soviet Union were invited to submit their applications before a set date. I did so without delay. Shortly afterwards I was invited for an interview.

I did not take chances and called on my friend at his home a day prior to the interview to prepare for the occasion. Based on his experience from previous years he briefed me on the type of questions I might expect.

Finally the day arrived. The interview was conducted in the premises of the Soviet Cultural Centre. As Yaw had already told me, the panel consisted of the executive members of the Accra branch of the Organisation.

One after the other we were called to face the panel. Each returned after about fifteen minutes. At last it was my turn. The moment I entered the room my eyes caught sight of my friend. I breathed a sigh of relief on seeing him.

The session was in the main a repetition of what I had practised with him the previous day: why did I want to study medicine and why had I opted for the Soviet Union rather than Ghana or somewhere else?

After about ten minutes, it was all over. I was asked to consult the general secretary a few days later to find out the outcome.

Though my friend had been at pains to assure me he would make certain I was selected, a certain degree of anxiety nevertheless crept into my mind as I left for home.

As I mentioned earlier, the telephone network in Ghana at that time was underdeveloped, so we could not communicate by way of the phone. The best way I could find out about the outcome of the interview was by calling on him personally at his residence. I did so a week after the occasion.

He met me with a smile. 'Congratulations, my friend! You have made it!" he exclaimed.

'Thank you Jesus!' I shouted spontaneously on hearing the news.

'You can now begin to pack your luggage!' he continued

'I will do!'

'Well, as we informed you during the interview, the list of the selected candidates will be forwarded to Moscow. There the beneficiaries will be distributed to various institutions of higher learning in various parts of the country. The final list, assigning each candidate to an institution, will arrive in Ghana a few weeks before your departure.'

'Do I need to prepare my own passport?' I wanted to know.

'No. Weeks before your departure, the GSFS will do that on your behalf. You will also receive a free plane ticket for Moscow.'

'Thank you very much for your help! I do not know how best I can express my gratitude.'

'Give God the thanks!' was his reaction.

The first person to hear about the latest development in my life was Grace. We had in the meantime become almost inseparable.

At church the following Sunday, as was customary, just before delivering the day's sermon, Pastor Mensah invited anyone who wanted to witness to what good things had happened in their respective lives over the week to come forward to do so to the glory of the Lord. About fifteen minutes was allotted for this.

Without hesitation, I stepped forward. First I informed the congregation about the dream I had a few weeks before. Prophecy was being fulfilled with my selection to study medicine in the Soviet Union. I continued by asking them to join me in giving thanks unto the Lord. Finally, I implored them to remember me in their prayers.

At that juncture our pastor joined in. He spoke very kind words about me to the congregation, praising my steadfastness in the faith. He was sure the Lord was going to use me for His good. After he prayed for me I returned to my seat.

If only I knew at that time what was in store for me! The Lord indeed had something ahead for me, something better than I had thought of. Before the crown, though, must come the cross.

Over the next several weeks my thoughts revolved around the imminent journey to the Soviet Union. I sent a message to Mpintimpi to inform my parents and the other relatives there about my impending departure from the country. In due time I travelled there to give them further details.

I was overjoyed by the prospect of leaving the country. First and foremost was the delight at the opportunity to take up my studies in my cherished field.

Equally important was the opportunity the scholarship offered me to leave the harsh economic situation prevailing in the country at that time.

Indeed, Ghana was going through very hard times. Inflation was running at astronomical rates. Alluding to the harsh economic situation prevailing then, some citizens coined the term Ogyakrom to describe their native land. The word is a Twi term which, translated, literally means 'the town on fire.' Anyone who physically could and had the means to do so wanted to leave the country. A friend of mine used to say: 'If there was any other place on the planet worse than here, then that place is hell.'

In my joy, one thought sprang to my mind from time to time, such as—what would happen to Grace should I leave Ghana first? Oh, she loved the Lord—there was no doubt about that. The reality on the ground was harsh though.

It was not the fear of backsliding that concerned me. My fear was that the harsh economic situation would lead her to decide to marry someone who didn't have the Lord at heart. The potential candidates were not few.

Among the problems we faced in the country at that time was transportation. One could queue a long distance for a tro-tro. Some of those who possessed private saloon cars took advantage of the situation.

Not on a few occasions she returned from a trip to the centre of the city to tell me about a wealthy person who had offered her a lift and who, during the ride, had expressed his interest in her. To that I would advise her to stand firm and not to give in to any opportunist.

Would she be able to resist such temptations once I was out of the country?

Of course I did not doubt the ability of the Lord to take care of her; it was necessary for her to do her part by running away from foreseeable danger, nevertheless. Under the conditions prevailing on the battlefield at that time, however, that was easier said than done.

About three months after my selection, I left home to attend the monthly meeting of the organisation, not suspecting anything. Shortly after my arrival one of the members approached me: 'Have you heard the latest news?' he inquired.

'What latest news?'

'I mean, the story regarding the revised list?'

'What revised list?' I began to feel uncomfortable.

'Well, according to well informed sources, the list of the selected has been revised!'

'Really?'

'Well, from my source, a new list has been prepared, leaving out the names of some of those originally selected.'

'You don't mean that!'

'That is what I have heard. I do not know whether it is true or not. That will emerge during the meeting.'

Unease began to fill me. I fought hard to suppress the thought that I could be among those whose names had been deleted.

At last the meeting got underway. After the initial greetings the chairman went straight to the point:

'I am sorry to announce the following: a serious overlap occurred during this year's selection process. The southern branch failed to take into consideration the applications of our comrades from the north of the country.'

A murmur began to go round the hall.

He continued after a while: 'Naturally the mishap needed to be corrected. The implication will surely not go down well with some of you. Since the number of scholarships placed at our disposal by our friends in the Soviet Union is limited we had no other choice than to remove the names of some of those selected from the south from the original list.'

He paused for breath. A deep silence filled the room as all eyes were directed towards him.

'I want to make one thing clear at this stage: contrary to the rumours circulating all over the place, neither favouritism nor nepotism played a role in the decision making. I also want to emphasize one point: no member of the executive received any bribe from anyone to keep that person's name on the list!'

Meanwhile the hands of several members were in the air.

'Yes, please?' he pointed to one of them.

'How do we know whose name has been eliminated and whose name has not?'

'I was about to address that issue. For the sake of discretion, I am not going to call out names here. After the meeting I will remain here. All those originally selected can then contact me one after the other to find out about their fate.'

That seemed to be the question on the minds of the others, for all hands went down after his answer.

He continued: 'I wish at this stage to assure those whose names have been eliminated of one thing: you will receive top-priority during next year's selection process. Finally, I want on behalf of the executive to apologise to you for what has happened. It could have been avoided. We take full responsibility for the unfortunate situation and wish to assure you that we will do our best to prevent a repetition in future.'

I could hardly concentrate to follow the rest of the proceedings. At long last the deliberations were brought to an end. As requested, I waited behind to find out about my fate.

One after another, the chairman called a candidate to a lone corner of the hall. After about five minutes' chat some returned with a broad smile on their faces whereas others could hardly hide the disappointment in their faces.

Finally it was my turn.

'Well, I am sorry to tell you that unfortunately you are among those the executive have decided to leave out this year!'

His words were like a sword slicing deep into my heart. For a while I was dumbfounded. Eventually I regained my composure.

'Why me?'

His reply was as shocking as the news regarding the deletion of my name. 'Please take it from me,' he continued. 'No one in the executive has anything against you. To be fair to you, you had one of the best grades among all the candidates. We decided to drop you on different grounds. As you walked into the room for the interview I noticed for the first time that you were limping on one of your legs. You have problems with your leg, I guess?'

He paused for a while as if to expect an answer. I was too stunned to say anything.

'Well, I have been to the Soviet Union myself,' he resumed after a while. 'The winters there are terribly cold, friend. Under such conditions your ailment could only worsen! So we decided to drop you. Indeed I would advise you to give up the idea of going there to study altogether!' Still he chose to be diplomatic: 'You go and ponder over what I have told you. In case you should still want to study there, you can re-apply next year. I strongly advise you against that idea, though.'

As I walked away I could hardly believe my ears—that my difficulty in walking could strike his attention!

Although my left ankle joint had been giving me problems ever since I resumed my schooling I had enjoyed relative calm over the last several months. On the day I attended the interview, it didn't offer me any discomfort at all. 'That man has the instincts of a forensic scientist or perhaps a routine secret agent!' I said to myself.

I decided not to accept the decision without a fight. I first thought of Yaw-Asante, who was conspicuously absent during the meeting. I wondered what was wrong with him. I decided to pass by his home to let him know what had happened and to find out why he could not prevent my name from being dropped.

He was present at home. He had been prevented by a running stomach from attending the meeting.

Yes, he had also heard about the latest development, he told me. As it turned out, he was not in Accra during the crucial meeting of the executive to revise the original list. Only on his return did one executive member pass by his home to let him know what had happened while he was away. On hearing that I was among those who had been dropped, he had tried to reverse the situation; but it had been too late—the final list had already been despatched to the Soviet Union!

What was to be done?

In the end I decided, in my desperation, to take my case to the highest ranking member of the organisation in the country, namely the National President. Coincidentally he happened to be the Navro-Pio, a traditional leader of a large ethnic group in Northern Ghana. He resided in Navrongo, the capital city of the traditional area.

Navro-Pio, I learnt, studied in the Soviet Union. While there he married a citizen of the host country. His wife accompanied him on his return to Ghana. He was credited with very close contacts to the representatives of the Soviet Union in the country. If there was any human being at that time who could help me out of the corner I found myself in, it was surely the Navro Pio, I reasoned. I decided therefore to consult him to entreat him to use his good contacts with the Soviets to work out an additional scholarship for me.

Navrongo is situated about 850 kilometres to the north of Accra. A journey between the two cities implied one literally crossing almost the whole of Ghana from north to south. By virtue of my job at the P&T external I had just enough money for the journey. I couldn't find a vehicle travelling directly from Accra so I had to travel first to Kumasi, located about a third of the distance I had to travel (Kumasi is about 270 km to the north of Accra).

I took the opportunity of the stop-over at the large central bus station there to make a surprise call on Ofosu, my most senior brother. He had such a love for the tailor's profession that he decided to learn that trade even before he could complete his first cycle education. On his insistence, father sent him to a well known tailor at Akuase, a small town about ten kilometres from home. After understudying the famous master for about three years he was declared good enough to work on his own.

Initially he set up his own tailor's shop at Mpintimpi. Later he moved the shop to Amantia. Five years before my journey, he moved his shop to Kumasi.

Apart from bidding him hello, I also had my personal interest at the back of my mind. The journey to the north had progressed at a pace slower than I had calculated. We got to Kumasi late in the afternoon, at a time when I originally thought I would be at my destination. It gradually dawned on me that the money on me would probably not be sufficient for the trip, for I would have to spend at least one night if not more at a hotel.

Fortunately, Ofosu's shop was not far from the 'transport station'. He was surprised and delighted at the same time to see his junior brother. We had not seen each other for several months. I informed him about the reason for my journey. He was disappointed at the sudden turn of events.

He had indeed rejoiced with me when the news got to him regarding my impending trip to the Soviet Union. He prayed that the distinguished person I was consulting would be able to help. When he got to know about the expected financial shortfall, he willingly contributed an amount that was enough to enable me to overcome any unforeseeable hurdle.

From there I went to the transport station to find a vehicle for my destination. The last vehicle leaving for Navrongo that day was a large passenger truck. As was usual with such trucks, it had two cabins. The front cabin was small and built with metal. It offered room for three persons, the driver and two others. The second cabin could be described as a huge wooden cage. Within it, arranged in rows of about seven, were long wooden seats.

Officially the vehicle had room for about forty passengers. On that occasion it carried not less than fifty passengers. It was about 5 p.m. when we set out on the approximately 580-kilometre journey to Navrongo.

We required about twenty hours to complete the journey! Wao! one might exclaim! I'll explain briefly the reason why the ride took that long. In the first place, the condition of the truck whose age I put at no less than fifteen years could only make a few kilometres in an hour. Added to this was the fact that it carried several tons of load beyond what the designers had expected the engine to be capable of carrying! Furthermore, the road we travelled on was not in the best of condition. About three quarters of it was tarred, the rest was not and displayed several potholes at several points.

Furthermore, the vehicle pulled to a stop at several places to allow passengers to disembark or new passengers to embark, or both

As if that were not enough, the vehicle pulled to a halt on several occasions for a very different reason! As it turned out, the driver of the vehicle as well as the great majority of the passengers on the truck were of the Islamic faith. That alone did not surprise me. My figures may not be very accurate. In any case, one can safely say that about sixty percent of the citizens of Ghana ascribe to the Christian faith, twenty percent are Moslems, whilst the rest have other religious inclinations—mostly traditional African religious beliefs. The great majority of the Moslem population dwell in the northern part of the country, in an area beginning about two hundred kilometres to the north of Kumasi and stretching to the northern border with Burkina Fasso.

Those conversant with some of the practices of Islam know that they are required to pray a number of times in the day with their eyes facing Mecca. The driver of the vehicle could be described as a committed Moslem, for he adhered very strictly to the principle of prayer in accordance with his faith.

Regardless of where we had got to, whenever it was time to say his prayer, he pulled his vehicle to a stop. After an announcement in his mother tongue that was like Latin to me, he took a small kettle from his cabin and began to walk away. (There are several languages in Ghana—some of the languages are dialects while others are entirely different from one another—like English is to Russia, Chinese, French, German, etc.)

I wondered what he was up to. Were the Moslem passengers on the vehicle aware that the driver shared their faith and also that he would give them the opportunity to pray during the journey? That was the impression they made on me, for almost all of them carried, like the driver, kettles filled with water (they used the water to wash part of their bodies before they said their prayers).

At that time of the day the road we were travelling on was almost deserted by traffic, so my Muslim co-travellers could go about their prayers—some did so in the very middle of the road—without fear of interruption.

Together, with a handful of passengers, I remained behind and waited patiently during these interruptions. As I reflected on what I was witnessing, it dawned on me how much freedom I enjoyed as a Christian. I could recite my prayer at my own choosing, at any place and in any position.

Finally, at about 3 p.m. the next day I reached my destination.

After I had asked my way a couple of times, I finally made it to the residence of the most powerful man in the traditional area. The meeting lasted only a few minutes. He repeated what I knew already—the final list of the selected had already been despatched to the Soviet Union. He was sorry there was nothing he could do for me at that stage. He would however direct the executive in Accra to give me top priority the following year.

It was late in the evening. There were no more vehicles travelling as far as Kumasi at that hour of day. What was I to do? An idea occurred to me. Navrongo also boasted of a state-owned second cycle boarding school, similar to those at Oda and Cape Coast.

I inquired about its location. I was told that it could be found a few kilometres from where I was. I got into a Taxi and asked to be driven there.

The school was on a short holiday recess. The majority of the students had as a result travelled home. Not so several of the students in the final year. They had stayed behind to prepare for an important examination only weeks away. Not long after I got out of the vehicle, I spotted two students at the corridors of one of the dormitories. I approached them and told them my story. They readily arranged to find me somewhere to lay my head for the night; besides that, they collected food from the school kitchen for me. I didn't have to pay for spending the night there.

The return journey was more comfortable. I travelled on a bus that at that time was run by State Transport Corporation. This time the vehicle did not have to halt at specific times to allow others to fulfil their religious obligations. All in all it was a tedious venture that not only depleted my meagre resources, but also strained me physically.

12

One step forward

In August 1979 the selected group from the GSFS left for the Soviet Union. I had entertained some hope, albeit faint, that somehow someone might not be able to make it and that I would be offered the vacant place. In a situation like that the executive had assured me I would be given top priority if it came to choosing a replacement.

For that particular year at least my hopes of making it to the Soviet Union had to be abandoned.

It did not lead me to doubt God, but I was puzzled. If I were to go Europe, and He was not sending me to the Soviet Union, then where else? As far as I was concerned, leaving to study in the Soviet Union was the most practicable alternative. I did not need to bother about acquiring a passport, a visa or a ticket. Being a scholarship holder I would be entitled to free boarding, lodging and tuition. Besides that, scholarship holders were given money for their books as well as pocket money to acquire other essentials of everyday life.

Pastor Ofosu stood by me in prayer and in encouragement. God works in mysterious ways, he was not weary of repeating. If He wanted to see me to Europe, He would work to bring things into fulfilment in His own time and in His own way. God makes all things beautiful, he added. Besides, all things work together for good for those who love the Lord.

What should I do? I was convinced beyond doubt that the dream indeed revealed God's plan for Grace and myself. Had God said He would do something and had He failed to do it? Our duty was to trust Him and wait patiently for His will to unfold.

God in His mercy opened my eyes to discern a ray of light amidst the darkness enshrouding me—the prospects of Grace leaving for Germany began to improve. Her relatives had to put one or two things right, they wrote. That would take a few months. Thereafter she would receive the green light to begin her journey.

◆   ◆   ◆

Waiting on the Lord to fulfil His promise can be very challenging. Not only do we have to fight our own doubts, the environment around us, through its attitude towards us, can also compound our woes. Relatives, friends, acquaintances began to put pressure on me. As expected, they could not understand what was going on in my life. As I mentioned earlier, apart from Pastor Ofosu, Grace and later our congregation, I did not reveal my dream to anyone else. Even if I had told them, would they have believed?

I heard people saying a whole lot of things about me. 'Instead of him concentrating on his study at the University, he is devoting his time to helping someone else realise her plans to travel to Germany!' Even my uneducated parents seemed to be baffled at the seemingly abrupt end to the educational career of their son in whom they had invested much hope. Although they did not understand the details of the educational system, they were at least aware that the next step after Mfantsipim would be a degree at the University. Reports they were hearing about me didn't indicate I was concentrating on my studies, however.

They probably wondered what was wrong with me. I could only alleviate their fears with vague words like, 'You do not have to concern yourself about me, for all will be well with me.'

Even Grace herself didn't make life easy for either of us. She was a woman who loved the Lord with all her heart, but she had a weakness—she could hardly persevere through uncertain times. One moment she would be very confident of the future, while the next small uncertainties set in and she would begin to waver. As the days turned to weeks and then to months and there apparently seemed to be no sign of her travelling to join her relatives anytime too soon in Germany, she began to lament her situation. In some respects I could understand her attitude.

The economic situation in Ghana in those days was harsh, to put it mildly. The money she earned from her work could hardly go round. In such a situation many a person was tempted to seek shortcuts to success. In her situation that would involve entering into an affair with one of the several well-to-do men in town going around hunting for attractive young ladies of her type. She was convinced that was not the right thing to do, for in many instances she would have been the second or third, if not more lover in the life of such a person.

Yes, many a well-to-do male in the society, particularly those who could boast of a saloon car and could drive the young ladies around town, took advantage of the harsh conditions persisting in the country to satisfy their lust.

She might might also have compared herself to one of her sisters and probably felt the clock of time was ticking against her. Indeed that sister, who was about two years older than her, was doing quite well in life. Married to a well educated man who had recently returned to the country after some years stay in Japan, she lived in a large detached family house in one of the prestigious districts in Accra. Her husband took advantage of his stay in Japan to acquire some of the latest household equipment: a sophisticated HI-FI system, a large Colour-TV, a large refrigerator, a deep freezer, etc. Their large hall displayed the best furniture. They also boasted of their own saloon car. Besides that, their marriage had been blessed with two pretty kids. Grace visited them regularly. On some occasions I accompanied her. Soon they got to know something about me and about my attitude to my studies at the University.

Why not say it to my face? I read their disapproval from their gestures as well as some of the comments they made when I was around. Clearly they didn't approve very much of my close association with their relative.

One evening, on one of my regular visits to Grace, I read from her gestures and the tone of her voice that her mood was low. Her business was not going well. She had so many financial obligations to meet. At the same time her relatives in Germany had not written for weeks. In one of the rare moments since our meeting in Accra, I realised the Christian soldier seemed not only to be running out of ammunition, but was also in serious danger of giving up the fight.

What could I do to arouse her fighting spirit? What weapon did I possess but the word of God? I recited some of the passages of scripture suitable for the occasion to try to rally her spirit. As in many instances in the past, I also pointed to my dream.

It began to dawn on me how difficult the office of the great prophets of old really was. When God in His grace reveals the future to His servants, He places them days, months or even years ahead of their generation. To convince others about an event that is to happen in the future is an uphill task, particularly when one considers the fact that the Devil never tires of sending his own prophets of doom to mingle with the crowd.

Before I left her that night, we knelt before her bed to pray. I took her Bible to look out for a passage to read before the prayer. Just as I got hold of it, it opened up at Isaiah Chapter 54. I decided to read it for the first time in my life:

> "Sing, O barren woman, you who never bore a child;
> burst into song, shout for joy, you who were never in labour;
> because more are the children of the desolate woman
> than of her who has a husband," says the LORD.

"Enlarge the place of your tent, stretch your tent curtains wide,
do not hold back; lengthen your cords, strengthen your stakes.
For you will spread out to the right and to the left;
Your descendants will dispossess nations
And settle in their desolate cities.
"Do not be afraid; you will not suffer shame.
Do not fear disgrace; you will not be humiliated.
You will forget the shame of your youth
And remember no more the reproach of your widowhood.
For your maker is your husband—
The LORD Almighty is his name—
The Holy One of Israel is your Redeemer;
he is called the God of all the earth.
The LORD will call you back
as if you were a wife deserted and distressed in spirit—
a wife who married young,
only to be rejected," says your God.
"For a brief moment I abandoned you,
but with deep compassion I will bring you back.
In a surge of anger I hid my face from you for a moment,
but with everlasting kindness I will have compassion on you,"
says the LORD your Redeemer.
"To me this is like the days of Noah, when I swore that the waters of
Noah would never again cover the earth.
So now I have sworn not to be angry with you,
Never to rebuke you again.
Though the mountains be shaken and the hills be removed,
Yet my unfailing love for you will not be shaken
nor my covenant of peace be removed,"
says the LORD, who has compassion on you.
"O afflicted city, lashed by storms and not comforted,
I will make your battlements of rubies,
Your gates of sparkling jewels, and all your walls of precious stones.
All your sons will be taught by the LORD,
and great will be your children's peace.
In righteousness you will be established;
Tyranny will be far from you; you will have nothing to fear.
Terror will be far removed; it will not come near you.

If anyone does attack you, it will not be my doing;
Whoever attacks you will surrender to you.
See, it is I who created the blacksmith who fans the coal into flames
and forges a weapon fit for its work.
And it is I who has created the destroyer to work havoc;
No weapon forged against you will prevail,
and you will refute every tongue that accuses you.
This is the heritage of the servants of the LORD,
And this is their vindication from me." (NIV)

That passage of scripture brought her out of the valley of despair and lifted her up to the hilltop of hope—not only for that night! From that day on, Isaiah 54 became her favourite chapter. Whenever despair seemed to overtake her, she turned to Isaiah 54; when her financial resources became scarce, Isaiah 54 offered her confidence of a better tomorrow; when others boasted about their stable marriages and their wonderful children, Grace countered with Isaiah 54.

♦ ♦ ♦

Towards the latter part of 1979 it became increasingly clear that Grace's relatives in Germany were desirous of fulfilling their promise to her. To underline their determination to help her settle in Germany they advised her to register for a course to study the German language at the Goethe Institute in Accra.

With my chance of studying in the Soviet Union shattered and the prospect of Grace making it to her relatives improving by the day, my interest began to shift to West Germany

West Germany, of course, was a more attractive alternative to the Soviet Union. Prior to my failed attempt to go to the Soviet Union, however, I had not considered it as an option. The most important reason for my attitude was the financial consideration. How could I pay for my ticket? How could I finance my studies? How could I sustain myself? This could change should my beloved sister-in-Christ make it there, I reasoned. Though she did not know what awaited her, she promised to do all she could to help me settle there as well the moment she got there.

With such considerations at the back of my mind, I decided to register together with her for the German language classes. Twice a week we attended lessons at the Goethe Institute. Our teacher was a German lady who was married to a Ghanaian national. She interested herself not only in the academic performance of her students, but also in issues like how her students got home after lessons. Indeed, during the whole time I was there, I never saw her drive home alone after classes. Instead she filled her VW Beetle with students who happened to live near the route along which she drove home.

We registered for a ten-week course. Apart from becoming acquainted with the German alphabet and some basic expressions such as 'good morning', 'good day', 'good night', 'what is your name?', 'how are you?' and so forth, the course did not advance me far in my attempt to learn the language.

I don't blame our teacher. Indeed, she was very dedicated in her effort to teach us her mother tongue. The true reason lay somewhere else.

Despite the trust I had in the Lord in regard to His promise, my mind was not free from anxiety. In the midst of a lecture, fear for the future would splash through my mind and for a while I was prevented from concentrating on what was being taught.

My time at the Goethe Institute boosted my determination to study in Germany even further. Our teacher did not restrict herself to only teaching us the language of Martin Luther, Goethe, Schiller—she also showed us films about her country.

'What a beautiful place to live in!' I said to myself when I saw the beautiful buildings and the tidy streets depicted in the films.

At the Goethe Institute I also received vital information regarding how a foreigner could study in Germany at that time. Most importantly, I learnt that tuition at the universities as well as other institutions of higher learning was free for everyone—including foreign students.

One had to pay for one's boarding, lodging, stationery, textbooks, however. But even on that issue, I was told, opportunities existed for one to apply for a scholarship. Another possible source of income for the student was by way of vacation jobs.

As part of my preparation towards a possible departure for Germany, I sought means to acquire a passport. Acquiring that document in Ghana in those days was a Herculean task. Without good contacts with people working at the Passport Office in Accra, it was almost impossible for ordinary citizens like me to own one.

Fortunately Grace had good contacts with a high-ranking staff member there. She had been issued one through his help. After she had discussed the matter with him, he eventually used his position to get me one as well.

◆   ◆   ◆

By the end of 1979 Grace's travel plans had reached an advanced stage. The plan was for her to accompany a much travelled businessman on one of his business trips to Rome. Whilst in Rome, she would stay in a hotel and wait for her sister-in-law. She would drive there to pick her up.

The whole cost involved in the journey—the fee for the Italian visa, the cost of the round ticket to Rome, the money to enable her to hang around in the ancient city for a few days, was borne by her relatives in Germany. Her relatives had made it clear to her that it was not advisable for her to travel on a German visa issued on their invitation.

At that time we couldn't understand the reason behind their thinking, but it became clear to me a few years later. With an official invitation she could not have overstayed her visit or seek political asylum without bringing her relatives into trouble with the immigration authorities

Grace finally left Ghana in February 1980. Almost the whole Kotobaabi Branch of the Open Bible Church was at the airport to see their beloved member off. Things went according to plan for her. After spending a few days in Rome her sister-in-law picked her up.

I was delighted to see her part of my dream come true. Her arrival in Germany strengthened my resolve to go there as well. I had no doubt in my mind that the Lord would fulfil my part of His promise.

Not long after her arrival I received a letter from her. I was delighted by it! She had after all not forgotten her promise to keep me in mind. I wrote a quick reply to her letter in which amongst other things I encouraged her to keep the faith.

Her first letter was followed a few days later by a second. This time she enclosed some pictures of herself. The pictures fascinated me—a few weeks in Europe had added more charm to the already attractive sister. One aspect of her pictures surprised me, however. Up until then we had held the notion that it was not fitting for a Christian woman to wear trousers. Whilst in Ghana, Grace had also held to that view. That only a few weeks in Europe had been enough to change her attitude in that regard made me nervous.

I became concerned for her. Would she be able to standup for her faith in the new environment? My concern was not without foundation. We had received regular reports regarding some citizens from the country who prior to their departure for Europe and North America were very deeply rooted in their

Christian faith but turned back on their faith on settling into their new environment.

I raised that issue in my next letter. She assured me she would not let the Lord down, particularly in view of all that He had done for her. On the issue of wearing trousers, she had chosen to adapt to the cold weather. So long as I had not experienced the weather myself, her argument did not counter all my reservations. It was when I got to Europe that my attitude changed for ever!

In her letters to me she did not mention specifically what she was doing for a living. On my part I did not find the need to ask questions in that direction. In line with the African custom where family members who are in the position to do so generally try to help other family members in need, I assumed her brother would take care of her—more so when I considered the effort he and his wife had invested to get her there.

Grace urged me in her letters to do all my best to get to Europe. She made it clear however that it would be a long time before she could be in the position herself to contribute financially to make that happen. Much as I would have liked to make it to Europe as soon as possible, my hand was bound financially.

I had an acquaintance who had good contact with a so-called 'connection man'. Such 'connection men' had made it their business to help so-called hustlers (people who were fleeing the harsh economic situation at home to try their fortunes in the rich industrial nations) acquire visas. Whether it was for visas to the US, Canada, Australia, or Western Europe, the 'connection men' were the first persons such hustlers contacted. The 'connection men' demanded substantial amounts depending on how attractive the end destination was.

My acquaintance talked to his friend. No problem! He could procure me a direct visa for West Germany. That would cost me about three thousand US dollars, the ticket included. If I was not in the position to pay that fee, I could make do with a visa for East Germany. From East Berlin I could then move on to West Germany. The fee was about seventy percent of that required for West Germany itself.

Even if they had demanded a hundred dollars, I would not have been able to afford it! Based on the exchange rate at that time, my monthly salary at the P&T external amounted to a few dollars. I did not give up my hope of making it to Europe one day, however.

The economic situation in Ghana meanwhile continued to deteriorate with each passing day. Thanks to my job at the P&T, I was managing to keep my head just above water.

A few months after her departure to Germany rumours began to spread to the fact that a certain gentleman who hailed from a town not far from Grace's hometown had performed the marriage rites on her.

Here I shall pause awhile to explain the issue of marriage rites within the Akan tradition to which both of us belong—for the benefit of readers not accustomed to our African culture. Traditionally the potential husband goes to seek the hand of the future wife from her family. After approval is given, the traditional marriage rites are performed. Basically this requires that the future husband pays an amount of money (usually affordable by the average person) to the family of the bride. In addition he presents the future wife as well as her family members with gifts. That is the basic step in marriage. In former times things ended there. Today some couples go a further step to register their marriages at the courts. Finally, Christians may choose to formally bring their marriages before the Lord in the form of a wedding. It should be emphasised that whatever one's social background or religious inclination, the Akan custom requires everyone to pass through the first stage of marriage.

Initially, I did not believe the story. Grace was so busy during the latter part of her preparation for West Germany that she could hardly have had the time to have gotten to know anyone. Shortly after the rumour concerning her marriage reached me, another story reached me to the effect that her alleged husband had even joined her.

Readers will please pardon me for my inclination to refer to the saying that 'behind every rumour is an element of truth!' I don't know the situation in regard to rumour-mongering in the society in which you might live, but one thing you can be assured of—rumour-mongering can be described as a kind of sport in the society I grew up in. Don't brush away such rumours when they reach your ears! Remember—behind every rumour is an element of truth, at least within our culture.

And so I decided not to brush aside the news or take it with a pinch of salt. But then, if it happened to be true, why had she kept it from me?

Well, I didn't have to wait for long, since a few weeks after the news first reached me, Grace wrote to inform me about the latest developments in her life.

Dan, her husband, she went on to explain, happened to be an old acquaintance of hers. Shortly before her departure from Ghana they met casually. Soon their friendship was rekindled. After a while she agreed to his offer of marriage and he had, in the meantime, performed the traditional marriage rites.

It was not surprising therefore that her brother offered to assist his brother-in-law in his effort to join his wife. Fortunately things worked favourably for them.

With the help of a 'connection man', he managed to obtain a transit visa for East Germany. He flew first to East Berlin. From there he moved on to West Berlin and finally Hamburg. She had in the meantime also moved to settle in Hamburg.

The first letter was followed shortly by a second one. In it Dan introduced himself formally to me. After his sixth form education, he had moved on to the University of Ghana at Legon where he had obtained a degree in economics.

With Grace married to him, I knew her attention would be divided. Truly, I could expect her to send me some gifts from time to time; but I should not expect a young couple who had just settled to build their family to go beyond that and offer substantial assistance. For the moment the prospects of my ever meeting her in Europe seemed to have gone with the wind.

Perplexing thoughts began to fill my mind. Not a few times I was tempted to doubt whether indeed the spirit of God was leading me. Couldn't the evil one have sent the dream to confuse me?

While not claiming to know how to read the mind of the Almighty God, I wondered whether He would allow the evil one to cross the plans of his children in such a manner. I had sacrificed the joy of family re-union in the village to spend my Christmas alone in order to become baptised. I had thereafter engaged in a fast in an attempt to draw closer to Him.

On the night I had the peculiar dream, I had not specifically prayed to God to see me to Europe. Instead I had only committed my future into His hands. I retired to bed that night not expecting anything. Then came the dream which showed the meeting between me and Grace on the streets of Europe. Would the Lord lead His children in that manner?

Gradually the dark clouds that had engulfed me began to dissipate. I began to see things objectively. I saw myself as the cause of the problem. Grace had not broken any promise. Indeed, she had from the very first day of our meeting made one thing clear to me—she was trusting God to lead her to her future husband. Why should I complain now that it had happened?

Neither could I also accuse God for breaking any promise. Yes, He had revealed the future events to me. Grace and I were to meet on the streets of Europe—no more. He didn't show her and myself exchanging rings at the altar as a married couple!

I better look on the bright side of things instead of grumble, I thought. With Grace already in Germany, fifty percent of the prophecy had been fulfilled! It was up to me to be obedient to God and faithfully trust Him to fulfil the rest of the prophecy.

Easier said than done! For a while the anxious thoughts continued to recur.

Dan wrote regularly. His letters were quite informative. He urged me to follow his example by obtaining a transit visa for East Germany. The moment I got to West Berlin, they would assist me to Hamburg. On the issue of studying there he only confirmed what I already knew from our German teacher.

Following on Dan's advice I decided to seek a transit visa for East Germany. Since I did not have the means to solicit the help of 'connection men' I decided to go to the embassy myself to try my luck.

Prior to that I embarked on a week of fasting and praying.

I still did not know where I would gather the necessary funds to purchase a plane ticket. My speculation was that the moment I was issued with a visa, I could get someone to grant me a loan.

After a week of fasting and prayer I headed for the East German consulate. Things were not as easy as I had imagined. I was asked to produce a substantial amount of hard currency before my application could be considered.

◆ ◆ ◆

Grace was gone; Dan had joined her; my interest in going to Germany had prevented me from giving the idea of going to the Soviet Union a second try; and now my attempt at the East German visa had also hit the rocks!

From time to time I saw the medical school bus transporting students from the university to the teaching hospital at Korle Bu, about ten kilometres away. Sometimes I saw some of my classmates at Mfantsipim on it. At times some of them saw me and waved heartily to me.

On other occasions I also came across some old mates, both from Oda and Mfantsipim on campus. One of them, on hearing my case, told me he had managed to change from Science to Agriculture and advised me to try the same. The latter field was quite attractive, he continued. After doing the first degree one stood the chance of gaining a scholarship to do further studies abroad, particularly in Australia or Canada. My mind was set, however—I wouldn't give in until I met Grace on the streets of Europe.

Still, every defeat plunged me into confusion, if only for a brief period. Though I continued to believe the leading of God in my life, on not a few occasions despair began to set in. One spell of anxious moments followed on another as the circumstances began to overwhelm me.

I read through the Bible, often, dwelling on passages that urge the Christian not to give up when faced with trying situations—such as:

> Count it all joy, my brethren, when you meet various trials, for you know that the testing of your faith produces steadfastness. And let steadfastness have its full effect, that you may be perfect and complete, lacking in nothing.—James 1: 2-4 (RSV)

Fasting became one of my best friends. It served two purposes. It helped me to save money and food, for both money and food were scarce in those days. More importantly, it sustained me in my fight with despair. In the fasting state my brain was spared the anxious thoughts that seemed to drive me mad.

God in His mercy placed other resources at my disposal. In particular, a Bible programme from the Oral Roberts Ministry in the US, shown every Sunday evening on national TV at that time, was a source of strength.

I took the keynote to the preaching of the renowned evangelist—'Something Good is Going to Happen to You!'—as a personal message from the Lord to me. I was confident something good would really happen to me. I beseeched the Lord to give me strength as I waited for that to happen.

13

Agege, here we come

Just as I was contemplating my next move, I bumped into Yaw, the old acquaintance with the extraordinary talent in painting.

The last time I met him at Kwadwo's hometown he was also doing his Sixth Form. At that time he spoke about his desire to study architecture at the University of Science and Technology in Kumasi, which is Ghana's second largest city.

'What are you doing on the streets of Accra!' I inquired after the initial exchange of greetings.

'I'm on my way to Agege!' (Agege is a suburb of Lagos—it came to stand for Nigeria for Ghanaians.)

'Agege!' I exclaimed, not believing my ears.

'You've heard me right, boy! I am on my way to Agege!'

'What for?'

'I'm going there to work to buy my ticket for the States!'

'For the US?'

'Yes, sir!'

'You have very big plans, boy!'

'Well, I want to move to the States to study architecture!'

'Do you know anyone there?'

'Yes indeed. My senior brother is a resident there. As a matter of fact he promised to get me the visa and send me a ticket! I've been waiting months for him to fulfil his promise—in vain. You know these big brothers and sisters! The moment they make it in life they forget everyone else! Well, I have decided to take my destiny into my own hands rather than wait on him. Who knows when he will make good his promise? By then I may be too old to study.'

'Do you really mean it?'

'Hey, don't you believe me? I am one hundred percent decided; as a friend of mine used to say: *eyes are red when things are bad.*'

'But where will you stay? Do you know anyone there?'

'Oh yes. I have an address in Lagos where several young men from our village are currently residing.'

'Indeed?'

'Yes. From my information it happens to be a construction site!'

'A construction site?'

'Yes, it happens to be a building still under construction.'

'How did they come to live there?'

'The owner of that building, an elderly woman, is a citizen of Nigeria and used to reside in our village. By chance a couple of young men from the village who happened to be stranded in Lagos bumped into her on the streets of the large city. When she learnt about their situation she decided to allow them to live in the half-completed building she was erecting for the purpose of renting out later. In the meantime the number of people living there, the majority of whom hail from our village, have increased considerably.'

Yaw's friends were not the only Ghanaians living in Nigeria at that time. Nigeria then was a great attraction, not only for Ghanaians but also nationals from the whole of the West African region. The reason was not difficult to fathom. The economy of the oil rich nation had received a big boost resulting from the sharp rise in the price of crude oil following on the oil crisis of 1979. The country was at that time literally swimming in petro-dollars. The favourable economic climate had rejuvenated the labour market. Several hands were needed to work on the countless building and constructing projects going on throughout the large country. The buoyant economy had also led the federal government to introduce free education for all. Several new schools had been established to cope with the increased number of pupils enrolling to go to school. The huge demand for teachers that had arisen as a result of that policy could not be satisfied by local staff alone. Ghana and Nigeria, being former English colonies, had a similar educational structure. Teachers from Ghana were thus highly welcomed in Nigeria. News soon spread to Ghana in this regard. Several Ghanaians left to take up appointments in the comparatively wealthy Nigeria.

I saw my chance! I would travel with Yaw to Lagos to work and earn money for my ticket to Germany. I stood a good chance of being employed as a teacher, I thought, and should that hope fail to materialise, I would be prepared to do any reasonable job that would help me achieve my goal of studying in Germany.

At the time of our meeting Yaw was already sitting on his packed luggage; his departure was imminent and only a matter of days away. But there was a stumbling block that needed to be overcome on my part—I didn't have the financial resources to enable me to pay for the journey! Yaw, while desirous to travel with me, could not assist me financially since he had just enough money to pay for his journey. (He was prepared to delay his journey only a few days for fear of spending the money at his disposal in Accra!)

So who could help me out at such short notice?

That evening I talked to Aduama, then my roommate at Legon, about my problem.

'I wish I could help you out myself!' he began after hearing my story. 'You are aware, however, how I am hard-pressed with money myself!'

Just as I was considering who to appeal to next, my roommate turned to me and said: 'Your situation will not leave me in peace!'

'That is very kind of you! I know you would readily help if you could.'

'Well, I have an idea. Give me up till tomorrow. I will travel to Accra to consult my sister on the matter. She is a trader and quite wealthy—she may be willing to help.'

'That would be great!' I replied.

As I lay on my bed that night I prayed to the Lord to use my roommate's sister to help me out of the situation.

As promised, Aduama left campus after lectures the next day to consult his sister on my behalf. I prayed and hoped that something good would come out of the meeting for up till then I had not been able to think of anyone who could help me out at such short notice. Finally, after he had been away for some time, the key to our room was turned and my roommate stepped into the room. His face was wreathed in smiles.

'How was it?' I asked as my heartbeat quickened.

'Well, I knew my sister very well to know she would help!' he beamed. 'Indeed, she has agreed to lend you the amount you need for the journey.'

'Thank you Jesus!' I exclaimed. 'I will repay her as soon as I find work.'

'You don't have to repay her by way of money!'

'In what form then?'

'She wants you to use the money she lends you to purchase her some pieces of java (cloth).'

'Really?'

'Yes, that is her condition for granting you the loan. As you are aware, these days one can hardly come across such items in the country. Even when one does, they attract very high prices. The situation in Nigeria is reported to be quite the opposite—the supply is said to overwhelm demand.'

'But it might take some time before I find a reliable person who will be willing to deliver the items to her. I could send them by mail, but where is the guarantee that they will reach her? Even if they do, they could attract considerable import duty.'

'You don't have to worry about time. She is prepared to wait—until the favourable moment arrives.'

Aduama left the next day to collect the amount I had requested—enough to pay for my fare and sustain me in my new environment for about a week.

And so the stage was set for the journey to Nigeria. Apart from my roommate, her sister and a couple of Yaw's relatives, no one else knew about my impending adventure into the unknown.

We woke up very early in the morning of Monday December 1, 1980. (We had arranged for Yaw to spend the night with us.) After we had said a short prayer with Aduama, each of us took a small handbag containing a few personal effects and got ready to go. Before I said the final goodbye to Aduamah, I entrusted him with my key and begged him to return it to the university authorities in case I did not return after about a week.

We joined a *tro-tro* from Legon to the Central Lorry Station in Accra, reaching there around 3:00 a.m.

The scene that confronted us on our arrival gave me food for thought. Even in those very early hours of the day dozens of would-be travellers to Nigeria had already queued up for their turn to board a vehicle that would take them to their destination. The majority of those present, like Yaw and myself, were young men and women in their early and mid-twenties. Shortly after we had joined the queue a young man standing a few metres ahead of us remarked: 'Hey friends, what will happen to the country when all the young adult citizens follow our example and leave the country?'

'This is not the time for such considerations,' someone in the line replied.

'I agree with you, friend,' a third person joined in. 'Look at me! See how lean I have grown. That was not how I used to be. Over the years I have witnessed successive governments come and go. "You tighten your belts a short while; things will soon change for the better!" Now I am squeezed up not only at the waist, but my whole body has become a pack of bones!'

Almost everyone present burst into laughter.

After standing in the queue for about half an hour, it finally came to our turn. We were to travel in a nine-seater Peugeot campervan. It was about a quarter past four when our driver finally set his car in motion.

Nigeria lies about 500 kilometres to the east of Ghana. Between the two former British colonies lie Togo and Benin, two comparatively small countries, both former French colonies.

After about one and a half hours drive we reached the Ghana-Togo border, about 200 kilometres away from Accra. The situation at the border was typical of that prevailing along the frontiers of several other African countries—a legacy of the African colonial past. The colonial masters drew borders to create countries (artificial) without any consideration to the ethnicity of the local population. The border between Ghana is cut between the Ewes who live there. The whole of Togo used to be a German colony. After World War I Togo was divided between the victorious England and France. The English added their part to the neighbouring Gold Coast which was their colony. The rest of Togo is what remains to this day.

After we had gone through immigration procedure on both sides of the frontier, our driver urged everyone to scramble on board so that we could continue our journey.

'Why the rush?' one of us asked.

'I want to get out of here before it approaches midday.'

'Why?' one of us inquired.

'That is the time when Eyadema, the long-ruling President of Togo, leaves the seat of government to return to his private residence for lunch. Long before his convoy sets off, all major roads in the vicinity of his travel route, including the main coastal road on which we are travelling, are closed to all traffic! Sometimes they remain closed for a considerable period of time.'

'That cannot be true!' someone remarked.

'That is the whole truth! The ritual is repeated every day the president works at his office! I have always taken pains to prevent having to go through an experience like that; on one occasion, however, I was overtaken by events and had to delay my journey several minutes.'

Fortunately there were a couple of hours before us and the President's lunch and so we managed to put Lome behind us without any difficulty.

After about an hour's drive we got to the checkpoint on the Togo-Benin border. It took us about another forty-five minutes to get through the immigration formalities of both sides of the frontier.

One aspect of Cotonou, the capital of Benin, was unique to all the other cities I had so far visited—there were just as many motor-bikes on the streets as normal vehicles (if not even more).

'There seems to be a competition between motor cyclists and normal automobiles here!' one of the passengers observed.

'Be careful whenever you happen to be driving here,' our driver cautioned. 'Over here the motor-bikes always have the right of way! In case of accident drivers of normal vehicles are blamed—no matter who in reality was at fault.'

About twelve hours after the onset of our journey we finally reached the Benin-Nigeria border. Several dozens of vehicles were already lined up on the border when we got there. The queue of vehicles inched forward at a very slow pace as the immigration authorities took considerable time to go about their duty.

The greatest desire of everyone on the van was that we got to our destination before darkness fell. The city of Lagos, according to stories reaching us back home in Ghana, happened to be an unsafe place, even for those acquainted with it. According to such reports the city was literally infested in many places with armed gangs who had little mercy for their poor victims. The situation was worse at night. Life was also said to be unsafe for pedestrians. Vehicles were said to travel at high speed even in the city, putting pedestrians at risk of being knocked down.

Unease was written all over our faces as it approached six in the evening and our vehicle was still metres away from the pass control.

Whoever lives in the tropics where the length of day almost equals that of the night will tell you the transition from day to night is very short indeed. Shortly after six in the evening it suddenly turns dark.

It was about 6 .30 p.m. when we finally put the immigration procedure behind us and embarked on the last leg of our journey. We still needed to drive about 100 kilometres to reach Lagos.

One positive surprise awaited us. Unlike the roads we had travelled along so far, this was a modern dual-carriage road. If the nature of this road was anything to go by, I told myself, Nigeria had surely left her sister countries on the West African coast far behind in the area of development.

After about an hour's drive we got to the outskirts of Lagos. Back at home in Ghana we had heard about the notorious traffic jams that plagued that city. I didn't have any idea of the severity of the situation until we approached its outskirts. The roads were jammed everywhere with cars of all brands, a good proportion of them being new models.

'Oil talks!' one of us exclaimed after seeing all the modern vehicles on the road.

Fortunately for Yaw and myself, we didn't have to travel far to the centre of the city. Yaw's friends had instructed him to make his way to a suburb at the outskirts of the city known as Mile 2, about three kilometres from the city centre.

We said goodbye to our co-travellers. Apart from a couple of them the majority were, like us, travelling to Nigeria for the first time. Did they all reach their destinations safely? Did they fulfil their hopes to make use of their stay there to earn money and return as soon as possible to Ghana to build their respective futures?

A very noisy spectacle confronted us as we stepped on the streets of Lagos. Shouts of 'Alaba, Alaba, Alaba *s-t-r-a-i-g-h-t!*' assailed our ears.

"Ojodi, Ojodi, Ojodi, last person!'

'Ajengule, Ajengule, Ajengule, come on board!' erupted from the throats of the assistants of the *tro-tro* drivers to fill the already noisy evening atmosphere.

To aggravate the situation, the drivers of the minibuses blew their horns incessantly and for no apparently reason. Several such vehicles, for the most part Nissan, Toyota and VW minibuses, were lined up in a large open place waiting for their turn to transport passengers. The scene was quite overwhelming, not that we were not used to such a situation back home in Ghana, but since the scale and the ferocity we were witnessing was in another league!

The word *Ajengule* struck Yaw.

'Come on friend!' he urged me. 'My friends asked me to join a vehicle heading for Ajengule.'

We hurried towards the vehicle a few metres ahead of us.

'Ajengule, Ajengule, Ajengule last person!' the driver's mate continued to scream.

'We are two!' Yaw shouted as we approached the van.

'Come on board!' the assistant, barely sixteen years old, signalled to us.

We clambered into the vehicle.

'*Ogah*, please push a little, I beg you!' the boy pleaded with a passenger in his mid-thirties to create some space for me to sit.

'Where do I push to, j-o-o-h?' he protested, not without justification for there was no empty seat left on the row he occupied.

'Please Oga, I beg?' the assistant persisted.

The traveller pushed further, reluctantly. The space so created was barely enough to seat a little child. I squeezed myself there. Hardly had my buttocks touched the seat than the order: 'Oya jale!' (Get going, friend!) issued from the throat of the assistant.

Soon the Toyota minibus was speeding away.

'You count the stops with me,' Yaw urged me. 'We are to get down on the fourth.' After we had travelled on the vehicle for about twenty minutes, we got down as requested.

After we had asked our way a couple of times we were finally directed to our destination. Pandemonium broke loose in the house when the news of our arrival became known. Yaw had sent a message through one of them who arrived about four weeks earlier to announce his intention to join them there. Since telephone links between the two countries was underdeveloped at that time, and also since no telephone link existed yet in the building, none of them knew he would arrive that evening. From all over the place, the residents streamed to the hall at the ground floor where we were. I counted no less than twenty heads.

A considerable proportion of the young male population of the village appeared to be assembled at the construction site! Apart from a few faces I had seen on my visit to Kwadwo, the majority of them were unfamiliar to me.

We were heartily welcomed. Within minutes of our arrival dinner was served to the new arrivals.

Throughout the greater part of the evening Yaw was milked empty of news, anxious co-inhabitants of his village wanting to know how relatives back home in Ghana were faring.

Yaw's friends were right to use the term 'construction site' to describe where they were. Only the ground floor and the first storey of what was to be a four-story building were halfway complete. There was no running water there. A dug well actually inside the house provided the inhabitants as well as the construction workers with water. The toilet facilities were not yet in place…a dug-in lavatory/toilet served us. The kitchen was not completed either. We made use of kerosene stoves to do our cooking. There were enough rooms to occupy us. We slept in groups of about five in rooms which were yet to be fitted with doors.

The unwritten constitution at the construction site could be fittingly summed up as 'each one for himself and God for us all Put in a different way—no form of laziness; no form of dependence on others, no form of parasiting on others was tolerated there.

Put in the nutshell—each resident was expected to work hard to earn money to support himself.

We earned our income through performing casual jobs on building sites. As I mentioned earlier, thanks to the booming economy, several construction projects—from the public as well as the private sector—were underway.

The larger projects were generally executed by well established construction firms from within and outside the country. They relied on workers they had regularly employed. Minor projects such as putting up new private homes or renovating old ones were on the other hand carried out by smaller firms or even by what could be called one-man contractors. Few of the small firms boasted of sophisticated machinery such as earth-moving machines, cranes, concrete mixtures, etc. Instead they relied mainly on manual labour. Hardly any of them had any regular worker on their payroll. Instead they made use of casual workers they hired on a day-to-day or in some instances on a week-to-week basis. It was to such minor firms that we looked for working opportunities.

With the exception of Sundays we left home early in the morning in small groups of three or four. Each carried a small polythene bag containing the work suite. We set out to visit one after the other, some of the several construction sites in the vicinity. When we got to a site and there was demand for workers that day, they asked for the number they required to begin work immediately. Sometimes there was work for everyone. Otherwise the unlucky ones tried their luck at the next available site. On some days luck could delay coming one's way—the oppo-rtunity to work often came at a late hour. In a situation like that one could be asked to work for a reduced wage, or if there was still the need, one was asked to report the next day. On some rare occasions one failed to find a job entirely on a particular day.

◆　　◆　　◆

The work we performed at the construction sites was tough, back-breaking work. As I mentioned, hardly any of the small building firms boasted of machinery such as digger excavators, concrete mixtures, cranes for conveying building material from one floor to the other. As a result, almost every stage of the work—concrete mixing, block-cutting, transporting building material from one point to the other—was carried out manually.

The day's work usually began with concrete mixing duty. The fine sand as well as the gravel needed was usually conveyed by special trucks to the site a day or two before the working day. As a first step the construction assistant had to help convey the quantity of cement that would be needed for the day's work to the building site. When we were lucky, we only needed to unload the cement from a truck that had pulled up at the site. That was the exception, though; usually the cement was kept in storehouses that the contractors had rented in the vicinity. Usually it involved walking a few metres; there were times, though, when the storehouse was located several metres from the construction site. We transported the bags of cement, each weighing about twenty kilograms, on our heads. Each was expected to transport one bag at a time, though some managed to carry two at a time!

The next stage usually involved filling a large container with enough water that would be needed for the day's work. In case there was a dug-in well in the vicinity, we were required to collect the water ourselves, using large plastic or metal buckets. There is no need to mention the fact that we carried the load on our heads. In the rare instances when there was no well around, the contractors bought their water from special firms that delivered the water in special tankers.

After we had gathered sufficient material we moved on to the construction work proper. With the help of shovels we mixed sand and cement together. If the material were needed for plastering the walls or the floors, water was added to it at that stage to help achieve the required consistency. If, on the other hand, the material was needed for laying the foundation of the building or for use in a building that needed to withstand a certain degree of resistance without giving in, gravel was added to the sand-cement mixture before water was applied to it.

It was every construction assistant's wish to be employed on a building site that had not progressed beyond the stage of the ground floor. As was to be expected, we didn't always get what we wished for. Instead we found jobs on a site that had got to the second, third or even a higher floor. Whatever the height of the building, the construction assistant was required to carry material on his head from the mixing sites below to the masons on the respective floor! Fortunately, it seems, my left ankle joint realised how much I depended on the money I earned from the building sites to survive in the new environment! Indeed, for the time being it decided to bear with me for a while and not go on strike!

At the end of each working day one's employer informed one whether one's services would be needed the next day or not. If not, the search for work was resumed the next day. When luck was on one's side, one could spend a whole week or even several weeks working on the same site.

In the course of time word spread to the contractors in the vicinity concerning several strong and dutiful young men from Ghana residing in a semi-completed house around the corner who provided reliable services at building sites. (As is usually the case, the local residents shunned the jobs we were desperate for.) In due time contractors in dire need of workers came to us, instead of the other way round.

The wage for working from around 8 a.m. to about 5 p.m. on the construction site was five Naira. Based on the exchange rate at that time, this was equivalent to about five US dollars. It was normally handed out at the end of each day's work.

Those of our friends who had been there longer than ourselves advised us to insist on outright payment at the end of each working day. Some employers, they warned us, became reluctant to hand out the money the moment it added up to a considerable amount. They cited several instances in the past when some employers had vanished before they could pay several hundreds of dollars due to their workers.

Not only Yaw and myself had big future plans. Indeed, if we lacked anything there, it wasn't big plans for the future! Nigeria was considered only as a transition by everyone I met there. The main reason we were there was to work to earn money that could help each one of us fulfil a cherished goal. Someone wanted to spend a couple of years there to acquire suitable machinery to set up a vehicle repair shop back home; another was there to procure a lumber machine; yet another inhabitant had plans to purchase an electric generator to set up an entertainment centre in the village, and so forth. As a result of our cherished goals, each one of us made great efforts to spend as little as possible from our earnings. The plan was to live on a day's wage every week and save the rest of the week's earnings for the future. We were not required to pay for living there—money was needed only for food and hygienic items: tooth paste, soap, cream, etc.

Everyone prayed for good health to enable him go out everyday to look for work. Although born into the African tradition where solidarity for one another is a widespread practice, the extraordinary situation at the construction site led us to abandon this virtue. It was only in extreme situations when one fell sick and could not work several days that one could count on the mercy of the rest. Even then, one was expected to exhaust one's savings first before one could expect help. This attitude was adopted to prevent others taking advantage of others. As I mentioned earlier on, everyone there had his own big plan for the future. We didn't want to tolerate others who would hide their money and seek to live on the sweat of others.

I regarded the construction work as a means to an end. Ultimately my goal was to find employment as a pupil teacher. With my three passes at A-Level my chances were not bad. Several Ghanaian teachers, including Kwadwo (he arrived in Nigeria about a year before me) were teaching in various schools in Lagos. Initially I attempted to find work as a pupil teacher in Lagos. I was unsuccessful. Most of the vacancies there, I learnt, had already been filled—mostly by Ghanaians.

A few weeks after my arrival in Lagos I came across a young man who happened to be a resident of Amantia. He told me he was living together with several young men and women from mother's hometown in a factory building not far away from where I was. Later I visited them. There I met no less than twenty residents of the village. Most of them were employed in the factory as factory-hands. The owner of the factory allowed them to live in a makeshift hut erected on the grounds of the factory.

Whilst there I learnt about another colony, also consisting solely of residents of Amantia, in Shagamu, a town about 80 kilometres to the north-west of Lagos.

That was good news for me. During my fruitless search for a teaching appointment in Lagos, I was advised to try my luck in Ogun State, Lagos's immediate neighbour to the north-west. I had planned to visit Abeokuta, the state capital, after the Christmas recess to make the necessary enquiries. Shagamu happened to be part of Ogun state and located a few kilometres from Abeokuta.

I made up my mind therefore to visit the colony in Shagamu at the beginning of January. Whilst there I would call on the schools there to explore the opportunity to work as a teacher.

Christmas 1980 was celebrated under the humble setting of the construction site.

I left Lagos as planned at the beginning of January 1981 for Shagamu. I found the colony from Amantia without difficulty. They welcomed me warmly into their midst. A few dozen young residents of Amantia lived there. They were literally crammed into a small makeshift wooden hut. I had money that could sustain me for a couple of weeks. It enabled me to concentrate my energies in the search for work as a teacher without the need to engage in casual jobs as a means of survival.

Shagamu had a population of about 80 000 people. There were several first and second cycle schools there. I went from one school to another and spoke to the headteachers about the prospects of gaining employment in their respective schools. After consulting about half a dozen of them, the headmaster of a second cycle school expressed the desire to sign me on. He gave me a letter of recommendation and asked me to forward it together with my certificates to the District Education Office at Abeokuta. I did as requested. After a short interview I was issued an appointment letter.

In the middle of January 1981 I assumed my duty as a junior teacher at the second cycle school called Shagamu Muslim High School. I was placed on a salary of about 100 Naira per month.

A Christian teaching at a Muslim High School! One might wonder why. Well, apart from its name, it was in fact secular. Originally a private school owned by a rich Muslim businessman, it had been taken over by the state a few years prior to my arrival there. At that time a nation-wide policy of free education for all was introduced. As part of the take-over arrangement, the former proprietor insisted that the school be allowed to maintain its name—and the state agreed.

Muslim High School was a good example of how people of different religious persuasions could learn and work peacefully side by side. The great majority of the pupils as well as the teaching staff shared the Muslim faith. Yet hardly any conflict arose on the basis of faith.

The teaching staff was international in constitution. About half were Nigerians. Of the remainder, around eighty percent came from Ghana. Nationals from India and Pakistan made up the rest. At the time I joined the staff, the headmaster was a Nigerian. Shortly before my departure he went on retirement—and he was replaced with a female expatriate from Pakistan.

I was assigned the responsibility of teaching general science in Forms One and Two. Though I soon developed a keen interest for my job, I did not allow that to distract my attention from my ultimate goal. I was determined to make my stay in Nigeria as short as possible. My plan was not to stay beyond a period of twelve months. Nigeria's currency at that time carried considerable weight; twelve months would be enough to enable me purchase my air-ticket.

Whilst in Shagamu, I worshipped with the Assemblies of God. I was warmly welcomed by the brethren there and soon felt much at home with them.

True to my calculation, by the end of October 1981 I had saved enough money for the ticket. My plan was to leave Africa by February 1982. Man proposes, but God disposes, so the saying goes! That saying would soon become a practical reality in my life.

One night in November I had a dream. In it I saw father at a cemetery, taking part in a burial ceremony of someone. I began to wonder on waking up what that could mean.. Throughout that day I pondered over the dream.

A few days later I was back from school and relaxing in front of my apartment house when I saw a young citizen of Amantia approaching the house; I knew him to be part of the settlement colony in Lagos.

'What are you doing here?' I inquired even before he reached me.

'I have come to visit you!' was his reply.

He who has lived in Africa before knows that unannounced visits by relatives, friends and acquaintances are nothing unusual. In line with that thinking I did not expect anything unusual from him. After I had offered him water to drink in line with our Akan tradition, I asked him to let me know why he had travelled from Lagos to see me. He hesitated for a while, something which made me uneasy.

'Please let me know why you are here!' I urged.

'I wish I were carrying some good news for you,' he began. 'I am sorry, though, for that is not the case!'

'Tell me—what has happened?'

'Well, someone arrived at the colony yesterday from Amantia. The bad news is that your eldest brother, Ofosu-Gyamfi, has passed away!'

At the mention of my brother's name my heart begun to accelerate. The last three words sent it beating even faster.

'What happened?'

'We do not know exactly. The messenger could only say that he died after a short illness.'

'Unbelievable!' I screamed, unable to control my emotions.

The visitor from Lagos did his best to console me. He couldn't stay for long, however. He needed to return to Lagos to pursue an important assignment.

Soon I was alone to fight with my emotions. My thoughts went to the young widow he had left behind as well as her five young children, the youngest of whom was barely six months old.

I asked myself, what could have happened so suddenly to end Ofosu's life at the young age of 38 years?

At the time the news reached me, he had already been buried. In line with our culture, final funeral rites still needed to be performed for him. This was scheduled between Christmas and the New Year.

What was to be done?

So long as I was in Nigeria, not very far from home, there was no way I could stay away from this very important family meeting. Failure to attend would have incurred the displeasure of the entire family, none of whom was aware of my real intentions for going to Nigeria in the first place.

I left for Ghana shortly before Christmas 1981 to pay my final respects to my late brother. This time I decided to go by air—the first time in my life I travelled on an aeroplane. The first thing I did when I got to Accra was to fulfil my part of the agreement with Aduamah's sister. I gave her pieces of clothes worth about double the amount of money lent to me.

Finally I set out on the approximately 250-kilometre journey to Amantia where the ceremony was to take place. It was a great family re-union and offered me the opportunity to meet the whole extended family. By virtue of my stay in Nigeria, I turned out to be ofi mmense help to the extended family in regard to the financial burden they had to carry as a result of the death of our member. The Naira was at that time strong against the Cedi, our local currency.

On exchanging a few hundred Nairas, I received enough local currency to meet all the expenses incurred regarding the death, burial and funeral of my departed brother.

14

Plans almost hijacked

I left the village a few days prior to New Year's Eve and returned to Accra to prepare for my return journey to Nigeria. Schools were to re-open in the first week of January.

Then came New Year's Eve 1981! I had gone to the city to get certain things done when suddenly news began to spread to the effect that the military were in the process of staging a coup d'etat. It turned out to be no unfounded rumour, for the sound of gunfire could soon be heard from some parts of the city. I took the next available taxi and hurried home. On reaching home I was greeted by the sound of military music emerging from National Radio.

Shortly afterwards Flight Lt. J. J. Rawlings came on air to announce the overthrow of the ruling government.

'One more time!' was my first reaction to the news. I was saddened beyond measure. I wondered how the country could possibly make headway under such unstable conditions. Indeed, the coup leader was not new on the Ghanaian political scene. About two years prior to the present military takeover he had returned power to the civilian government he was now overthrowing. He staged his first coup to overthrow a military regime that had ruled the country for over seven years. At that time he ruled the country only for a few months.

Much as I was against the forceful takeover, I was at the moment too preoccupied with my own personal well-being to be bothered much by matters concerning the nation as a whole. What influence, after all, did I wield to alter the situation?

I could only hope that the new developments would not disrupt my plans, to enable me leave the country in time to be at my post in Shagamu.

Soon it would dawn on me that I had made my plans without taking the strategies of the coup-makers into consideration. Not long after I arrived home, an announcement was carried on the air announcing the sealing offof all our national frontiers—land, sea and air!

Initially that did not bother me much. Having lived to witness several coup d'etats—both successful and unsuccessful ones—I was aware of one of the very first measures adopted by all the coup-makers—to seal offall entry and departure points in the country. Based on past experience, I reckoned with a re-opening of the borders after about three days.

Another announcement followed on the heels of the first to dampen my optimism. 'Anyone wishing to travel out of the country will require a special exit permit. For the moment these permits will be issued only at the National Sports Stadium in Accra!'

For the moment I thought I was not hearing properly. No, I did, for the same text was repeated several times on National Radio!

January 1st being a National Holiday, all offices were closed. I left home early on January 2nd to apply for the exit permit. The scene that confronted me when I approached the vicinity of the national stadium brought me almost to the point of tears. Tens of thousands of would-be travellers had assembled in the morning sun. They had lined up in several queues leading to the various gates of the Stadium. Some of them stretched back several hundred metres, winding and winding as they progressed along the alleys bordering on the traffic ways.

The coup could not have come at a worse time for the majority of nationals living outside the country, in particular Nigeria, who had travelled home to celebrate Christmas.

Without exaggeration, something in the neighbourhood of two hundred thousand people had already gathered before the stadium when I got there. Initially it was thought the idea of the exit permit was to prevent the working force from leaving the country. As it turned out, however, that was not the case. Rather, it was introduced to prevent the leading figures of the deposed regime from leaving the country. It threatened to jeopardize my plans for the future, however.

The permits were issued at a snail's pace. On the first day I stood in the tropical heat for hours, only to return home in bitter disappointment. Having joined the queue about five hundred metres from the stadium gate, I could move only a few metres forward!

The second day was no better than the first. Come the third day and there was still no progress in acquiring the permit that would allow me to leave the country.

I was filled with anger mixed with despair. Judging from the rate at which the permits were being issued, I realised it could take several weeks before I could obtain the permit. That could surely lead to the termination of my appointment in Shagamu.

I began to shiver! Would the coup shatter my hope of ever making it to Europe to study medicine once and for all?

I prayed to God for a way out. As in many instances in the past, I drew inspiration from the fateful dream. I would meet Grace in Europe one day, come what may, I assured myself.

On the fourth day I returned home as usual without the important document.

Ransford met me at the door. Though a soldier himself, he had been infuriated by the coup from the word go. Since then he had not stopped to heap insults at his colleagues for, in his own words, plunging the country into chaos.

'Did you get the permit?' he inquired

'Negative!' I replied.

'Disgusting, totally disgusting! Why should they cause such inconvenience to ordinary citizens like you?'

'Well, you better write to your own people!'

'What's driving me even more crazy are the rumours spreading in town. Should they turn out to be true, it will make a mockery of all the military have avowed to do, check bribery and corruption as well as bring accountability and transparency into government!'

'What rumours?'

'Well, rumours have it that travellers without the exit permits you have spent four days in vain to acquire are being allowed to cross the border at Aflao after being made to pay substantial amounts of money as a bribe!'

'That cannot be true!'

'Well, as I said, they are only rumours. I have reasons to believe them, however. I can imagine some of the border guards recognising in the present situation their chance to make some money!'

Initially I found it difficult to believe what I was hearing. This was particularly so when I considered the brutal force the soldiers in Accra were applying against the so-called enemies of the revolution—former ministers, members of parliament, high ranking civil servants, etc., suspected of corruption as well as ordinary traders accused of inflating the prices of their goods.

The experience I had made trying to acquire the permit led me to heed Ransford's advice to travel to the border and find out the truth for myself. Because of the uncertainty in regard to the substance of the rumour, I took only my vital documents as well as a small bag containing a few personal belongings.

Behind every rumour is an element of truth! Not long after I stepped out of the vehicle that drove me to the Ghana side of the border, a young man, about my age, approached me.

'Excuse me, please,' he began. 'Do you want to cross?'
'Yes—can you help?'
He looked around him to make sure no one was near us.
'Yes. Not for free, though.'
'How much?'
'100 Naira.'
'That is too much! Won't you accept fifty?'
'No bargaining is allowed, sir!'
'Please!'
'No. They won't accept anything less!'
'Who?'
'The border guards, on both sides. They share the lion's share of what we earn among themselves. We, the go-betweens, receive only a small portion.'

Realising his mind was fixed, I decided not to waste time but to consent. He then went on to give me a short briefing on how the 'escape' along the 'green frontier' was to be executed! For readers not conversant with the situation on the Ghana-Togo border at that particular frontier, I shall offer a brief description. The frontier passes through the two coastal towns, Aflao, on the Ghana side, and Lome, on the Togo side. At many places, the two towns can hardly be separated from each other—particularly by the stranger to the place. To show some symbolism, border guards from both sides have been posted between the buildings at some points where the two cities converge.

The plan was this: in order not to attract attention, I should appear like any of the young men on the streets. Some were dressed in worn-out T-shirts over equally worn-out jeans, shorts or trousers. To protect their bare feet from the streets heated by the scorching sun, many wore home or beach sandals made of plastic, popularly known locally as *charley-wate* ('let's get going friend').

Towards that end, he led me away from the main street, and to an area of the town which, judging from the nature of the buildings, was inhabited by people of the lower income bracket. Hidden from all sides by the buildings, he asked me to take off my shirt and the pair of shoes I was wearing. Next, he helped me to roll up my trousers to the level of the knee.

'That is great! You follow me,' he said.

I walked barefooted alongside him over a distance of about two hundred metres, my belongings in my hands.

Finally he turned to me and said: 'We are almost there. Do exactly what I tell you, okay?'

'Alright.!' I replied, excited beyond measure.

Just as we walked past a building, I saw to my surprise, a border guard sitting under a coconut tree a few metres ahead of us. He held his gun firmly in his hands. A few metres from where he kept his post, several children were enjoying a game of football on an open field on the Ghana side. Form time to time one of them would run from Ghana to Togo to pick up the ball! The children seemed quite unconcerned by the presence of the guards there. That was the situation the officers took advantage of. The moment we got there the go-between began: 'I have brought a customer.'

'Has he paid?'

'Not yet.'

'Gentleman, your money, please!'

I handed the officer the 100 Nairas.

'You take this ball,' he said and handed me a large plastic ball that happened to be lying beneath his seat.

Next he turned to his co-worker.

'You move ahead a few metres into Togo with his belongings.'

He did as requested.

He turned to me again:

'You are good at the game of football, aren't you?'

'I used to be a goalkeeper of the Mpintimpi Youth Team!' I replied.

'Mpi—what?' he asked, a surprise in his face.

'Mpintimpi,' I repeated.

'Where on earth is that place?'

'It is a small village not far from Nkawkaw.'

'My goodness! What a peculiar name! Now to business. Give the ball a kick into Togo territory, and run after it.'

Moments later the ball was flying in the air.

'Run and fetch it boy!' he shouted to me.

'I will do!' I shouted back.

Soon I was running into Togo, leaving my turbulent native Ghana behind me. Quickly I put on the rest of my clothes as well as my shoes.

Moments later I was walking briskly on the streets of Lome, my small travelling bag firmly in my hands. I headed for the bus station. Soon I joined others on a minibus heading for Lagos.

As I sat in the vehicle once again on my way to Nigeria, I pondered over what I had just gone through. Whereas the self-proclaimed saviours of the nation were making noises all over the country, the officers at the border posts were enriching themselves!

The rest of the journey to Shagamu was uneventful.

I was warmly welcomed by the few Ghanaian colleagues who remained behind over Christmas. As it turned out, I was the first to make it back. As expected, they were inquisitive to know at first hand what was happening back home. In the next several days others stranded in Ghana arrived. Everyone on our staff eventually returned.

Not everyone was so lucky. As we learnt from other schools, some returned too late, to find their appointments terminated. Yet a few never made it back at all. My short trip to Ghana exhausted almost half of the savings I had made towards my adventure to Europe.

With the experience in Ghana fresh on my mind, I was determined to leave for Europe as soon as possible. The coup in Ghana brought home powerfully to me the unstable nature of the body politic in Africa. It was then the turn of Ghana; the next day it could well be that of Nigeria.

I was determined to leave latest by June that year. I sat down to plan.

Barring any unforeseeable event occurring once more to disturb things, I would be able to save almost all the money I needed for the ticket by the end of April. I planned to embark on the journey at that stage. But what about the money for other expenses—visa, pocket money, etc? Since it involved a regular one-year ticket, the return ticket would be refundable. If only I could get someone to lend me about a quarter of the amount needed for the ticket! On my arrival in Berlin I would return the ticket. Together with an authority note, that person could claim the refund as re-payment.

I thought about Kwadwo who was still at his post in Lagos. I paid him a visit to discuss my proposal with him and appealed to him for a loan to make up the rest of the money I needed. He agreed to my proposal and lent me the money I requested.

Things went according to plan. At the end of April 1982 I purchased a ticket from Balkan Air, the Bulgarian National Carrier, for a round trip from Lagos to East-Berlin.

With that ticket I went to the East German Embassy in Lagos and applied for a transit visa for East Germany. After paying the required visa fee, and showing them a few hundred US dollar notes, the requested visa was issued to me.

15

See you later, Africa

I was all set to leave Nigeria. The thought of leaving my pupils whom I had gradually come to love, made me sad. There was no time for emotion, though.

May 11, 1982, the day I had to embark on my adventure to Europe, finally arrived. The flight was scheduled for 8 p.m. local time. I left Shagamu around 3 p.m. for the hour's drive to Lagos.

Mr Imbeah, popularly known as OK, who at that time had become my closest associate among the Ghanaian staff, accompanied me there. A lawyer by profession, he had given up his practice in Ghana to join the exodus to Nigeria. He was the leading English teacher at the school.

I asked him to inform the headteacher the next day about my inability to attend class. As a precautionary measure against a possible immediate repatriation from Europe, I urged him to conjure up an excuse that would enable me to be excused for a couple of days. He could let the cat out of the bag should I not return after a week.

Apart from him, only a couple of staffmembers from Ghana knew about my plans. The hour's ride to Lagos was free from any incidents. After spending some time with me at the airport, OK begged to leave—just in time to get back home before the fall of darkness.

Soon the order came for us to check in. The majority of those checking in were Europeans. A considerable number of Africans were present also and I wondered where they were heading for.

Finally, the plane was set in motion. A look at my watch read a few minutes past 8 p.m. After taxiing along the runway for a while the plane lifted up into the dark tropical skies. I took a look through the window. Spread beneath us, illuminated with innumerable bright sources of light, was Lagos, the large metropolis on the west Africa coast—the city with many faces, wealth and affluence on one side and on the other slums, violence and crime. I was gradually leaving Nigeria and Africa behind me.

Scarcely a year after my departure from Nigeria, the order came for the Ghanaians living there without residence permits to leave the country at short notice. Between half a million and a million people were affected. Although teachers were not directly affected by the deportation order, many of them, including almost all the Ghanaian staff at my former school, decided to leave voluntarily for their own safety. The environment, OK wrote in a letter, had all of a sudden turned hostile towards them.

It was the second time in my life that I was flying. In contrast to the last flight with the Ghana Airways to Ofosu's funeral ceremony, the destination this time was unfamiliar. Besides that, I did not know what awaited me on touchdown at my final destination. Would I be arrested and placed on the next available plane back to Lagos?

Even if that did not happen, where would I end up? In Hamburg? In Berlin? If I should remain in Berlin, where would I spend my first night? Where would I eventually find accommodation?

Grace and Dan made it clear prior to my departure that owing to their legal status in the country they would not be in a position to meet me in Berlin. They asked me, however, to call them immediately I arrived there. They promised to do what they could to help me. At that time I did not fully understand why they couldn't travel to Berlin. Things would become clear to me later.

As I mentioned earlier, about a dozen other Africans checked in at Lagos. Because the plane was about half full, the seating arrangements were not strictly adhered to. In the course of time all the dark-skinned travellers on the airplane gathered in one corner of the Russian-made jetliner. It turned out that, with the exception of only one person, all the Africans on board were from Ghana. Even the exception was not perfect. Although the person involved was Nigerian by nationality, he had lived most of his life in Ghana. Only the booming Nigeria economy had led him to leave Ghana for Nigeria a couple of years before.

One after the other, each one of us in turn began to tell the group where we were headed for. It soon became apparent that I shared several things in common with everyone present. To pay for the journey to Europe, each one of us had come to work in Nigeria for a while. We were all heading first for West Berlin with the intention to move to West Germany.

Each saw in West Germany a symbol for a better future. West Germany was seen as a place where one could work to earn the means to enable one to establish a living on one's return home. With that, one would be able not only to cater for his nuclear family but the extended family at large. Hardly anyone wished to live there all his life.

We were all travelling on transit visas for East Germany; none of us possessed a visa for West Germany. Each one of us intended to apply for political asylum on our arrival in West Germany. None of us expected anyone to meet us on arrival.

Apart from one person in the group who was embarking on his second adventure to Europe, the rest of us were travelling there for the first time. According to him, he had returned voluntarily to Ghana a couple of years before after staying in West Germany for a few years. On his return he had established a small retail shop in his hometown. With his business now almost collapsing, he had decided to sell the shop and return to Europe for the second time.

We tried to encourage one another. 'We shall make it!' the young man sitting next to me began. 'Other Ghanaians left for Europe under similar conditions. If they succeeded, why not we too?'

'You are right, my friend!' chimed in another.

'I didn't take the pains to apply for a West German visa. Why should I when it was crystal clear to me that the application would not go through?'

'These Europeans! Who demanded a visa from them when they first came to us? Not only did they come without permission; the moment they arrived they began to scramble for our land! Soon they became our colonial masters!'

'You realise how smart they were? They just took advantage of the kind hospitality of our ancestors!'

'But our ancestors were stupid! The Europeans just bought their loyalties with things like alcoholic drinks, pieces of clothing as well as bread and butter.'

Everyone in the group burst into laughter.

'Don't just blame our ancestors! Cast your eyes around Africa of today and the immediate past. Consider people like Mobutu of Zaire, Bokasa of Central Africa, Idi Amin of Uganda, Acheampong of Ghana—my goodness, what brand of rulers!'

'Still, I think the Europeans have the moral responsibility to help us; you think about the amount of resources—gold, diamond, timber that they looted from Africa.'

'Don't expect them to help you, friend! Where else would they obtain their raw materials? Where else would they find markets for their manufactured goods?'

'Well, if they are not willing to help us develop so that we can survive where we are, what other option do we have than to join them where *they* are!' I joined in the discussion.

'Africa, Africa, Africa! Friends, do you think Africa can ever get on her feet?' one of us asked in a tone laced with despair.

Our lively conversation was interrupted by a stewardess who had arrived to serve meals.

What a self-confident bunch of young men! Our average age was barely 25 years. Poverty coupled with the hope of a better tomorrow had forced us to leave family and friends to embark on this journey into the unknown.

We made a short stopover on the island of Malta. From there we continued on to Sofia where we landed in the early hours of May 12, 1982. There the instruction came for everyone to disembark.

A bus came to pick us up from the tarmac to take us to the airport building. Passengers on transit were sent to a special hall to await their connecting flights. The flight to East Berlin, we were told, was to take off around midday local time.

The Sofia Airport did not impress us. It could not match the Lagos International Airport both in size and beauty. Another fact struck us—almost all the workers at the airport wore faces that seemed to betray their dissatisfaction with their lot.

'What is wrong with these people?' one of us wondered.

'The answer is communism,' the co-traveller on his second journey to Europe remarked.

'But they give us a different impression in Africa!' I observed.

'Well, you will see things for yourself. The difference between the West will become even more clear when we get to Berlin.'

Around midday local time, we took our seats in the plane that would take us to our final destination.

I was glad when we finally put Sofia behind us: firstly because of the reason given above and secondly because the stay there was a strain on my nerves. If we had to make the step into the unknown, then the sooner it was done the better.

Apart from the fact that the second airplane was a lot noisier than the first, the short flight from Sofia to East Berlin was uneventful. It was around 2 p.m. local time when we began our descent to Berlin. It was a bright cloudless day in spring. From the windows of the airplane I enjoyed a clear panorama of the world beneath. From above, the city of Berlin seemed to have no bounds.

As I mentioned earlier, each of us possessed a transit visa for East Berlin. The fact that none of us possessed a destination visa did not appear to bother the East German immigration officers. Instead, they seemed to be particular about something else—our proper identity. Under the pretext that all the Africans on the flight seemed to be travelling on false passports, they asked us to wait in one corner. I was surprised at the accusation, for there was nothing wrong with my passport.

Our companion who was travelling to Europe for the second time soon understood the message. Calling us together, he said: 'Do you know their true intention, friends?'

'What do you mean by that?' one of us inquired.

'Well, they want us to do something.'

'Do what?' I joined in.

'My friend, you are from Ghana? Assuming you are arrested by the police and they ask you to do something what would you read from that?'

'You don't mean to imply that these people want to take *money* from us?' I inquired, dumbfounded.

'That's exactly what they're after!'

'That cannot be true! Bribery and corruption does not exist in the communist world,' I stated emphatically.

'Who told you so?'

'I used to be a member of the Ghana-Soviet Friendship Society. These are some of the things we learnt there!'

'Well, you are experiencing the hard realities of life. That is exactly what I experienced the last time I was here.'

'Incredible!'

'Friends, be quick, and don't let us waste precious time here.'

'How much will they accept?' someone in the group wanted to know.

'The last time I was here, each of us placed twenty dollars in the passport; so please, everyone, be quick and place twenty dollars in the passport. Those who do not have dollars may give them ten pounds or twenty DM.'

I placed twenty dollars in my passport and the others followed my example. Next, our co-traveller collected all our passports and handed them in bulk to the immigration officers. Our 'gesture' changed everything! Soon we were through with the immigration formalities.

I pondered over my experience for a while. That one could bribe one's way through in a socialist country was beyond belief! I was shocked beyond measure.

This was not the time to dwell on emotions, however. The uncertainty regarding what awaited us overwhelmed everything else.

16

Finding my way in a divided city

At the time of our arrival in Berlin, Germany was still divided—the result of World War II. West Germany was Western, democratic and capitalist. East Germany, on the other hand, belonged to the Eastern Block of communist countries.

Berlin, which before World War II was the capital of Nazi-Germany, was divided after the war among the Allied Forces. The three Western Powers—the US, Britain and France—were in charge of West Berlin. East Berlin came under the control of the Soviet Union.

West Berlin assumed a unique status in Cold War Europe. It became a capitalist enclave surrounded completely by communist East Germany.

To travel from West Berlin, part of the federation of West Germany, one had to travel about two hundred kilometres through East German territory. Travellers from West Berlin to West Germany and vice versa were allowed to do so only by way of a few specified Highways. The so-called *Transitstrecke* were placed under intense surveillance by the East German security forces. They did so not only through their physical presence—in the form of patrols, hidden observatories at several points on the roads—they also made use of modern electronic surveillance apparatus.

Apart from doing so at filling stations specially constructed to serve travellers on the Transitstrecke, it was strictly prohibited for vehicles to stop anywhere else on the highways linking the two countries. In case of breakdown, the ubiquitous East German secret police arrived in no time to supervise things and make sure the rules and regulations governing the use of the special highways were strictly adhered to.

There was also a rail link between West Berlin and West Germany. There, too, the East German security service frequented the trains during the journey through their territory to ensure none of their citizens used that means of transport to flee to West Germany.

Finally one could travel from West Berlin to West Germany and vice versa by air.

On August 13, 1961, the Communists built a wall between East and West Berlin. This was mainly to stem the flight of their citizens to the West. What eventually happened to that wall is part of history.

By virtue of its geographical location West Berlin served as a suitable point of entry for people seeking to apply for political asylum in West Germany. As in our case, the refugees first arrived in East Berlin before moving on to the West.

Was it due to economic considerations?

A good proportion of the refugees travelled on the East German National Airline—Interflug. The refugees needed a transit visa before they could be allowed into East Berlin. The East German consulates abroad on their part demanded hard currency, US dollars, before issuing the refugees such visas.

Was it political calculation aimed to create internal unrest and dissatisfaction in West Germany? Was it a way of conveying a message to the wider Western world? It was in the middle of the cold war, remember. The western democracies had written it on their banners to provide refuge to all running from political and religious persecution. The East German authorities, on behalf of their comrades in Moscow and elsewhere, seemed to be saying to their arch-enemies in the West: 'Hello, you avowed champions of the cause of freedom! Here you are with tens of thousands of others yearning for the virtue you so passionately uphold!'

Whatever the reasons behind their attitude, the Communist authorities in East Germany did nothing to stem the influx of refugees to the western part of the city. One could even safely say that they condoned and connived at it by regularly driving the refugees on special buses from the East Berlin Airport to the checkpoint at the Friedrichstreet.

◆ ◆ ◆

Dan had advised me to join the train that commuted between the International Airport and a place in the city known as Friedrich Street. Friedrich Street, he told me, served as border crossing between the divided city. There, he pointed out, my passport would be checked for the second time by the East German authorities. After I had passed that check-point I should follow a staircase that led to the Underground. I should then join the Underground train and come out at the first stop. I would then be in West Berlin territory. From there I should call him for further instructions.

A pleasant surprise awaited us the moment we left the airport building. We had scarcely walked a few metres in the direction of the train station when we saw a group made up of four Africans walking towards us.

'Hurray!' I exclaimed to the rest. 'In the midst of this strange environment here at last are people we have something in common with! Maybe they can help us find our way.'

The group meanwhile had reached us. The surprise became perfect when the strangers began to talk to us in the Twi language! '*Moye Ghana fo*? (Are you Ghanaians?),' one of them inquired.

'Yes!' we replied in unison. How, I wondered, did they know we were Ghanaians and for that matter Twi-speaking?

'That is great—welcome to Aburokyire!' they said as if with one voice.

'Is anyone coming to meet you?' one of them inquired.

'No,' we replied simultaneously.

On hearing that, they began, literally, to scramble for us. 'The four of you come with me,' one of them, who gave the impression of being the leader, began. 'You three share the rest among yourselves!'

'That is not fair!' his three companions protested as if with a single voice. 'We should distribute them equally among ourselves.'

'Okay, I will take three; the first three follow me!' he responded, pulling three from the group to himself. Like lost sheep that had found their master, the selected individuals readily followed him.

Eventually I came to be possessed by a young man of about my age. I followed him with mixed feelings.

Dan had warned me to beware of such 'connection men'. They were themselves asylum seekers. Having resided in the city for a while, they knew the environment quite well. Not permitted to work in view of their status, they had made it their business to travel to East Berlin regularly to meet flights arriving from Ghana and Nigeria. At that time, they were sure to meet anything between half a dozen and a dozen new arrivals per flight. The majority of the new arrivals, like ourselves, did not know where to go. We were like ships lost on the high seas without any navigational equipment. Their services were thus highly welcome.

To facilitate their work they had studied the schedules of the airlines in question. In order not to provoke the suspicions of the East German police, they arrived at the airport just in time to meet potential clients. Some of them had brought disrepute to their colleagues by duping unsuspecting new arrivals of all the money on them. Others were said even to have gone to the extent of forcing newly arrived women, some of them on their way to their spouses in West Germany, to sleep with them!

If there was any characteristic my mentor lacked, it did not include eloquency of speech.

'Don't be afraid,' he said. 'I am only here to help you. You have to be bold and smart, however. There are so many secret agents mingled with the pedestrians. Do not do anything to raise their suspicions or they could present problems for us.' Soon we got to the train station. A commuter train was already waiting. Our 'mentor' asked us to wait for some time while he went to buy the tickets. He returned after a few minutes.

'Get on board, friends,' he urged us.

Not long after we were seated the train was set in motion. After about half an hour's ride, our mentor asked us to get off at the next stop. 'When we get to the check-point, do not create the impression I am travelling with you, okay? I will go through the formalities ahead of you. I will then move forward and wait for you near the staircase leading to the underground. I will position myself in such a way that you will find me.'

We didn't encounter any difficulty at the check-point. Soon the group was complete. As we waited our mentor handed us the tickets he had purchased.

'You will need these tickets for the ride on the Underground train. Keep them well. Show it to the ticket collectors in case they enter the train to demand them.'

We then followed him along a long stairway that led downwards.

'You will soon be in *Aburokyire* proper,' he remarked as we followed him. 'What you have seen so far in East Berlin is nothing to compare with it.'

Not long after we got to the underground platform, a long train, coloured bright yellow and tidily kept, emerged from the dark tunnel.

We were struck by its large size, beauty and the immaculate seats inside; the train we had travelled on from the Airport to the Friedrichstreet hardly came close to it in quality and comfort. As we sped through the underground channel, I was fascinated and impressed by the train's smooth efficiency and comfort. Not only that, I was also astonished by the extraordinary feat the human spirit had accomplished in creating such an underground rail network. We changed trains a couple of times. The fact that we could do so deep below the surface of the earth impressed me very much.

Our mentor noticed the surprise written on our faces. 'Are you fascinated at what is unfolding before your eyes? This is only the beginning! Be ready for more surprises. As I said earlier, you are now in Aburokyire proper.'

One thing also struck me. Everyone on the train seemed to be preoccupied with their own business. Some read from newspapers, others read from books. Hardly anyone spoke to the other.

My eyes were cast back home. Imagine a train of that nature travelling in Accra—people would be heartily chatting with one another, cracking all sorts of jokes and making all sorts of noises.

We changed trains a couple of times. The fact that we could do so deep below the surface of the earth still amazed me.

After we had travelled about thirty minutes our patron got up from his seat. 'Get ready, boys, we have to get offat the next stop.' We followed his example and got up. I had difficulty balancing myselfi n the moving train. This did not escape the attention of our helper. 'Here come the bushmen from Africa!' he laughed. I was not amused by his remark, but I kept quiet. How could I afford to say anything that would infuriate the only person in the group who knew the way in this strange environment?

Moments later the train pulled to a stop. The automatic doors slid open.

'Be quick boys!'

We sprang out of the train, our bags hanging on our shoulders.

Despite the speed at which events were unfolding I took notice of the bold inscription written on the walls of the station: DEUTSCHE OPER.

'Follow me quickly,' our helper charged us.

He walked briskly and we had difficulty keeping pace with him.

When we emerged from the underground I was fascinated by the beautiful scenery that confronted me. Before us was a large concourse stretching a distance of about two kilometres. Lined on either side of the broad dual-carriage road were several magnificent and neatly kept buildings. The street was unbelievably tidy. As far as my eyes could stretch, I could not detect any litter lying anywhere—not on the pavements or on the street itself. Are the streets swept clean everyday, I wondered?

I had entertained fantasies of what Germany was like prior to my arrival. The scene that now confronted me—on the Bismarckstreet, as I later realised—surpassed all my previous imaginings. 'Africa, you really need to buck up!' I said to myself.

After we had followed our guide for about a hundred metres along the Bismarckstreet, we saw our protégé press the knob on one of the buildings lined up along it.

'Who is there?' the sound boomed from the microphone fixed to the door.

'It's me!'

Moments later we heard a shrill noise at the door. At the sound, Charley (our guide) pushed the door and it opened! I was fascinated.

'Follow me!' he urged us. We did his bidding and he led us to a room on the second floor. The room measured about five metres in length and four metres in breadth. At one corner were two small beds. It had a built-in kitchen. At another corner was a small enclosure which contained a toilet and a shower. Later I got to know that this building used to be a hotel. It had been converted to a hostel for asylum seekers.

There were two young men, about Charley's age, in the room.

'Welcome to Aburokyire!' one of them, who was relaxing on one of the beds, greeted us in Twi. 'At long last your dreams have come true!' He smiled broadly. 'How are Rawlings and the rest faring?' he went on.

'At the time I was leaving there, it was all chaos!' I replied.

'These soldiers! When will they learn that the country is not their property to handle the way they wish!'

'Charley, we made a mistake in life!' exclaimed the other young man, who was seated on a sofa and watching TV.

'What do you mean?'

'We should have joined the army ourselves. We could have taken our guns one day, headed for the seat of government and proclaimed ourselves leaders of the country!'

'Imagine America Man ruling a country!' Charley burst into uncontrolled laughter.

'Don't laugh, friend—I would do only good things for the country—free education for all, free medical care for all, provide cheap accommodation for all…'

'Free mansions for his dozens of girlfriends!' Kofi, the first man who had spoken, interrupted him.

'Oh, friend, I am not the womaniser you take me for!'

A short silence followed. It was broken by Kofi.

'I hope you will not be too soon disappointed by the hard realities of life here!'

He turned the attention back to the new arrivals.

None of us uttered a word. For my part I was too confused to say anything.

Kofi then walked towards the corner of the room containing the built-in kitchen. He pulled open a small refrigerator and removed some soft drinks. Next he opened a small wooden cabinet and pulled out three cups made of glass. He placed them on a small centre table.

'Here you are—you may serve yourselves,' he invited us.

We seemed to be reluctant to help ourselves to the drinks.

'Hey, don't be shy, friends! Feel free to serve yourselves!' he urged us.

'Don't be shy about food and drinks here in Europe,' America-Man joined in. 'They are in abundant supply—and at a price you can afford to buy.'

'You enjoy yourself! Very soon we will serve you hot food—typical Ghanaian dishes—fufu with groundnut soup and plenty of chicken! Look how lean you all are. You eat and grow fat. Even if you are sent back home with nothing in your pocket, you could boast of having returned with your good body!' That was Charley.

'You show Kofi respect!' America-Man advised us. 'He is the cook here—a wonderful one, for that matter!'

'Hey, who made me cook here? You better learn how to do so yourselves. Hope you've not forgotten that I will be leaving you soon!'

Shortly after that Kofi got up to prepare fufu. About an hour after he got to work, the meal was ready. If the taste of the fufu we were privileged to enjoy was anything to go by, America-Man was right in his comments about his roommate. For the first time since I stepped on European soil, I felt very much at home.

After we had finished with the meal Charley got to business: 'I want to know your plans,' he began after he had called for our attention. 'As it is, there are two options at your disposal: either you submit your application for political asylum here in West Berlin or you travel on to mainland West Germany and submit your applications there. From my experience many new arrivals prefer the latter alternative. So please let me know.'

One after the other we all expressed the desire to continue on to mainland West Germany.

'Do you have any idea how much that will cost you?'

'No,' we replied with one voice.

'400 DM. That will be required to buy the air ticket and pay for the "connection-fee". Can you afford to pay such an amount?'

The two with me replied in the affirmative. Their relations in Germany were ready to bear the cost. They only needed to call them to make the arrangements for transferring the money to Berlin.

Charley then turned to me: 'What about you, friend?'

I hesitated a while.

'You heard me clearly. Are you in a position to pay for the "connection" to West Germany?'

'Will you please give me some time to contact my friends in Hamburg?'

'Are you sure they are ready to help?'

'Well, they gave me vague promises. They would do their best to help the moment I got to Berlin.'

'Did they mention categorically that they would pay for the connection to West Germany?'

'They promised to offer any help possible the moment I arrived in Berlin.'

'That doesn't sound convincing, friend. I would advise you to apply for asylum here. I have been in this business long enough to know. There have been several instances in the past when even close relatives have reneged on their promise to help their relatives the moment they got here. Money is hard to come by here. Hardly anyone is willing to hand it out easily.'

'You still need to give me time to contact them first. They may otherwise accuse me one day of not having consulted them first.'

'Do you have money for the call?'

'I have only dollars on me.'

'Oh, I even forgot to consider that issue!'

He then turned to the group in general.

'All of you give me your foreign money! I will hurry and change it at the bank—at a bank two stops away from here.'

One or two of us looked sceptical.

'Hey, friends! You don't seem to trust me? Has anyone of us stolen anything from you? Has anyone of us collected any fee from you for helping you? Since your arrival we have fed you and done everything to make you feel happy. If money was our priority that would have been the first thing we would have demanded from you! Well, if you cannot trust us with your money you better take your bags and leave us!'

Which of us could afford to do that?

I handed him all that I had, around 100 US dollars as well as few British Pounds. The others did likewise.

'You wait for me. I will be back soon. The bank is not far from here.'

He returned a short while later and distributed the money.

Later I had the opportunity to find out myself the then DM equivalent of the dollar. From my calculation he kept about ten percent of what he got for himself. What was that compared to the services he provided?

Armed with German money, Charley accompanied the three of us to a nearby telephone booth. One after the other he gave us the opportunity to contact our people in West Germany. My two companions were not disappointed. Their relations promised to send them the needed amount per special priority mail the next day.

In regard to myself, Charley's prediction came true.

Grace and Dan advised me to apply for asylum in Berlin; after all, that was exactly what I would do when I got to Hamburg. There was thus no need for me to take the extra risk to attempt to join them in Hamburg with the connection passport.

I didn't want to give up trying. Next I decided to contact another close associate. Kwasi had arrived in Hamburg a few months prior to myself. He was staying with his brother who had lived in Hamburg for many years. I didn't expect Kwasi to be able to help but harboured the distant hope that he could convince his brother to lend me the needed money.

No, they were also not in a position to help me.

Charley read the disappointment written all over my face.

'Don't be disappointed, my friend. That is part of life. Maybe Berlin will in the end turn up to be a blessing.'

I spent my first night in Berlin with mixed feelings. I was, in the first place, thankful to God that I had not faced immediate deportation. On the other hand I was disappointed that I had not made it to Hamburg, to join my friends there. For the moment I felt like someone left alone in an African jungle with no landmark to guide me to safety.

The relations of my two companions kept their word and despatched them enough money the next day to pay for their connection to mainland West Germany. Charley set out to organise their journey. Things proceeded smoothly, enabling them to leave the following day to join their relations.

Our ways have since that day not crossed again. I have wondered—did their dreams come true?

17

Surviving in a crazy world

With my two companions having left, Charley and his two friends could now dedicate more time to me. They began to question me to know more about my background. When they got to know my desire to study, Charley shook his head.

'You have come here to waste your time, friend!'

'Why?'

'They won't allow you to study! I know a couple of others who came here with the intention to study. No way! They were denied the opportunity to do so. As an asylum seeker you won't be allowed to study. One of them was lucky. His sister in the US organised a "connection" for him to go there.'

'If I will not be allowed to study once I seek political asylum, is there no other way I could live here to await a possible admission to the Uni?'

'What way?'

'I mean, any other way apart from seeking political asylum!'

'This guy must be a dreamer! Do you think anyone of us would have put ourselves in such a tight corner if we had any alternative? Listen—the only way you can legalise your stay here is to apply for political asylum. This place is not like Nigeria where you can walk freely on the street and go everywhere in search of work! Over here no one will employ you unless you possess a residence and a work permit. Who is going to issue you with a residence permit? You can count yourselfl ucky that the police have so far not stopped you on the street to demand your permit! Without such a permit the police will sooner or later arrest you and place you on the next available plane bound for Ghana! Even if we agree to harbour you, we could also be arrested by the police and charged with harbouring an illegal immigrant!'

He paused for a while, apparently to study my reaction. I remained still.

'It should be clear to you by now that you have no other choice than to apply for asylum. Or do you need more lecturing from my side?'

At last I opened my mouth. 'What do I need to do then?'

'Simple. You sit down to write a statement!'
'What kind of statement?'
'The statement you want to base your asylum case on. We know a couple of Ghanaians who have made it their business of writing such statements for the illiterate and semi-educated arrivals for a considerable fee. A person with your educational background should be able to write his own statement, shouldn't he?'
'Of course I can.'
'Okay then—get down to work, sir! Many asylum seekers from Ghana claim they were traders. The government banned them from selling their products. They demonstrated against that. Subsequently Rawlings sent soldiers after them. Sensing danger, they fled for their lives. Under cover of darkness most of them made it through the forest to Togo, later to Nigeria and to East Berlin and then West Berlin.'
At that point he burst into uncontrollable laughter.
'What's the matter?' Kofi inquired.
'My goodness! If Rawlings ever got to hear about such stories! Auto mechanics from Kumasi Magazin! Illiterate and semi educated farm labourers from Dormaa Ahenkuro, Akim Oda and others as well as beach boys from Labadi—all of them claiming they were being chased by Rawlings!'
'My friend, you be quiet! What story did you tell yourself? Was it not the same demonstration thing?!'
'Stop it, friend! My story was really sophisticated. I was a leading member of the NPP in my town. I wrote a petition to the district commander of the Peoples' Militia to protest against the indiscriminate arrest and torture going on in the town. A few days later they despatched a group of officers of the Special Forces to arrest me. Fortunately for me, minutes before their arrival I left home to obey nature's call. They waited a while for me to return. Fortunately my wife managed to send someone to warn me about the danger to my life. I hurriedly sought refuge in the house of a friend. Later in the evening my wife sent me money and advised me to flee. I first fled to Togo and finally to East and West Berlin.'
'What is sophisticated about that?'
'If you don't find that sophisticated you can go to hell!'
Everybody present burst into laughter.
'Now think about your own story. It's a matter of survival, my friend. We live in a crazy world, you know!'
I got down to work.
I was a first year student of the University of Ghana, Legon. Being a convinced democrat I joined a group of students to demonstrate against the new military

regime. The peaceful demonstration was forcefully repelled by the military. The ring leaders of the uprising were arrested. The authorities would not leave things like that. Later they went about arresting ordinary participants. Sensing danger, I decided to flee the country along the classical route of escape mentioned above. I was appealing to democratic West Germany to offer me protection.

I gave my statement to Charley to read. He began to read it aloud.

The whole room burst into laughter once again the moment the word *demonstration* fell from his lips!

Early the next morning Charley begged Kofi to accompany me to the offices of the immigration authorities responsible for receiving asylum applications. We left home early in a bid to avoid waiting too long in the queue. Our wish was partly fulfilled. Even at that early hour of day, several dozens of asylum seekers had already lined up to present their applications. The majority of them were people of Asian descent. Later I got to know that quite a good proportion of them were nationals of Afghanistan, Sri Lanka as well as Pakistan.

Moments after joining the queue, Kofi tapped me on the shoulder: 'Take good care of yourself—I'll see you later,' he said to me and turned to go.

'I thought you were going to accompany me through the whole procedure!'

'Friend, this is Europe! You will have to learn to fend for yourself. You just watch what the others are doing. When it's over, you will be given a ticket for the Underground. Ask the officers to give you the route plan to the Deutsche Oper Station. In case you get lost don't hesitate to ask any police officer you meet for directions.'

'Won't they deport me?'

'Don't be too scared by the police! The moment you submit your paper you will be issued a visa. From then on, your stay is legal. In the worst-case scenario, when you are completely unable to find your way, you give us a call. You have our number, don't you?'

Moments later I lost sight of him as he disappeared between some of the numerous vehicles parked on the streets.

In time the queue grew behind me. Around eight in the morning the officers opened the main gate to let us into the main compound of the building complex. Shortly afterwards they began to attend to us. After waiting in the queue about two hours, it finally got to my turn.

I submitted my application to a middle-aged officer. He asked me to hand in my passport. I obliged. Next I was instructed to take a seat for a while in the corridor.

Moments later I was called into a small room. Mounted at one corner of the room was a big camera. With it an officer took several pictures of me, from all possible angles. Next I was directed to another corner of the room. Fingerprints were taken, not only of my two thumbs, but also of all the fingers of my two hands. I felt uncomfortable. For the moment I felt as if I were a hard-core criminal under arrest.

I was then asked to wait outside for a while. About ten minutes later the officer who served me at the beginning called me to the counter. He handed me a document folded in two in the middle. He asked me to unfold it. I obeyed. Fixed to the right upper corner was one of the passport pictures taken a few minutes before. He asked me to place my signature in a space earmarked for it. I obeyed.

'That is your stay permit for West Berlin, for the meantime!' the officer told me in accented English.

'Where is my passport?' I inquired. (This was actually a redundant question for Charley had already told me what would happen to it—they would confiscate it until my case had been decided on.)

'We will keep it until a decision is made on your asylum application,' the officer replied icily. He then directed me to a nearby building. There I would be given the address of the hostel that would accommodate me.

I did as requested. After I had submitted my residence permit, I was given a sheet of paper containing the address of the hostel where I was to stay pending further development in my asylum case. In addition to that I was given a few German Marks together with a one-way ticket for the Underground.

I headed straight for the Bismarckstreet. I found it without difficulty. My new-found friends allowed me to spend the night with them.

The next day, Charley accompanied me to my new hostel. Thereafter I visited them a couple of times. In the course of time my contact with them broke completely.

I wondered, what remained of the dreams that led them to Europe?

18

The Asylum procedure

For a better understanding of subsequent events, I want at this stage to give my readers a short insight into the asylum process at the time of my arrival in West Berlin.

Asylum seekers, after they had submitted their applications, were given temporarily accommodation in the city. The files were then submitted to the Federal Agency in a city in the federal state of Bavaria called Zindorf, entrusted with the processing of asylum applications nationwide.

After a few weeks stay in the divided city, applicants were distributed, based on a quota system, among the then existing eleven states of the Federation.

The next stage in the process was the interview. The time that usually elapsed between the submission of application and the invitation to attend an interview varied greatly. As I learnt on my arrival from others who had been in the system for some time, in former times it could take months if not years for one to be called to be heard personally on one's case.

With an ever-increasing number of refugees arriving in the country to seek political asylum, the government of the day came under increasing pressure from the population to take appropriate steps to curtail the influx. Among the measures adopted in response to the new development was the speeding up of the processing of the individual cases.

Thus at the time of my arrival the time between the submission of applications and the invitation for interview had been reduced to a few months, if not weeks. The interview was followed by a decision of the federal agency to grant or reject the request of the applicant. In the great majority of cases, particularly with regard to applicants from Ghana, the outcome of the interview was usually a rejection.

One had the right of appeal. Hardly anyone failed to make use of this right. Not that anyone had any illusions about the ultimate outcome. The appeal served to buy time for the applicants.

The lower courts rarely overturned decisions of the federal agency. In some cases one was given the chance to challenge the decision of the lower courts at a higher court.

As I mentioned, in previous times the process could take several years to pass through all the legal instances. At our time matters had changed for the worse—from the viewpoint of the asylum seeker, that is. Two years was the maximum time most of us gave ourselves to legalise our stay through other means or else face deportation.

19

A back yard of flowers

My first official address in West Berlin was along the street bearing the name Schoeneberger Ufer, in a suburb known as Schoeneberg.

It was a hostel operated by the German Red Cross and carried the name BLUMESHOF which, translated, literally means *a backyard of flowers*.

A large six-story building-complex, it boasted several rooms—sleeping rooms, offices, a large dining hall, etc. In addition to that it had a large kitchen as well as a large laundry to cater for its residents.

It was a men's only hostel and provided accommodation for several dozen asylum seekers from various parts of the developing world—from Pakistan to Afghanistan through to Lebanon and right down to Ghana. One could well describe it as a mini United Nations of the developing world.

Every resident was issued with an identity card. These were left at the porter's lodge when residents left the hostel for the city. Officially no one was allowed to leave or enter the building after 10 p.m. A porter kept guard throughout the night. For those yet to be assigned to a particular federal state, Blumeshof was only a provisional accommodation. For residents who had been stationed in the state of Berlin it was an end station. It was only in the rare instances when an asylum request was granted that such an inmate could leave there to find private accommodation.

Not that it was the cheapest means of accommodation available to the state to house these dependants on the taxpayers' money. Generally four refugees were housed in a room occupying an area of about sixteen square meters. Judging by the money, which from our information, the state paid for four people to live in that room, it would have been cheaper for them if they had allowed us to rent private accommodation. Economics, however, were apparently not the main deciding factor.

The hostel arrangement appeared to be part of the strategy of the authorities to make the status of an asylum seeker as unattractive as possible which, in turn, would, they hoped, help to stem the influx of such people into the country.

I was assigned to a room on the sixth floor, to room 601. I shared it with three other asylum seekers from Ghana. Okuobi and his friend Jerry as well as Seidu (name changed) had all made a stopover in Nigeria on their way to Europe. Okuobi had a very good sense of humour. That, combined with the fact that our room happened to be adjacent to the staircase, helped to turn it into a kind of meeting point for other Ghanaians living in the hostel, in particular those sharing the floor with us.

Breakfast was served at 7:30 a.m. One had up till 8:30 to break his fast. Lunch, the only time when hot meals were served, followed between 11:30 and 1:00 p.m. During lunch dinner packets were handed out. These consisted of a litre off resh milk, small containers of butter, cheese, marmalade, as well as a large pita-bread.

Although at the time I arrived there about a third of residents were from Ghana and Nigeria, the meal served was about 90 percent Asian and 10 percent European. For a while we did not complain. Eventually, however, we protested to the authorities about the unequal treatment.

They were not unaware of the situation, they admitted. They had until then not addressed it because they had no idea how they could satisfy our taste. In the end a solution was found. A few residents from Ghana were signed on to help prepare a couple ofl ocal dishes for lunch. This arrangement didn't bring complete satisfaction to everybody. This is because the meals offered did not include the popular local food, fufu. Residents were strictly forbidden to cook on their own. The love for fufu led not a few to find ways to break the rule. Notwithstanding the regular searches carried out by the porters to check for those attempting to smuggle small, mostly used electric cookers into the hostel, such items abounded in the hostel. It was not difficult to acquire those items. Every Saturday and Sunday a flea market was organised near the vicinity of the hostel. They were sold at affordable prices.

In the evening, at a time when the official staff had left the hostel, the scent of boiling soup emerged from several rooms to fill the corridors of the building. That was the time when some inhabitants, for the most part Ghanaians, were busy preparing their local dishes.

At home in Ghana fufu is pounded from a combination of boiled plantains and cassava into a ball. In Europe we substituted these two main ingredients with powdered potato und powdered starch respectively. The pounded stuffis swallowed in small balls. To facilitate the swallowing one requires soup .The soup could be prepared from palmnut, groundnut or tomatoes. Fufu is eaten with soup containing meat or fish or a mixture of both.

Needless to say, money was a scarce commodity among the residents of Blumeshof. We had to seek the cheapest way to prepare the cherished meal. Soon word spread among the Ghanaian community in the hostel about a large supermarket in the central part of the city, Kadewe, where the bones of pork were being offered for sale for almost nothing.

Whenever we planned to prepare fufu in Room 601 we sat down to make an estimate of how much it would cost. Each contributed equally towards raising the amount. With part of the raised amount one or two of us left for Kadewe. In time our faces became familiar to the sale assistants at that particular point of the supermarket complex. The moment anyone of us got there, even before he had time to utter a word, the sale assistant on duty removed a polythene bag and began to fill it with the bones. Occasionally they would cast an eye towards the direction of the African customer for a sign that the quantity of bone in the bag was enough for the day.

From there we passed by another counter to purchase the remaining ingredients. In the evening we went about the business of preparing our meals.

Naturally we could have survived in Blumeshof without fufu. Preparing the meals served an important function, however—it became a social event no one wanted to miss. With entertainer Okuobi ever willing to dig into his archives to bring out a joke to crack that would send everyone around bursting into uncontrolled laughter, the ritual was a welcome change to what was otherwise a monotonous life at the hostel.

The precautionary ban imposed by the authorities in regard to cooking meals in our rooms was not without justification. On one occasion, one of the electric cookers short-circuited in one of the rooms, leading to an outbreak of fire. Fortunately it happened during the daytime, facilitating a quick evacuation of the whole building. Apart from some minor bruises some of us incurred from falling on the stairway as we ran for our lives, the fire on the whole caused only minimum damage.

20

'Africaman' in Europe

An asylum seeker was generally condemned to idleness. As I mentioned earlier, such persons were forbidden to work, study or learn a trade.

Besides that, they were not allowed to travel beyond the district of their posting. We learnt from acquaintances sent to West Germany that they didn't always keep to the regulation and risked travelling beyond their places of residence to visit relatives, friends and even look for work!

By virtue of West Berlin's geographical location and its political status, however, those of us stationed there were forced to stay within the boundaries of the city.

The day of the asylum seeker in Blumeshof usually began with breakfast at 7:30. Some spent the time between breakfast and lunch watching TV. At that time all the programmes were in German. Since hardly anyone had any knowledge of the language, we sufficed ourselves with watching the moving pictures. Others went for a walk in the neighbourhood. Since lunch followed almost on the heels of breakfast, most of us confined ourselves to the vicinity of the hostel till lunch was over.

Between lunch time and 10 p.m. when everyone was expected to be back at the hostel, we were free to do whatever we wanted. The large, metropolitan city offered many places of attraction to visit. One could, for example, move from one of the numerous and well-stocked supermarkets to another to watch and admire the goods on display. On such visits I would stand in the midst of the abundant wares on the shelves and wonder. Such scenes led me to reflect on the inequalities of the world we live in. If only in Ghana we could have access to even a small proportion of the goods on display and at a price affordable to the proverbial common man on the street!

In those days it was customary for any first visitor to the city to pay a visit to the Berlin Wall. The situation was not different with me. Our hostel happened to be situated about one kilometre from the wall. Several important historical buildings and structures in the vicinity of that particular portion of the concrete demarcation which stretched for a distance of approximately 155 kilometres, contributed to make that area of particular interest to sightseers. First was the Reichstag building with its tumultuous history. Between 1871-1918 it served as the parliament of the then German Constitutional Monarchy. On November 9, 1918, the first German Democratic Republic was born there. On February 27, 1933, the building was set on fire by a lone left-wing activist. Historians credit that event as serving as a springboard that would lead to Hitler's rise to power. Severe fighting is said to have taken place there towards the end of World War II. Hitler is said to have committed suicide there.

The Division of Berlin left the Reichstag on the western side of the city. Not so the Gate of Brandenburg, a few metres away. Built between 1789 and 1791, it served as the symbol of the city until its division. The communist closed the Gate when they erected the wall. Tourists could view the historic structure only by means of a ramp that had been erected on the Western side to allow a view over the wall which rose to the height of about three and a half metres.

Also of attraction was an enclave in the vicinity of the Wall, on West Berlin territory, on which a monument to the memory of the war-dead of the Soviet Union had been erected. By virtue of a special arrangement, soldiers from the then arch-enemy of the Cold War were allowed to keep watch there. From several meters away the passer-by could see some of them, as they, like human statutes, stood motionless in honour of their war-dead.

What I saw on my first visit to the area would occupy my mind for several days. When I entered the Reichstag building, a documentary on World War II was running. That was my first real confrontation with the suffering of the war that eventually led to the division of Europe. Days after watching the film I kept on reflecting on it. That human beings could be capable of inflicting such terrible suffering on their fellow human beings was something beyond my understanding.

I went on pondering. I tried to compare the human being, the crown of God's creation, to the beasts—the lion, for example. The lion will kill to satisfy its hunger. So long as it is satisfied, it rests for a season. What about the human mind taken over by the devil? You better run away, friend! For it can never be satisfied until it has destroyed and destroyed—*and* destroyed. One thing makes such a person even more fearful—he or she may have the means of destruction that our so-called civilisation has invented—machine guns, and bombs, whether conventional, chemical, nuclear, or biological.

Then there was the scene of the East German security forces keeping guard from small cubicles raised to a height that enabled them a good view of the area bordering on the wall from their territory. That the guards could go to the farthest extreme to prevent their citizens escaping to the West was brought home to me after I inquired about the several crosses that had been erected on the western side of the wall, near the Reichstag building.

'Each cross stands for someone who has been shot trying to climb over the wall in an attempt to flee to the west!' I was told.

After days of pondering on my experience on my first visit to the area just described, I decided to sum up my experience in the form of a prayer: *Heavenly Father, please have mercy on Humankind for we do not know what we do!*

I was impressed by the extreme discipline of those I met on the streets. For example, at the traffic lights everyone waited patiently for the lights to turn green before venturing on the streets, even when no traffic was around. I was astonished at the patience the drivers had for pedestrians and bike riders. At zebra crossings and special pedestrian crossing points regulated by traffic lights, the vehicles were brought to a halt when the lights turned green for pedestrians to go. I wondered if the same degree of discipline would have been shown in other places of the world I was familiar with.

Another aspect of my new environment struck me. Rarely did the drivers of the numerous vehicles on the streets blow their horns! That was in big contrast to what I was used to. In Ghana, worse still in Nigeria, blowing the horn of a vehicle seemed to be a hobby for many a driver, particularly taxi and tro-tro drivers.

Next were the tidy streets! I observed pedestrians with litter in their hands who actually waited until they got to a bin some metres away before dropping it!

Another aspect about the city that struck me was the way everyone seemed to mind their own business and seemed not to be bothered about what was going on around them. This was particularly evident on the Underground. Almost everyone in the Underground trains seemed to be concentrating on doing something—reading the newspaper, knitting the components of what would later be a pullover or something to decorate their rooms. Those who seemed to have nothing to do remained still in their seats.

I needed only a few days to draw my own conclusions about my new place of residence: this must indeed be a country of very disciplined residents!

◆ ◆ ◆

It soon dawned on me that I couldn't afford travelling with the tube for long. The fares they demanded, while not being substantial for an average worker, was a lot of money for a person like myself who had very scarce resources. Besides the monetary consideration, there was another reason why I was not keen on using the Underground as my main means of transportation. I wanted to be conversant with the city; using the Underground for the most part could only be a hindrance to achieving that goal.

On the other hand I realised the city boasted excellent bicycle paths. I thought of the bicycle as a good practical means of achieving the objectives outlined above. I had a handicap though—I did not know how to ride a bike!

I decided to overcome that hurdle. Who was there to help me do that? I talked to Dadzie, a Ghanaian resident of the hostel who I knew had the ability to ride. He expressed his willingness to help me acquire the skill.

The following Saturday I visited the flea market near the hostel in search of a second-hand bike. In the process I acquired a medium sized one for almost nothing. That very afternoon, my trainer accompanied me to a nearby park. After falling several times and sustaining bruises here and there, I finally succeeded in balancing myself on the unstable two wheel-travelling device and managed to move a few metres without falling! The training continued for the next few days.

About a week after I began my training I had such confidence in my riding ability that I decided to venture into the city centre on it—a little prematurely, as it turned out. As I approached a traffic lights at a busy crossing, the lights suddenly switched from green to yellow and then red. In my attempt to come to a stop, I applied the front breaks—too forcefully, as it turned out! Moments later my body went flying through the air. Fortunately, I landed on the side lanes. All eyes were directed at me. Some of the passers-by rushed to my assistance. But before they got to me I was already on my feet. Moments later I was back on my bike and speeding away. Rarely did I travel on public transport thereafter.

◆ ◆ ◆

A few weeks after I had submitted my application, word came for us to report to the authorities for our postings. Though I had been in Berlin only a few weeks, I had developed a great affection for the city. Not only that, I had made contacts with several people. My prayer therefore was for the Lord to allow me to stay there. My prayer was heard. Seidu and myself were stationed in the city. With tearful eyes we parted from our 'entertainer' as well as Jerry, his friend, as the order came for them to leave West Berlin for West Germany. Shortly after their departure Gyasi and another refugee of about his age, both Ghanaian, were sent to replace them.

◆ ◆ ◆

With the onset of autumn, and with the trees that lined the streets shedding their leaves, the authorities organised what came to be known as *Soziale Arbeit* (community duty). The asylum seekers were employed to tidy the city. The policy, as already mentioned, was to make the status of asylum seeker as unattractive as possible. To this end we were permitted to work only a few hours every month. Furthermore, only a token wage of a few German marks was paid per hour. Finally, only a small proportion of what we earned was handed down as cash; the greater proportion was handed out as coupons that could be used to buy only selected articles—mainly food and hygiene items in a few specified shops.

I still recall an incident that happened one day as we cleaned the streets in a northern district of the city. As we worked, a middle-aged man watched us from the window of his house. In the course of time we grew thirsty. When faced with a situation like that in Ghana, particularly in the village, one could approach a neighbour to ask for water. Jerry and myself, thinking the same custom applied in our new environment, approached the man: *'Wasser, bitte; Wasser, bitte!'*—thus we made use of the little German we commanded. But he was not moved. Thinking he might not understand our broken German, we made signs with our hands to make our intentions clear. To our surprise he closed the window in our faces and never re-appeared.

'He must be a very wicked person!' Jerry concluded.

On other occasions we were sent to clean Old Peoples Homes.

◆ ◆ ◆

My greatest desire on realising I would remain in Berlin for a while was to establish contact with the Ghanaian student community there as soon as possible.

A few days after my arrival, Dan gave me the telephone number of someone he knew there and instructed me to contact him in case I needed help. I did so without delay. Tony, who happened to have arrived there from Ghana several years before, was very forthcoming on the phone, assuring me of assistance when and where he could. During our first contact he told me about a cultural dance the Berlin Branch of the Ghana Students Union in Germany was organising that weekend. He gave me the address of the venue where the concert was scheduled to take place and urged me to do my best to attend. He would also be there. It would be a good opportunity not only to get to know each other, but also to meet some of the Ghanaian students in the city. I thanked him for his tip and promised to be there.

I left Blumeshof early, to be at the meeting on time. After travelling on the underground about forty minutes I finally got off at the station indicated by Tony. After a short search I located the students' hostel mentioned by him. I entered it and began to look for the hall on the ground floor where the event was to take place. Just then the doors of the lift, about ten metres from where I stood, opened. An African male person whose age I estimated to be about 35 sprang out. I decided to seek his help.

'Excuse me, sir,' I began as I approached him, 'could you please direct me to the hall where the Ghana Cultural Evening is taking place?'

'You want to attend it?'

'Yes.'

'You have come too early, friend!'

'But I was told it was to take place about this time!'

'Forget it! That's what they have advertised on paper! In reality it won't begin any time soon. Even the organisers themselves are yet to arrive!'

'But I heard people keep to time in Europe!'

'Well, when our friends have appointment with Europeans they take pains to be punctual. When it comes to events like this involving ourselves, people choose to be late; everyone thinks the other will arrive late so they decide not to be punctual! In any case, I'll show you the place. You can hang around and wait for them.'

I walked beside him. After we had gone a few metres he turned to me. 'Your face is not familiar to me. How long have you been in Berlin?'

'Less than two weeks.'

'A fresh arrival from Africa?'

'Yes.'

'How was Ghana?'

'I left there at the beginning of January; my general impression was that the majority of the population were not amused at what's going on.'

'So it took you five months to get to Berlin!'

'Well, I was teaching in Nigeria.'

'Really?'

'Yes. I left my post because I wanted to move on to study here!'

'Oh indeed! So you arrived on a student's visa?'

'No! I came on a transit visa for East Germany!'

'Oh, you did? And then?'

'Well, we were picked on in East Berlin by some Ghanaians. I had indeed wanted to move on to Hamburg. In the end I ended up applying for political asylum here.'

'You really have?'

'Yes. Those we came across told me that was the only way I could legalise my stay.'

'They are right. Since you didn't come with a proper visa for West Germany that is the only way out.' He pondered for a while. 'How far have you come in your education?'

'I have three passes at the GCE 'A'-Level.

'Why didn't you study in Ghana?'

'Indeed I was admitted to Legon to do science—pure science. Throughout my life however my desire has been to become a doctor. I made up my mind to come to Germany to try my luck here!'

'You really want to study medicine here?'

'That is the main reason why I embarked on my adventure!'

'I wouldn't like to discourage you, friend. I am afraid, though, it will be very difficult if not impossible to realise your goal. In the first place, I understand the authorities are preventing asylum seekers from studying! And even if they didn't, the chance that you could be admitted in a strongly contested area such as medicine is very slim indeed.'

We had in the meantime reached the hall where the event was to take place.

My countryman was right. Apart from some music instruments that had been set in place, there was nothing to show something was going to take place.

'What about the language?' he went on. 'Do you have any idea?'

'I attended the Goethe Institute in Accra for some time. I don't want to mention it to others, for apart from a few words and expressions, I have practically no idea of the language.'

'How will you study here then?'

'I am determined to learn the language!'

'As I said, one of my policies is not to discourage others by what I say. Though almost impossible, there could still be a way out. I will advise you however to begin immediately to study the language. In order for anyone to consider your application, you have to show a proof of adequate knowledge of the language. After you have acquired adequate knowledge of the language, you could then apply for admission. You may have to apply first for a less competitive field. You could then switch to medicine at later date. As to the issue of a student's visa, I am confident the moment you are admitted by a University, the visa authorities may decide to issue you one.'

He paused for a while.

'Be assured of one thing,' he continued, 'you can count on my full assistance. Whenever it is in my means to help, I will not hesitate to do so.' Just then he took a look at his watch. 'Oh, I have to leave you now. My girlfriend will otherwise be angry with me. But feel free to contact me. I live in this hostel. You will find my name at the main gate.' At that moment he took a pen from his pocket. 'Do you have some paper?' he inquired.

'No.'

Together we began to look round for a piece of paper.

Eventually he pulled a small piece from the pocket of his coat. He then wrote something on it. Finally he handed it to me.

'You can reach me on either of the two numbers. The first is my own. The second is that of my girlfriend. If you don't get me at home, you may try my girlfriend's.'

Soon he was on his way.

His open-mindedness and generosity surprised me. I had heard about many a citizen from Ghana who, on moving to the West, became influenced by the economic system prevailing there. They tended therefore to think about themselves only and not to bother about what was happening in the other's courtyard. The first impression Emmanuel (that turned out to be his first name) made on me was that he was a notable exception.

Later I got to know more about him. He arrived in West Germany about ten years before me. After completing a language course, he gained admission to the University of Kiel in the north of the country. There he did a first degree in Agricultural Science. From there he moved to West Berlin to do a postgraduate course in Agricultural Engineering. In due time he introduced me to Anna, his then girlfriend and later wife. Both first met when Emmanuel was a student in Kiel. A nurse by profession, she gave up her job in northern Germany to follow him to Berlin. She had in the meantime found work in one of the hospitals in the city.

At the time I got to know them they were living apart—he in the students' hostel, and she in a staffhostel of the hospital where she was working. Was it by coincidence or design that Mensah—or Anna—became a friend to a person who displayed just the same degree of openness and kindness? About the same age as Emmanuel, Anna not only displayed the characteristics I referred to but was also exuberant, energetic and selfless.

Emmanuel spent more time in Anna's apartment than in his. I soon became their regular guest. On such visits he, an accomplished cook, treated me to various Ghanaian dishes.

Through Emmanuel I learnt about other details concerning the admission procedures to German universities. Then, as now, most German Universities as well as institutions of higher learning admit students twice a year—in summer and winter. Applicants for the summer semester beginning April 1st have up to January 15th to submit their documents. In the same way those wishing to be admitted for the winter semester beginning October 1st have to submit their documents by July 15th.

When the time came for me to fill the admission forms, he provided useful tips as to how best to go about it.

Apart from Anna and Emmanuel, Tony and his family also provided support. I visited their home a couple of weeks after my arrival in West Berlin. They lived in an apartment building in the district of Kreuzberg. He had been trained in the field of industrial printing and had found work with one of the leading publishing houses in the city.

21

German for Beginners

For a while my desire to study appeared to have hit rock bottom. Nevertheless I decided not to allow the seemingly impossible situation to deter me from my avowed goal to study medicine and use my position as a doctor to serve the Lord.

Rather than resign to the situation and do nothing, I resolved to work towards the realisation of my goal. Of one thing I was convinced—if it was His will that I became a doctor, then it surely would be so.

I agreed with Emmanuel that a good command of the German language was essential if I wanted to get any closer to the realisation of my goal. As a first step, therefore, I decided to dedicate the greater part of my time to learn the language. The best way I could learn the language was to register for an intensive course with a private language school. The laws did not prevent that.

I set out to make the necessary enquiries. In the process I got to know that such institutes demanded a considerable amount of money from their students. As a result I ceased to pursue that path.

Another option was for me to register to take part in state sponsored adult education classes. Even there my meagre resources did not allow me to afford the token fee demanded.

The only feasible alternative left for me was to teach myself the language!

Towards that goal I travelled to the central part of the city to look for suitable material. After I had searched through a couple of bookshops, I found in one a book titled *German for Beginners*.

German for Beginners was to turn out to be an invaluable asset in my effort to master the German language. A teach yourself book, it was intended for people with a command of the English language desiring to study the German language on their own. Every line in German, be it part of a passage, be it an example in sentence construction, be it lessons in the correct use of words, carried a colloquial or idiomatic English translation immediately beneath it.

Armed with this I set out to learn the language on my own. Working through the book was such a pleasure! The moment I got hold of it I did not want to leave it.

My roommates, realising how much time I was devoting to my new companion, began to make fun of me. 'Friend, we came to Europe to look for money. It is work we are looking for, work that will enable us to earn money to establish ourselves back home,' one of them informed me. 'Why waste your time learning such a difficult language?' the other countered. 'After all, the laws forbid us from studying!' Another added bitterly: 'I will not waste one second to learn the language of these wicked people!' Yet another said sarcastically: 'Leave the bookworm alone to do whatever he wishes to do!'

In some respects, I could understand their attitude. Apart from only one of them who had made it to the GCE O-Level, the rest were so-called dropouts. How could I expect any of them to harbour the ambitions I had?

Still, I found it unfair that they wouldn't leave me alone to do what I considered important for my future. In any case I was so determined in my goal of studying at the university that none of their sour or bitter comments could distract me.

I mentioned elsewhere that our room was a meeting point for several other Ghanaians living in Blumeshof. In time it became increasingly difficult for me to concentrate to work there. Fortunately our hostel happened to be located near a large public library, so, whenever the atmosphere in room 601 became unsuitable for academic work, I put on my clothes, placed my *German for Beginners* in a polythene bag and left the noisome room for the library.

The discovery of the library brought me an important advantage. I made use of some of the leading national and international dailies as well as magazines supplied to the library to improve my skills in the language I sought to master. My strategy was the following: first I went through a story making headline in English. Next I tried to understand the story in German.

The German language, in my opinion, cannot be classified with one of the easy-to-master languages—should such a language exist! The fact that I did not receive any intensive lessons in it haunts me from time to time. This is particularly the case when it comes to the fine details and nuances of the language. For this reason I wish I had undergone a period of intensive study in a classroom context.

◆ ◆ ◆

Later I contacted the Free University personally to find out more about their admission requirements. There it was officially confirmed that I needed to provide proof of sufficient knowledge of the German Language, at least at the GCE 'O'-Level.

How could I overcome the hurdle? Once more I contacted Emmanuel and Tony. They advised me to contact some of the established language schools in the city to find out whether I could sit for the exams with them.

Eventually the International Translators School provided the answer. They organised such exams on a regular basis for a UK based examining body, the Associated Examining Board.

The next GCE at Ordinary level was scheduled for November. A registration and examination fee of about two hundred German marks was required.

Again, how was I to overcome the financial barrier? Again I contacted Emmanuel and Tony for advice.

My two friends pointed their fingers in the direction of the Ghana Students Union. They were aware of a social fund that had been set apart to meet exigencies such as the present one. They advised me to discuss the issue with the executive members of the organisation.

Without delay I rang the general secretary.

'Well, we have some money in the bank,' he began when I told him the reason for the call. 'I cannot decide alone, however. As you know, we shall be meeting in about two weeks' time. I would advise you to attend personally and present your case there.'

Fortunately the closing date for registration at the Language School was well beyond the scheduled date for the meeting.

I was among the first to arrive at the meeting that day. A few days prior to the meeting I had set out to call the leading members to lobby for support. As usual the meeting began with discussion on the bigger issues; the political situation at home, the situation of Ghanaian students in particular and that of the Ghanaian community in general in Berlin.

Towards the end of the deliberations, the general secretary brought up my case, stressing his personal conviction for the need to help me out. The money should not be declared a gift. Instead it should be given as a loan that should be repaid at an unspecified date. Members were given the opportunity to air their views on the issue. Speaker after speaker followed and the idea of granting me the loan received support from the plenum.

Just as the motion was about to be put to vote, one of the leading members raised his hand.

'Do you want to comment on the issue of the loan or do you want to talk on something else?' the chairman inquired.

'The issue of the loan, please!'

'But I thought we were done with it?'

'Who told you we were done?'

'Okay, please let your opinion be heard.'

'Well I want to air my strong opposition to the whole idea of granting our relatively new member a loan!'

A murmur went through the hall.

'Well, I am not against the principle of helping our countrymen and countrywomen who find themselves in difficulty. In this particular instance, however, I want to appeal to members to reconsider their decision to grant our fellow member a loan.'

'Why?' the chairman inquired, surprised.

'I will cite three reasons to support my case. In the first place, I am only prepared to invest money in someone when I am convinced my investment has the chance of yielding good results. Now we are all aware that the authorities these days strictly forbid asylum seekers from working or studying. In the second place, how can we be sure that our friend will be able to pass the test? Finally, where is the guarantee that he will be able to make re-payment?'

He then took his seat. I turned my head in his direction.

Shortly after that the motion was put to the vote. Thank God the majority did not follow his argument but voted in favour of granting me my request.

The following Monday, the financial secretary arranged for me to meet him at the bank. After he had withdrawn the money he handed it to me.

Without any waste of time I hurried straight to the offices of the International Translators' Institute and registered for the GCE O-Level examination for November 1982. I then set out to prepare for the test. In November 1982 I sat for the exam. A few weeks later the result was released. I had obtained a Grade C pass.

Several years later I repaid the loan.

22

American Lutheran Church in Berlin

Besides establishing contact with the Ghanaian student population, one issue high on my priorities was to find a congregation where I could worship. Owing to the language barrier, my prayer was for the Lord to lead me to an English speaking church.

A few weeks after my arrival, I undertook one of my regular sightseeing tours to the city. I went by bike. When I got to a popular area of the city, a place known as the Zoologischer Garten, I fastened the bike to a lamppost and began to stroll along the streets. The beautiful weather had attracted several people into one of the most attractive areas of the city.

Whilst strolling around my attention was drawn to a tall Victorian-style church building partly destroyed at the top. A few metres next to the old building was a modern one. The cross it bore on its roof revealed its use.

Later I got to know some historical facts about the partly destroyed church. Built between 1891 and 1895, it was partly destroyed during a bombing raid on Berlin in 1943.

After the war, the authorities suggested the ruined building be completely demolished. The proposal met with protests from the population, who wanted to leave the ruined building as it was to serve as a lasting reminder to succeeding generations of the destructive power of war.

The protest yielded results; the partly destroyed building was allowed to remain. As a compromise, a new church building was built beside the old one.

Like many of the people roaming that area of Berlin on that beautiful day in spring I decided to enter the old building to view it from within. While admiring the splendid work of architecture my attention was drawn to a table placed at one corner of the hall in the mighty building. When I got closer I noticed some bundles ofl eaflets that had been placed on it. I took a closer look at the leaflets. They all seemed to be in German. Just then my attention was drawn to a set written in English. I removed a sheet and began to read it:

> The American Church in Berlin wishes to invite English speaking visitors to the city to join them in Sunday worship. For further information please contact the pastor on the number below.

I saw the opportunity I was looking for! I folded the sheet and placed it in my pocket. Next, I looked out for a telephone booth. After a short search I found one. After placing a few coins in it, I dialled the number on the sheet.

I was greeted heartily by a male voice, that of the resident pastor.

As expected, Gary (that turned out to be his first name) was delighted to learn the reason for my call, and took great pains to instruct me on how I could get there by way of public transport.

My bike had by then become my best travel companion, however, and the following Saturday I left Blumeshof after lunch to look out for the church. After missing my way a couple of times, I finally located it. Everything was thus set for my first church attendance in Berlin the next day. I was delighted at the idea though I didn't know what to expect.

From my information so far, the typical German church was poorly attended. My source went on to say that churches were attended mostly by elderly people. The young, on the other hand, hardly had any time for such issues. Imagine my surprise, therefore, when, on my first visit, the church was completely filled!

As I found out later, my first attendance coincided with the once a year joint worship service of the American church, a church with a Lutheran tradition, and its German sister church, the Paulus Lutheran Church of Berlin-Zehlendorf.

I realised later that the issue of church attendance that I mentioned applied in the main to the traditional churches—the German Lutheran Church and to some extent the German Catholic Church. On the other hand the American churches as well as the German Pentecostal churches were well attended.

I was heartily welcomed by the congregation. As far as the members could recall, I was the first African to worship with them. After service they invited me to remain for cookies and tea. Several members approached me to find out more about me. As I cycled home that day my mind was made up—so long as I remained in Berlin, I would worship with that congregation! Indeed, though in later times I came in contact with some German Churches, I only attended such churches on a visiting basis.

Later I introduced several other Ghanaians to the church. In the end it became quite known to the Ghanaian refugee community in Berlin.

My contact with the American Church in Berlin subsequently brought me into contact with Kurt, the pastor of the German sister church. Kurt and his American wife Karen would later be of invaluable help to me.

23

The three-way friendship

An account of my stay in Berlin would not be complete if I failed to give some attention to the peculiar relationship that developed between a teenage girl and her grandmother on one hand and myself on the other.

On my second Sunday at the American Church I learnt that the church would embark on a picnic after service. I was told the event took place every year in summer. Gary and several other members encouraged me to join them. I decided not to miss the opportunity to get to know members of the congregation closely.

I joined some of the worshippers in a small bus to drive to the venue, a resort park in the midst of a large forest about five kilometres from the church. Abundant and rich food was served. On the basis of what members termed 'Potluck Dinner', most families had come with ready-to-serve meals to share with others.

Apart from the opportunity to sample some of the delicious meals available, one could take part in various games—table tennis, volleyball, American football, etc. Although my left ankle prevented me from engaging in any sporting activity that required moving quickly from one place to the other, I tried to participate in some of the activities. Was it because I was new in the group? Was it because I was the only African around? Whatever the reason, members went to great lengths to make me feel at home.

'Robert, come join us to play volley ball!' one would invite me.

Hardly had I left that game to relax and a new invitation would reach me: 'Robert! Are you familiar with America football?'

'Not at all!'

'Never mind—just join us! We'll teach you the rules!'

Moments later, someone else wanted me to join in table tennis.

In due course my attention was drawn to a tall, attractive girl.

It was quite easy to make her out. Apart from being tall, her features suggested she was the product of a marriage between an African and a European. Apart from her, an Indian couple and their three children as well as myself, all the rest of the group happened to be pure European in appearance. I tried to estimate the tall girl's age based on her physical appearance and thought she must be about 20 year old. Indeed, I was way out! As I later found out, she had turned 14 a couple of months before.

During the games one thing struck me. The strange girl seemed to follow me most of the time. If I moved to play volleyball, she followed; if I joined in table tennis, she would show up there a few minutes later. Finally I decided to talk to her.

'Excuse me,' I began, 'how do you do?'

'Fine,' she replied with a broad smile.

'You're enjoying your time here, I suppose!'

'Very much!'

'It's a nice congregation; everybody seems to be so kind!'

'That's right. That's why I decided to join.'

'Have you been a member for long?'

'Well, I'm not a full member yet. I only attend from time to time, with my Grandmother.'

'With your grandmother? Is she around?'

'Yes. You see that elderly lady with the short blonde hair, sitting about fifty metres away, beneath a tree?' She pointed in the direction.

'Yes I do.'

'She is my grandmother.'

'She is indeed?'

'Yes.'

I could not wait long to satisfy my curiosity as to why the colour of her skin differed from that of her grandmother. I tried an indirect approach.

'Are you American?'

'No, I am German!'

'But you speak very good English!'

'Well, my father is an American.'

'Is he around?'

'No,' she replied.

I realised she was not at home with that question so I decided to change the topic.

'Would you like to tell me your name?'

'Of course. I am Nina (name changed). What about you?'

'Robert. You can call me Robert. Of course, I have an African name. Since my arrival I have realised the residents here have difficulty pronouncing my African name. Being fed up with always trying to teach them the proper pronunciation of my name I have decided to introduce myself simply as Robert.'

"That is typical of the people here!' she exclaimed. 'Many have just made up their minds never to learn anything that's not familiar to them—particularly when it happens to originate from Africa!'

Nina seemed to have waited for the opportunity to establish contact with me. From that moment on she never left my company. Before we departed that evening she gave me her telephone number. She asked for mine as well. She was disappointed when I told her I had none.

'Don't worry,' I tried to calm her. 'I will call you from time to time.'

I kept my promise and called her the next evening.

She was delighted by my call and was reluctant to end the conversation. From then on I called her regularly.

We met in church the next Sunday. She took the opportunity to introduce me to her grandmother, Margarethe (name changed), who turned 60 a few months after our first meeting. As was the case on our first meeting, her grandmother accompanied her on every occasion we arranged a meeting. Later Nina told me more about herself and her family.

Her father happened to be an American soldier who used to be stationed in Berlin. (Up until German Unification in 1990 several American soldiers were stationed in West Berlin.) Her father on his part was the product of a relationship between an American of African descent and an American of Indian descent. While in Berlin, he met her mother. In due course an affair developed between the two. Just about the time his term of duty in Berlin was about to end, her mother became pregnant. Her father tried to persuade his pregnant girlfriend to accompany him to the States. According to Nina, her mother had wanted to follow her lover.

'No!' her grandmother had objected.

Her grandmother seemed to have had a great deal of influence on her daughter, for her daughter decided to heed her advice and remain in Berlin whilst her American lover left for home.

Was it out of frustration for having lost contact with her lover? Was it out of anger towards her mother for having contributed to the situation? Nina could not say. One thing was certain, however—shortly after Nina's eyes saw the light of day, her mother deposited her with her grandmother and refused to take her back!

The duty then fell on the middle-aged woman to nurse her few days' old granddaughter. A strong emotional bond had since existed between Nina and her grandmother. For example, she used the word *Mutti* (Mum) to refer to her instead of *Oma* (Grandma). When her grandfather passed away, she was left alone with her Mutti.

At the time I got to know them they lived in a three-room apartment located in a southern district of the city.

As she grew up Nina became increasingly fascinated with the American way of life. She invested extra energy to learn the English language. Towards this goal she became a regular listener to the American Forces Radio based in West Berlin.

At the time of our meeting I was astonished by her good command of the English language. This was against the background that Mutti, with whom she spent most of her time, had almost no knowledge of English. As I learnt from Nina, she used to worship with the Paulus Gemeinde, the German sister church. After one joint service with the American congregation, she opted to remain with the Americans. Mutti joined her, although she scarcely understood what went on there. Indeed, Margarethe barely let her 'daughter' out of her sight.

Soon my friendship with Nina became a three-way relationship. There was barely anything we undertook without her grandmother; be it a bike ride through one of the many forests in the city, be it a walk through the parks, be it a stroll through the city, Mutti almost always expressed the desire to accompany us!

We travelled for the most part by way of our bikes. Soon Mutti realised my old, worn out bike, was a hindrance rather than a help in our undertakings. One day during one of our rides she turned to me and began: 'I have a surprise for you, Robert!'

'What then?'

'I won't reveal it now. Let's meet tomorrow about the same time—at the supermarket around the corner. Do not come with a bike this time. Instead you travel by way of public transport.'

We met as scheduled the next day. When we entered the shop they led me to the area dealing in bicycles.

'You choose one of these bikes,' Mutti began.

I was lost for words.

'Yes, choose one! Nina and I have decided to present you with a new bike to facilitate your movement!'

Eventually I settled for a green bike with the brand name 'HOLLAND LOOK'.

When I cycled on it to Blumeshof that evening, my roommates could hardly believe their eyes!

If anything happened that could be described as a climax to my friendship with Nina it came during the annual German-American Friendship Day of 1982. As Nina told me, it was a street festival held once every year by the American forces in the city. It was organised on a big open compound near a shopping complex that served the American forces and their dependants there. Nina and I decided to attend and, as usual, Mutti accompanied us.

After visiting various stands we were drawn to an area from which some of the latest pop music seemed to be emanating.

'Let's find out what's happening there,' she urged me

I followed her. It happened to be the stand of the American Forces Radio.

Not long after we got there, it was announced that a dancing competition was about to take place. The contest was open to all. Single individuals could not enter. In fact, contestants could only enter as male and female couples.

'Come on Robert, let's try our luck!' Nina urged me.

I knew her to be a good dancer. One of her pastimes was to dance to loud music in her room. On one or two occasions her neighbours had complained to her Mutti about the noise!

And me? I could not remember the last time I engaged in something like that. Even before I could utter a word she had jumped up to the dance floor and had begun dancing. I did not want to leave her there alone! Soon I was also on the dance floor shaking my body in some form of a dance, my movement hardly in tune with the rhythm of the song.

Was it because we were what could be described as an exotic pair? Was it because we were brightly dressed? I wore a bright red T-shirt, a pair of ash trousers as well as a blue-white pair of canvas shoes. Nina on her part was wearing a white T-shirt and a blue skirt as well as a white pair of canvas shoes.

Whatever the case, we were favourably judged by the jury who selected us first for the semi-finals and subsequently for the finals! To my amazement we were in the end declared winners! And the dramatic turn of events would not end there! The MC handed us the microphone in turns and allowed us a few minutes to introduce ourselves on live radio!

As a prize, each of us received a long-playing record of a leading pop singer as well as a T-shirt with the inscription of the American Forces Radio Berlin.

On my return to Blumeshof I told my roommates what had happened. On hearing the news they grasped me and carried me on their shoulders! They rejoiced with the *Osofo* (Twi for Pastor) who in their words had at long last been involved in some of the things of this world!

In spite of its peculiar nature, the three-way relationship brought me many advantages. Mutti treated me like a son. Eventually I became a regular guest to their home. I was invited there not only on ordinary days but also on special occasions such as the respective birthdays of the two, Christmas-Eve (Germans regard Christmas-Eve as a very solemn occasion; only close relatives and friends are invited home on such occasions) as well as New Year's Day.

Apart from the material advantage, my friendship with Nina offered me a good opportunity to practice my oral German. As I mentioned earlier, Mutti was not at home in English. I was thus forced to speak German with her.

Realising how much favour had come my way since joining the American church, some of my acquaintances at Blumeshof accompanied me from time to time to also worship with them.

Eventually Seidu, my long-time roommate, expressed his desire to worship with me. He came from the northern part of Ghana. The distinction is important. As I mentioned earlier, the great majority of residents of northern Ghana adhere to the Islamic faith. That was the case with him too.

I was particularly delighted about his decision. He had acquired a second-hand bike which was in quite good condition. One Sunday we cycled together to church.

As was customary in the church, all those attending for the first time were invited to stand up and introduce themselves. Seidu did as required, mentioning that he shared the same room with me and that I had led him there.

At the end of the service I introduced him formally to Nina and Mutti. After he had exchanged a few words with them we left for the hostel.

In the ensuing weeks, Seidu occasionally accompanied me to church. On one such occasion he engaged in a long conversation with Mutti. In the process she gave him her number and address and asked him to contact her when he needed help. Eventually I realised something was developing between the two.

I suspected his intentions. His asylum case had in the meantime been rejected. Though he had appealed against the ruling, he knew, like anyone else, that it would only serve to prolong things for a short while

The news had dawned on other asylum seekers in the hostel that marriage to a German citizen or a citizen from one of the member states of the EU was the best guarantee for gaining a residence permit. Many asylum seekers in fact were desperately looking round for a marriage opportunity. Some made it their policy to frequent the discos, while others visited the pubs; yet others went on regular walks through parks looking for the opportunity of a chance encounter with a likely partner.

Seidu had a German girlfriend who was about his age. However, from what he told us about her, she didn't seem to be in a hurry to marry. And so it became clear from his conversations with me and others that he saw in Mutti someone he could use to regularise his stay in Germany.

I decided to warn her to beware of him—a measure which, unfortunately, was to bring about the demise of the friendship!

Acting according to the principle that 'if you don't want me to progress in life, I will do my best to ensure progress doesn't come your way either,' Mutti set out to systematically destroy the friendship between me and Nina. Some of the methods she adopted included banging down the phone, refusing to open the door of their home to me, forbidding Nina to turn up for an appointment with me. Soon I lost the privilege I enjoyed in their home—the favour that enabled me to enjoy the delicious dishes she prepared every Sunday.

Just as I was suffering under her disfavour, Siedu, who she had in the meanwhile begun to refer to as her 'future husband', was basking in the luxury of her favours. To enable him to drive her around, she paid for his driving school. Days after he received his German driving licence, she bought him a middle-class saloon car. Soon they set about to procure the necessary documents he needed from Ghana to enable him to marry in Germany. Barely six months after they got to know each other they were married. Married to a German citizen, Siedu was soon granted a residence permit.

With the substantial capital that is purported to have come from his wife, Siedu began a small business, buying used cars from Germany and re-selling them in Ghana.

Although I maintained contact with Nina for a while, it eventually broke down completely.

24

At the mercy of the 'gods' in white

Well did the executive member of the Soviet Friendship Society in Accra advise me to avoid exposing my left ankle to the winters of Europe!

Throughout spring and summer of 1982 the weather in Germany was very friendly. Daytime temperatures remained far above 25°C. That led my roommates and myself to wonder whether the reports reaching us in Africa regarding the cold European whether had not been unduly exaggerated after all.

Our conclusion turned out to be premature .With the arrival of October the cold weather gradually set in. The fall in temperatures led me to experience pains from my left ankle joint once again. As the cold intensified, so also did the pains. Frustration with the situation gradually gave in to anger.

As if in conflict with part of my body I would say to my leg, 'You left ankle joint! When will you cease to torment me! Ever since I was young you have continued to be a thorn in my flesh! Having prevented me from studying in the Soviet Union, you want to make life difficult for me here as well!'

Initially I tried to suppress the pains. In due time however the pains became unbearable. Finally I informed the social worker at Blumeshof about the situation.

As an asylum seeker, she informed me, I was entitled to free medical care. After consulting the yellow pages she directed me to a General Practitioner not far away. I consulted the physician without delay.

Eventually he referred me to an orthopaedic surgeon. He requested an X-ray. On taking a look at the picture he began to shake his head.

'What is wrong?' I inquired.

'Not very good,' he replied. 'How did it all start?'

I gave him a quick summary.

'Well, I will first try to inject some medicine into the joint. Maybe it will help. If it doesn't you should come again.'

He then instructed the assistant to prepare the injection. Finally, with the secure hands of a person who seemed to be very confident in his field, he injected a white solution into the joint.

The medicine seemed to work wonders! Shortly after it had been injected all pains seemed to have vanished to nowhere!

'That is Germany, indeed!' I said to myself. Long before I stepped on the soil of Germany, I was aware of the reputation West Germany enjoyed in the field of medicine. I did not need any further proof of that.

A week passed; two, three; I hardly experienced pain. Had German medicine finally cured me? Not yet, as I would soon realise.

As temperatures kept falling towards the end of the year, the discomfort began to re-surface. The pains seemed to increase in intensity directly proportional to the falls in temperature!

Finally, at the beginning of January 1983, I was forced to consult the orthopaedic surgeon once more.

He repeated the therapy of the last consultation.

'I hope all will be well with you,' he said after he had safely injected the same type of solution into my joint.

No, all would not be well with me. This time the injection relieved the pain for only a couple of days. Soon I could hardly walk. I called on my doctor the third time

'Well, I thought I could help with the injections. As it is, that is not enough. You will need an operation.'

'An operation?' I inquired in disbelief, as if I did not hear him right.

'Yes; that is the only way out. Indeed I thought as much the very day I saw the X-ray picture. Part of the bones forming the joint appears to be dead.' He pointed to an area on the film. 'The injections were a last minute attempt on my part to avoid the inevitable.'

He paused for a while, probably to give me some time to think about his proposal. He didn't have to! Indeed, after the initial surprise on hearing his proposal came the swift resolution—if that was the only way I could overcome the thorn that had afflicted me over the years, then so be it, and quickly!

'Do you agree to the operation?' he inquired after a while.

'Yes,' was my reply.

'Good. You will need to exercise some patience while I make the necessary arrangement.'

Saying that, he reached for the telephone on his desk and dialled a number. A long conversation with the person on the other end ensued.

My German was enough for me to get a gist of what was going on—he was trying to book an appointment with a hospital where I was to undergo the operation.

Finally he replaced the receiver.

'Well, I have talked to a colleague at one of the leading orthopaedic hospitals in the city. They are trying to fix you into their busy schedule. As soon as they can admit you they will let me know. I suggest that you call my secretary in about two days' time to find out about the latest development in that regard.'

I called his secretary three days later as required.

She asked me to call there personally the next day. Her boss had something for me.

'Well, you have to report in the first week of February at the Oscar Helene Heim in a district of Berlin known as Zehlendorf. I have asked my secretary to give you the address and directions to the place. It is an Orthopaedic Clinic affiliated to the Faculty of Medicine of the Free University Berlin.'

'Will you be operating yourself?' I wanted to know.

'No, I won't be there. I am not aware of the medical system in your country. Over here I am in charge only of out-patient cases. The doctors in the hospitals are responsible for the patients I refer to them—until their discharge. Don't worry though; you will be taken care of by some of the best orthopaedic surgeons around.'

At the beginning of February 1983, I was admitted to the Oscar Helene Heim. My first contact with a German Hospital left a favourable impression on me. First there was the extremely neat environment; next was the staff—from the cleaners, the kitchen staff, the nurses to the doctors—everyone went about his or her duty with a sense of duty that amazed me; finally they seemed never to be in short supply of any material they needed to carry out their assignment.

The stay at hospital was a welcome change to life at Blumeshof. The quality of meals served was far better than I was used to in Blumeshof. Apart from breakfast, lunch and dinner, we also had the privilege of enjoying cakes between lunch and dinner.

A look in the mirror at the end of a few days' stay there led me to say to myself: 'Boy, pray that your stay here lasts for a few more months!'

I resolved to take advantage of my stay in hospital to improve my German, in particular the spoken part. At the beginning the staff struggled to communicate with me in English. 'No, you may do so in German,' I told them one after the other. Naturally it was the option preferred by the majority. Later I realised that a few among them saw in me an opportunity for them to practice their English!

A day prior to the operation, I was lying in bed pondering over what was ahead of me when one of the nurses entered the room. 'The doctor in charge of the ward has asked me to come for you,' she began.

'What for?'

'I suppose you have to appear before a doctors' conference.'

'A doctors' conference?!'

'Well, as far as I know, from time to time they meet there to discuss some selected cases prior to the day of operation.'

Without any further questions I put on my clothes and followed her. The nurse led me to a small conference room on the ground floor in the building. Already assembled were about two dozen students and lecturers. All of them were dressed in white—a white pair of trousers, a white shirt or T-shirt, and over it a white coat. Each carried a stethoscope—either hanging loosely around the necks or emerging from the large pockets of the coats.

Seated at one corner of the room were about five other patients. Shortly after my arrival the session got underway. Based on the X-ray pictures from the respective patients one of the senior doctors discussed the cases with the students. Before each case was addressed, the patient was asked to give a short history of his illness. In the middle of the discussion the students from time to time sought further information from the patient involved.

I was fascinated by the medical terms I was hearing. Even as I sat there, I wished I was one of them!

At last it was my turn. Here, too, I requested that the questions be put in German. I provided the information requested to the best of my knowledge.

The leading doctor explained what was to be done—they intended to remove dead bone from two bones that formed the ankle joint at one point. The endings of the two bones would then be joined together and allowed to grow into one another. I would have to spend several weeks in hospital after the operation.

The operation was conducted in the second week of February. When I awoke from the anaesthesia, I could hardly believe what I beheld. Two surgical pins, each about five centimetres in diameter, penetrated my leg in two places—one directly through the middle of the ankle joint, the other about ten centimetres proximal to the first. After its journey through my body, about ten centimetres of each pin was allowed to hang in the air on either side of my leg. To keep them stable there, two other pins, each about double the size of those just referred to, had been screwed to the free endings that emerged from my ill-fated leg.

Quite a cumbersome construction, I found. To have a proper idea of how things looked, the reader might picture a rectangular metal construction through which my left leg from below the level of the knee-joint passed. Besides the metal construction, the whole left ankle as well as a great deal of the left leg was in bandage. As I later found out, the bandage covered two wounds both of which stretched from the area of the joint to about 10 centimetres above it.

As the junior doctor told me in answer to my question, the metals were meant to stabilise the new ankle joint that had been created from the old to prevent it from dislocating.

On the question as to how long the metal construction would be in place, he replied that it would only be dismantled after X-ray pictures had shown sufficient growth had occurred at the newly created joint—which could take several weeks. Only when the metals had been removed would I be discharged, he explained.

My new-found friends—Emmanuel and Anna, Tony and his wife Joyce, Nina and Margarethe, Gary and Kurt, and several residents of Blumeshof as well as some members of the American Church—visited me regularly in hospital.

I took my Holy Bible with me to the hospital. As it is my custom, I read it regularly. It was even more needed to provide comfort at a time when I was hospitalised in a strange land several thousand kilometres from my home.

I never realised that what I considered a normal custom would attract someone's attention and open the way for much blessings in the future. A few days after the operation I was being attended to by Ilse, the physiotherapist assigned to me. All of a sudden she said: 'I want to confess one thing—since I started working in this hospital several years ago, you are the first patient I have seen reading a Bible!'

'You don't mean that!' I replied, really taken aback.

What was so unusual about reading through a Bible from the hospital bed? She could visit any hospital in Ghana to find a confirmation of that, I thought to myself.

'Well, I don't know how long you have lived here. Sadly, few residents in this society wish to be associated with the Bible. Only a few shame themselves to be seen reading the Bible in such a public place!'

Throughout much of the day I reflected on Ilse's words. I was so amazed that reading through the Bible had become something special or unique in Germany—in Germany, of all places, the birthplace of Martin Luther, the person who at risk to his own life stood against the authorities of his time and invested such energy and effort to translate the holy scriptures so as to make it readable for his people! I prayed for the Holy Spirit to descend on the land to open the eyes of the residents to behold Divine Truths!

The meeting with Ilse turned out to be a great blessing. Through her I came into contact with several German Christians who not only enriched me spiritually but also provided me with material assistance.

◆   ◆   ◆

A few days after the operation, the doctor in charge of the ward entered my room accompanied by a nurse. It was an unusual time of day for him to visit me. The daily ward rounds were already over.

I could judge from the look in their eyes that they had something important to impart.

'We have to isolate you, Robert!"
'Why?' I asked, surprised.
'We now know the cause of your condition.'
'What is it?'
'It is a tuberculosis infection of the bone!'
'Really?'
'Yes.'
'How did you know?'
'As a matter of routine we sent a specimen of bone tissue from your operation for examination. We have just received the result. It has revealed that your ailment was due to a tuberculosis infection. Over the next several days you will have to undergo several additional tests. We will have to find out whether the infection had been restricted to your leg and that it has not affected other important organs such as the lungs and the kidney. In the meantime we will have to isolate you.'

'That is not all that bad, Robert, you will get a single room!' the nurse tried to comfort me. Soon action followed words as I was wheeled into a single room.

True to the word of the junior doctor, several tests were conducted on me thereafter—including an X-ray of the lungs.

Fortunately, the germs seemed to have been satisfied with my left ankle and had decided to restrict themselves to that part of my body! Nevertheless, I was immediately placed on anti-tuberculosis medication. The doctors told me I would be on it for a minimum of six months, if not a whole year. I was relieved that at long last the cause of the ailment that had tormented me well over the last several years had been detected.

I wrote to my parents to inform them about the new development in regard to my leg. But would they understand? They knew that TB could affect the lungs.

But that it could be behind *my* problem—particularly in the light of all they had heard from the various healers?

◆   ◆   ◆

A few weeks after the operation I began to write to various universities to request application forms. I wanted to apply for the winter semester beginning in October. From what the doctors told me, by then I would be in the position to walk sufficiently freely to be able to attend lectures should I be selected. In all, I applied to about ten universities, including Berlin, Düsseldorf, Hannover and Kiel. I used Tony's address.

Not long after I had despatched the letters, the application forms began to arrive. Tony brought them to me during his visits. I set out to fill them in without any waste of time. Notwithstanding the fact that it was generally thought to be almost impossible to be selected, I selected medicine as my first choice in all the Universities.

During major ward rounds one day, the eyes of the head of department caught sight of the forms spread on my bedside desk.

'What are those for?' he inquired.

'They are university application forms!'

'Oh, I see. You want to study?'

'Yes sir,' I replied.

'What then?'

'Medicine!'

'Sure?'

'Yes, sir.'

'That is an ambitious aim!'

'I have decided to aim high!'

'Why not? That is a good philosophy of life! In any case I wish you all the best in your endeavours.'

'Thank you, sir.'

The eyes of the dozen or so doctors, nurses and physiotherapists accompanying him were directed at me!

There was one practical problem that needed to be resolved before I could despatch the completed application forms: all the universities required recent passport-size photographs, something I didn't have. The forms had to reach the universities latest by July 15. I could not wait until I was discharged before going to take the pictures. It was around April and the doctors were still ambiguous regarding the approximate time I would be discharged.

I discussed the matter with Emmanuel and Anna on one of their visits. Emmanuel offered to help to push me in a wheelchair to a photoshop about one kilometre away. The only precondition was that the doctors wouldn't be against it.

The doctor responsible for my ward, on hearing my request, gave me the green light. I needed to sign a declaration, though, that I was going at my own risk. The stage was thus set for Emmanuel to help me to the photoshop. One afternoon, just after lunch, he arrived to fetch me.

Having obtained the pictures, I set out to despatch the completed forms. By the middle of June the last form had left my desk. I had done my part—it was left for the Lord to let His will be done.

I remained in hospital until July. Finally the time came for me to be discharged. Apart from a small screw that the doctors had decided to leave in my body for some few more months, all metals had been removed from my body. My left leg was placed in a cast which had been constructed in such a way as to permit walking with it.

I still needed to attend the out patients department from time to time. In taking the circumstances into consideration, the social worker contacted the authorities responsible for housing me to discuss the possibility of finding me accommodation in the vicinity of the hospital. (Blumeshof was about ten kilometres away.) The authorities responded positively to the request and housed me in a hostel about two kilometres away from the hospital.

Another issue needed to be tackled. As I mentioned earlier, I needed to take the anti-tuberculosis drugs for a while. Whilst I was in hospital, the hospital was responsible for placing the medication at my disposal. The moment I left the hospital, the medication had to be prescribed by a family doctor. There was therefore the need for me to find a General Practitioner in the neighbourhood where I lived.

Before my departure the social worker, after consulting the yellow pages, wrote out the addresses of three such doctors in the vicinity where I was being sent and asked me to find out which of the three could take me on.

25

My difficult neighbour

I was housed at a hostel on a street called Elvirasteig in Berlin-Zehlendorf.

It had beautiful surroundings. The street bordered on a large forest that boasted of several recreational parks. Only a stone's throw from it was the Krumme Lanke, a large lake. Particularly in summer the lake attracted several holidaymakers, some of whom came there not only to swim, but also to sunbathe on the green grassy fields along its shores.

The relative peace I had enjoyed at Oskar Helene Heim came to an abrupt end, however. In Blumeshof there were several Ghanaians so the hostel owner could house us in small groups in the same room. The situation was different in my new hostel. At the time I moved there, I was the only African. The majority were Asians—from Iran, Pakistan, Sri Lanka, amongst others. Eventually I was allocated a room occupied by an asylum seeker from Iran. As I later learnt, prior to my arrival, no one had been able to stay with him beyond a few days.

What made the well educated person so difficult to live with, I wondered? Later he told me more about himself. He used to be married to a German citizen with whom he had two children. Later the marriage broke up. The woman left with the children to settle in a town in Holland, not far from the German border. According to him, she adopted various tricks to prevent him from seeing his children. Not able to bear the situation, he had resorted to alcohol.

That, in any case, was the reason he gave to explain the situation he found himself in—a terrible one, for that matter. He spent almost all the meagre resources at his disposal on alcohol. He could buy a package containing half a dozen cans of beer, each containing half a litre of the alcoholic drink. In no time my roommate, who was about 175 cm tall and weighed not less than 140 kilograms, poured everything down his throat!

That was the first stage. Next he consulted the corner where he kept his cigarettes. One after the other he set about to smoke without taking his non-smoking roommate into consideration. After he had smoked several sticks, he turned his attention finally to the refrigerator in an attempt to satisfy his hunger. In that regard, he never minded whether the items it contained were his or mine—his hunger needed to be satisfied, that was all that mattered to him. Woe unto me if I protested! If I did he would bombard me with a barrage of insults.

What was to be done? First I complained to the owner of the hostel.

'I am sorry,' he replied, 'I do not have anywhere else to house you. The only alternative is to ask the authorities to house you somewhere else.

That was easier said than done. First there was no such hostel apart from Elvirasteig in the vicinity. Secondly, the bureaucracy involved would have resulted in a long delay. In the end I decided to follow a Christian principle which admittedly is not easy to abide by unless with the help of the Holy Spirit: 'Do not be overcome by evil, but overcome evil with good'—Romans 12:21(KJV).

The first strategy I adopted in that regard was to avoid doing or saying anything that would provoke him to anger. Second, I would not react to his incessant outbursts of insults, however offending.

Not long after I had made this resolve, he returned late in the night after a spree through the city. He assumed I was asleep, though I certainly wasn't. Shortly after his arrival he consulted the refrigerator. There was nothing there for him. That made him furious. 'The foolish African has eaten everything!' he burst out. 'Hey, you glutton! Next time you've got to leave something for others, okay!' He continued his barrage ofi nsults for a while, making use of one derogatory term after another.

When he realised I wasn't responding, he said to himself: 'Poor soul—he must be deep asleep!'

After a while he retired to bed. Moments later he was snoring loudly. His snores were of such an intensity that they threatened to shake the whole foundation of the building. I refrained from mentioning anything of the previous night the following morning.

Eventually, I invited him to accompany me to church. Indeed he did accompany me on several occasions. In the course of time I also introduced him to Ilse. Together we did our best to show him Christian love and help him whenever we could. In the end a cordial relationship developed between us. He stopped his verbal attacks, didn't attempt to take anything that belonged to me, and even tried to share some of the food he purchased with me.

In his desire to see his children, he left the hostel one day to travel to an acquaintance living near where they supposedly were. His hope was that his host would be able to arrange a meeting between him and his children. He never returned.

26

On the verge of success

From the information I got from the universities, latest by the middle of August applicants would have been notified about the outcome of their applications. Successful foreign students, unless they had attained a certain level in the German language, would be invited to sit for a German language test towards the end of September. Those who passed the test could matriculate as official students at the beginning of October.

As the middle of August approached I grew nervous. An admission to the university was essential not only for my academic future but also in regard to my stay in Germany in general. I had no illusion as to the outcome of my asylum application—that it would be rejected was a ninety-nine percent certainty, and I knew it.

I had used Tony's address to apply. Starting from the middle of August, I called there almost every evening for the latest news. The first University to write was the Free University in Berlin. Unfortunately, owing to the large number of applications they had to consider, they were unable to offer me admission, they wrote. About five additional rejection letters followed close on the heels of the first.

Spells of despair mixed with the fear for the future descended on me from time to time. Meanwhile August had stretched to the 22nd day.

I lifted up my eyes towards the Hills to look for help—and help seemed nowhere in sight. Finally one Monday evening in late August I made my usual evening call to Tony. I had meanwhile become used to his reply: 'No, nothing has arrived.'

Contrary to what I had tuned my mind to expect, Tony this time was excited. 'I just returned from work so I have not been able to read my letters. This time, though, a letter has arrived from the Medizinische Hochshule in Hannover which differs from all the others that have arrived so far,' he continued. 'This time it involves a big brown envelope. You hang on whilst I open it.'

A few tense moments followed during which my heart seemed to jump out of my body as the excitement hormones poured into my bloodstream.

'Are you still there?' Tony's voice filled my ears again.

'Of course I am. Any good news?'

'Yes indeed, you have made it, boy! Hannover has offered you admission!'

'I will be there in a few minutes!' I screamed at the top of my voice.

'We shall await you—hurry up…!'

I didn't wait for him to finish and hurriedly replaced the receiver. Before long I was hurrying to the nearby Underground Station, Krumme Lanke, on my way to Tony's home at Kreuzberg.

Tony met me at the door. 'Congratulations!' he exclaimed. 'That is a superb achievement!' He led me to his sitting room and handed me *the large brown envelope!*

Contrary to all expectations, the Medizinische Hochschule in Hannover, MHH for short, had decided to offer me admission for the Wintersemester 1983/84! The only precondition was for me to pass a German language test which was to be held in about four weeks' time.

I began to see my dreams come true. I saw in my mind's eye myself sitting in the lecture hall listening to lectures: anatomy, physiology, biochemistry. I continued to fantasize. I saw a picture of myself with a stethoscope on my shoulder, taking part in ward rounds, everywhere Europeans, myself the only African around!

After the initial excitement came the realisation that a major hurdle needed to be cleared before I could begin my studies.

As I mentioned earlier, my passport was taken from me when I submitted my asylum application. Not only did I need the document to travel to Hannover, I needed it also for the registration at the Medical School.

How could I convince the authorities to return my passport to me? Throughout that evening this thought occupied my mind.

The next day I called Emmanuel as well as several leading members of the Ghana Students Union to discuss the issue with them. The gist of the advice I received was the following: The authorities might only consider my request if I could convince them I had the financial resources to live on. In this regard I was advised to find an individual of influence or an organisation to issue me a statement of sponsorship. The admission letter backed by the statement of financial support might move the authorities to hand me back my passport.

Even if they didn't want to as a matter of policy, financial considerations alone might lead them to think otherwise—as an asylum seeker I lived at the expense of the taxpayer; as a student that would no longer be the case.

Who was I to consult for the statement of sponsorship? Two persons came to mind—Gary and Kurt.

Eventually I decided to consult Kurt first. Being in charge of a German Church, his letter should carry more weight before the authorities, I reasoned.

Kurt was delighted about what I had to tell him. As a result of my association with the American Church, our ways had crossed on several occasions. A relation bordering on friendship had in the meantime developed between us. On the issue of the sponsorship letter he asked me to give him some time to consider his decision. At the appointed time I called on him again. The letter was ready!

Armed with the admission letter and Kurt's statement, I approached the authorities and appealed to them to return the passport to me. The negative reply was prompt and decisive.

Foreigners, the officer told me as a prelude to his lecture, were heartily welcome to study in Germany; asylum seekers, on the other hand, were not permitted to do so, so long as their cases had not been decided on. The reason, he continued, was not difficult to understand. It was possible that their application might be rejected midway through their studies. That would mean the applicants would have to abandon their studies halfway through—amounting to a waste of time and resources! To avoid a situation like that, asylum seekers were advised to wait until their cases had been decided before attempting to do anything.

A dutiful civil servant he clearly was. He would not end his speech without pointing me to the other option at my disposal. Under the circumstance, he continued, I could also consider withdrawing my application. I could then travel out of the country and try my luck at any German consulate. Perhaps one of them would be willing to issue me a student's visa. Armed with such a permit, I could re-enter the country and take up my studies.

His advice was a non-starter for several reasons: The doctors were yet to decide when to remove the cast. The last X-ray taken a few days before had not shown enough bone consolidation to warrant a removal. Furthermore, the officer was aware that hardly any German consulate would issue me with a visa when it became known that I had been living there as an asylum seeker. Finally, even if these two factors didn't exist, I still didn't have the financial means to embark on such a venture. Even if I found a German consulate willing to issue me the visa, for procedural reasons, it could take several days before they could do that. How could I pay for a stay in a hotel?

For the next few days I was very disheartened. Yet I didn't allow the circumstance to overwhelm me for long and pondered on the next step to take.

One evening I visited Nina and Margarethe. Both had shared in the joys and sorrows of the last few days.

'I have an idea, Robert!' Margarethe began shortly after we were settled for dinner.

'Go ahead, I'm listening,' I replied.

'As I told you some time ago, the Minister for Internal Affairs of the Federal State of Berlin happens to live on the other end of this street. I am considering writing to him on your behalf to solicit his help. I will emphasise in my letter the fact that you are handicapped with your left leg and implore him to use his position to help you on humanitarian grounds.'

'That is very kind of you. I am sceptical though. From some of the reports I have been reading about him, I doubt whether he will be willing to help me.'

'Well, there's no harm in trying. Maybe when he realises that the letter was written by a street neighbour he would want to help.'

Saying that, Margarethe took pen and paper and got down to work. The next day the letter was ready to post.

Margarethe did not have to wait long for the reply of her street neighbour.

The Minister for Internal Affairs of Berlin found his hands bound by existing laws and could not make an exception for me—not even on humanitarian grounds.

27

Face to face with West Berlin's Governor

Though I did not reckon with the help of the Internal Minister, when he finally turned down our request, my disappointment was beyond measure. Just as I was resigning myself to my fate, I visited Nina und Margarethe early in September. The moment I took my seat Margarethe approached me with the day's edition of one of the leading mass circulating newspapers.

'I want to show you something,' she said and turned the pages. Finally she pointed to a passage.

'What is that?' I asked.

'You read it yourself.'

I read it reluctantly. It was a small announcement from the city administration. The general public was being notified about an open day being organised by the Governor of the city. Residents could bring their problems, petitions and other issues that they thought fell under his sphere of influence before him.

'Have you got the message!' Margarethe inquired after a while.

'Yes, of course.'

'Why don't you go and talk your problem over with him?'

'Ach Margarethe!' I said smiling. 'The notice referred to citizens **of Berlin**. I am only a guest!'

'Come on! So long as you are resident here you are also a citizen!'

'A third-class citizen for that matter!'

'If not a fourth, Robert!' Nina cut in. As a result of the discrimination and prejudice she said she had experienced by dint of the colour of her skin, she had grown highly sensitive to such issues.

'Do you want to see him or not?' Margarethe pressed on.

'Yes, of course! As the saying goes, there is no harm in trying.'

'Herr Weizacker is a kind person. I am sure he will use his influence to help you,' she added.

Thus I decided to take my case to the highest authority in the city on the open day which was only two days away.

Margarethe gave me a tip which turned out to be useful. From her experience, she told me, such open sessions were well patronised by the public. Timing there fore would be a deciding factor—whether one got the opportunity to meet him or not.

Naturally, I did not want to miss what I regarded as my last best opportunity to enter the university that year. Consequently I left home very early for the session.

The cast had still not been removed. I also possessed a pair of crutches. As far as the crutches were concerned, the doctors had given me a lot off reedom in regard to their use. Based on the intensity of pain I experienced, I could do away with them completely, or else resort to one of them or both.

On the day of the meeting I could as well have done without them. I decided nevertheless to make use of them—if only to add some degree of drama to the spectacle. A dark skinned resident, not in the best of clothes, carrying a white cast on one leg, supporting himself with a pair of crutches, the expression on his face betraying the considerable pain he was enduring in a purely European setting…Such was the scene many a playwright might introduce to elicit the sympathetic response of his audience!

Yes indeed, I was determined to carry my plight in the most forceful of terms, even in a manner that would help leave a lasting trace in the archives of the Governor's memory—in the very arena where the most striking scenes that confronted him during his tenure of office as Governor of West Berlin were enacted.

The session was to be held at the Rathaus Charlottenberg, a magnificent building which at that time served as seat of government. I arrived around six in the morning. The session was to begin around eight. True to Margarethe's predictions, several others had already lined up to the entry of the building at the time of my arrival. Not long after my arrival, numbers were distributed. I was delighted to find I was among the first ten.

'Come what may, I am to meet the Mayor of Berlin face to face!' I encouraged myself.

Soon the numbers began to swell behind me. In time several additional numbers arrived. Finally the security decided to shut the main gate to prevent anyone from entering.

We waited in a large hall. I was the only African—if not the only foreigner present. From time to time I took a look around me. On these occasions my eyes met those of others directed in my direction. The inquisitive faces seemed to inquire: 'What does this poor African want from our Mayor?'

I was not perturbed; I had acquired a number that would enable me to bring my plight to the mayor of the city—that was more important to me than anything around me.

Finally at around 8 o' clock, the first person in the line was asked to follow a tall man aged about 45 years. After about twenty minutes it was the turn of the next person. The session proceeded steadily as one after the other those lined up were called to meet the honourable Herr Weizacker.

It was around 10 o'clock when the person just ahead of me was called in.

'Very soon it will be your turn,' I said to myself. 'How are you going to present your case?'

Several ideas went through my mind as I considered the best way to present my case. I knew from various sources that the mayor spoke perfect English. Initially I considered using English. On second thought I rejected that idea. Instead, I opted to meet him in his own mother tongue. My German, while not perfect, was proficient enough to enable me to express the reason why I was there.

Would I emerge from the meeting victorious?

I had no idea. A sense of pride filled my heart though. I counted myself a winner, whatever the outcome of the meeting. I had been able to bring my case to the highest authority in Berlin. Posterity could not accuse me of not having tried all that was in my power to do as a human being.

Finally, the tall middle-aged man asked me to follow him. Supporting myself on the pair of crutches, I got up and followed him.

He led me into a large room. Seated behind a large wooden desk and dressed in an elegant dark suit befitting his high office was the highest personage the city could boast of.

The moment he caught sight of me he sprang out of his seat and headed towards me. On reaching me he held me tenderly under the shoulder and accompanied me the remaining few metres to a chair placed opposite his own.

I could read the embarrassment written on the face of the official who had come to call me. Was it an expression of guilt for having failed to show the gesture of kindness towards me the way his boss had?

After I was seated comfortably, Mr von Weizacker kindly asked, 'What can I do for you?'

'I have come to express my gratitude to the government and people of Germany for the help they have accorded me so far,' I began. 'In the first place they have given me somewhere to live as a refugee. Secondly, I have been privileged to receive free medical care for a condition that had afflicted my left ankle joint for several years. In the meantime I have been admitted to the Medical School in Hannover. I need my passport to go there. This was taken from me when I applied for asylum. Unfortunately, when I contacted the authorities to get it back, they turned down my request. I have come to appeal to your high office to help use your influence to get it back. Much as I have been helped medically by your doctors, I remain physically handicapped for life. That is all the more reason why I want to study, for I am incapable of performing any job that requires physical exertion of the body.'

I ended my speech on that note. I congratulated myself for the ability to say all that I wanted to say clearly and boldly.

All the time I spoke Mr von Weizacker listened with the utmost attention. If the expression on his face was anything to go by he seemed very much at a loss himself with the intricacies of the laws governing asylum seekers in his country. He did not reply immediately I had stopped talking. Instead, he sat down for a while, considering the situation.

Finally he turned to his subordinate.

'The young man should be given the chance to take up his studies,' he said. 'Wherein lies the difficulty?'

'Well sir,' his subordinate countered, 'the decision not to return the passport to him is exactly in line with the rules and regulations governing asylum seekers. The law forbids them to work or study so long as their cases have not been determined. The gentleman should have been aware of that from the outset!'

'Is it not possible to make an exception in this special case?'

For a while the official was silent. Finally he turned to me. 'Well, young man, you come to see me at my office tomorrow. I will see how best I can help you.' He then handed me a sheet. 'That piece bears my name. If you arrive, ask the ladies at the Information to direct you to me.'

Just as he had done on my arrival, the Governor of Berlin got up again to help me to the door.

Not long after the meeting, Herr Weizacker was elected to the position of President of the Federal Republic of Germany. Though a purely ceremonial post, it is a highly respected position. Among other things he has the power to appoint and dismiss the Federal Chancellor as well as Federal Ministers, sign legislation passed on the Federal level into law, and also appoint and dismiss federal judges and civil servants. Herr Weizacker brought a considerable degree of respect and flair to his office during his eight years of service.

Whenever I saw him speak on TV, read about him in the newspapers or heard him performing other duties as President, my thoughts went back to my meeting with him. In such a situation, I would say to myself: 'Does he still remember the meeting with the poor, handicapped asylum seeker from Ghana?'

I called on the high ranking civil servant the following day as requested. The bitter disappointment after that seemingly promising meeting is still fresh in my memory. Seated alone before him, with no superior to take into consideration, he could speak his mind freely. Looking at me sternly he began his tirade: 'You and these asylum seekers! How long do we have to tolerate you! The moment we offer you one centimetre you demand a metre! You are parasiting on the resources of the state, a big burden to the taxpayer! If only you would stop there! But no, you also want to block the chances of our children to study. My daughter, for example, very desirous to study medicine, has been waiting in vain for years to be admitted!' He shook his head. 'No, I cannot help you. If you still wish to take up your studies, you can withdraw your asylum application and travel back to Ghana. There you can apply for a student's visa at the German embassy.' He ended his address with a threat! 'I really do not understand why some universities still choose to admit people like you. I will write to them to advise them to stop doing that.'

On the way home I pondered over his speech. To allege that I was blocking the chance of his daughter was a distortion of the facts. He should know that as part of his government's Development Aid Programme a certain percentage of admissions to various fields of study in universities and other institutions of high learning were allocated to students from the developing countries. My information was that the quota for medicine at that time was around five percent. Thus her daughter did not have to compete with me for admission.

While I was disappointed with the first part of his speech, it was the last part of his address that really troubled me. Indeed, over the next several days it occupied my mind. Would he make good of his threat and write to Hannover? Would the authorities there listen to him?

My last hope of being admitted to medical school that year was thus forever shattered! What was to be done?

About a week before the scheduled language test, I called the authorities in Hannover to thank them for the offer of admission and regretted I couldn't honour the offer for reasons already known to the reader.

They sympathised with me for the unfortunate turn of events. They told me that unfortunately it was not in their power to reverse things. One thing they promised to do, though—they would give me a second chance the following year. It was their hope, they added, that by then I would have found a solution to my problem. For the sake of formality, however, they asked me to re-apply formally. Not long after the conversation I received a fresh admission form from them. Without delay I filled it in and returned it.

28

I wished I were a privileged foreigner

Have you ever found yourself in a situation when everything seemed to go awry in your life? Did you observe a peculiar phenomenon that I observed? It is a period when one is bombarded with all kinds of advice!

One should not necessary doubt the intentions of those offering such tips. Many do offer their counsel out of a genuine desire to help a loved one out of a tight corner. Much of such pieces of advice are in most instances well intended; but because of the burden of trying to sieve through the flood of information to determine which is relevant to the situation, the multitude of tips could end up having the opposite effect to that intended—to compound one's woes instead of helping to build one up.

The weeks following my unsuccessful attempt to persuade the authorities to return my passport saw me in a similar situation as pieces of advice poured in from friends and well-wishers as to the best way I could manage to make it to Hannover the following year to pick up my studies.

In the course of time I got a deeper insight into the laws relating to the rights and obligations off oreigners in Germany at that time. In particular, I got to understand the concept of 'the privileged foreigner' in the definition of the legal status of some foreigners from Ghana and other countries who are resident in Germany. While not claiming to be an authority here, I wish at this stage to give readers an insight into the terminology 'privileged foreigner.'

The foreigner with that status in Germany could reside anywhere in the country and do almost anything provided his or her activities did not go contrary to the common laws of the country. That person could, for example, study, learn a trade, work and in some cases even establish a business.

To attain that status a foreign national needed to satisfy one of three criteria: (1) That person should be a citizen of one of the member countries of the European Community. (2) That person should be a foreigner who had been granted political asylum or recognised as a refugee in line with the Geneva Convention. (3) Finally, the spouse of that person should be a German national or a national of one of the countries of the European Union with permanent residential status in Germany.

As expected, I began to explore the possibility of attaining that status as a solution to my problem. On account of citizenship, the first criterion was a non-starter. I also refused to give any thought to the second criterion. As I mentioned earlier, the chance of an asylum seeker from Ghana being granted asylum in Germany in those days was so insignificant as to be negligible. It was the third criteria that was feasible, if only theoretically.

If only I could become married to a German lady or someone from the EU, all my problems would be solved. Many a person who heard about my problem urged me towards this solution.

'Don't keep your mouth shut on the streets—anywhere the opportunity comes your way—in the Underground, in the parks, at the bus stop, in the church, try to establish contact with some of them. The moment you get married to one of them your problem is over!' Thus was I advised by some of them.

'You've got to frequent the discos in Berlin, especially the Black Discos. Any lady you meet there is interested in an African, otherwise they wouldn't be there in the first place...'

Yes indeed, I was tempted to seek such short cuts to success.

As I mentioned elsewhere, the teachings of Pastor Ofosu Mensah had been engraved deeply in my psyche. 'Make every effort to become married to someone who shares your faith. In particular avoid the temptation to look out for your partner in a disco. Contacts made in the disco often break up in the disco. You might as well eventually lead such a person to the Lord. It is a risky adventure that should be avoided, particularly by those who themselves are not well established in the Faith.'

I was not prepared to rush into marriage just for the sake of being able to stay and study in Germany.

Theoretically it was Nina who came somewhere close to fulfilling those conditions. But it was a non-starter for a lot of reasons; among others, she was 16 and fully under the control of her grandmother...

Others suggested I entered in a marriage of convenience. I do not know the personal opinions of my readers on the issue. I want to be honest with my readers and not to pretend to act like an angel—for indeed, in view of the circumstances I found myself at that time, I didn't completely rule out that option.

What was worse? To return to Ghana with my handicapped leg to an uncertain future, or pay money to someone to engage her in a marriage of convenience that would enable me pick up my studies in Hannover?

Yes indeed, if I had to make a choice between getting married to a person I didn't love just for the sake of getting the chance to study, and paying money to undergo a contract marriage, I would choose the latter.

Marriage of convenience as far as I was concerned was the response of the creative human mind in reaction to the restrictive immigration laws of many a rich country—regulations whose sole purpose is to ward off the influx of the poor to the rich countries.

As one of my roommates at Blumeshof used to say: imagine the parents of Baby Jesus fleeing the death threats of King Herod having to wait for a visa from the Egyptian Embassy before being allowed to flee there!

I declined to pursue that option, not because I was against it in principle, but for a very different reason.

In the first place, I did not have the financial means required for such a venture. Those familiar with matters relating to such contract marriages told me I would need no less than ten thousand German Marks to engage in something like that. This was made up of the fee to be paid to the potential bride, for the services of the go-between or connection man, for suitable clothes to be worn on the occasion as well as the rings to be exchanged at the wedding.

Some even asked me to make provisions for the services of a professional photographer as well at a party service which would serve snacks after the occasion.

Here, too, they quoted me the Akan proverb I referred to earlier—if you decide to tell lies, tell the lie in such a way that it will bear some resemblance to the truth!

Even if I had the money to entertain this strategy, I was yet to come across either a reliable candidate or a reliable go-between.

Caution was essential—several stories were circulating regarding people without any scruple who had taken advantage of the situation to dupe others of their hard-earned savings. Some of these stories spoke of go-betweens who after receiving part or all of their payments vanished into thin air without leading their clients to their promised candidates. In some instances the connection people did their jobs and led their clients to potential brides or bridegrooms. After all the formalities concerning the marriage—fixing the marriage date, acquisition of rings, purchase of suitable clothes, invitation of witnesses, etc., were completed, candidates vanished with the monies collected.

Some even allowed the arrangements to proceed until the very day of the marriage. Just as everybody was assembled at the registry the 'future' partner simply failed to turn up!

29

Passport Number Two

The first few weeks following the realisation that I could not move to Hannover that year have been some of the most difficult times in my life. I just tried to figure out why things had failed. I began to think it was probably not God's will that I studied medicine.

Okay and good. The other alternative was to go to Bible School. Even then I needed my passport. In Germany, as anywhere else, I would also need financial support.

Did God want to teach me more lessons in humility? Did he want to break everything up so that when He joined everything together one day I would learn to trust only in Him and not in my own strength?

Looking back, I'm convinced that was probably the case.

On numerous occasions I was so overwhelmed by circumstances I could not see any way out. I pictured myself as someone who had been thrown into a deep abyss. All around me was deep darkness. A way of escape seemed nowhere in sight.

I read through Holy Scripture a lot, in particular through portions where God led some of his children out of tight corners. One instance was Abraham and Sarah being promised a son at the time when they were very advanced in age! From the human point of view there was no way that promise could be fulfilled. But because the promise had come from the Lord who knows the end from the beginning, the promise was infallible. Then the same Abraham being asked by God to sacrifice the very child of the promise on the alter! How God intervened at the very last moment to save the situation is another testimony to His integrity. Another instance was that of Daniel who didn't compromise his faith even when he was threatened with being thrown into the den of lions—and see how the hand of God delivered him! And see how Shadrach, Mischach and Abedinego survived in the burning furnace.

Apart from Holy Scripture one book was a source of immense help. E.G. White's *The Desire of Ages* was presented to me a few months before I left Accra to embark on my adventure to Nigeria. Written by one of the architects of the SDA church, I received it from an acquaintance of Grace, a convert to the SDA. Together with his family they lived in an apartment house near the Open Bible Church . We visited them often after church.

The Desire of Ages was an invaluable help to me in trial and uncertainty. Two passages from the book were especially inspiring. I read through these quite often, so in the course of time I could recite both passages almost word for word.

Of Christ's second temptation the author writes:

> It was in the time of greatest weakness that Christ was assailed by the fiercest temptations. Thus Satan thought to prevail. By this policy he gained the victory over men.
>
> When strength failed, and the will-power weakened, and faith ceased to repose in God, then those who had stood long and valiantly for the right were overcome. Moses was wearied with forty years' wandering of Isreal, when for the moment his faith let go its hold upon infinite power.
>
> He failed just upon the borders of the Promised Land. So with Elijah, who had stood undaunted before King Ahab, who had faced the whole nation of Israel, with the four hundred and fifty prophets of Baal at their head. After that terrible day upon Carmel, when the false prophets had been slain, and the people had declared their allegiance to God, Elijah fled for his life before the threats of the idolatrous Jezebel. Thus Satan has taken advantage of the weakness of humanity. And he still works in the same way. Whenever one is encompassed with clouds, perplexed by circumstances, or afflicted by poverty or distress, Satan is at hand to tempt and annoy. He attacks our weak points of character. He seeks to shake our confidence in God, who suffers such a condition of things to exist. We are tempted to distrust God, to question His love. Often the tempter comes to us as he came to Christ, arraying before us our weakness and infirmities. He hopes to discourage the soul, and to break our hold on God. Then he is sure of his prey. If we would meet him as Jesus did, we should escape many a defeat. By parleying with the enemy, we give him advantage.

Then the second passage:

> Christ did not fail, neither was he discouraged, and His followers are to manifest a faith of the same enduring nature. They are to live as He lived, and work as He worked, because they depend on Him as the great Master Worker. Courage, energy, and perseverance they must possess.
>
> Though apparent impossibilities obstruct their way, by His grace they are to go forward. Instead of deploring difficulties, they are called upon to surmount them. They are to despair of nothing, and to hope for everything. With the golden chain of His matchless love Christ has bound them to the throne of God. It is His purpose that the highest influence in the universe, emanating from the source of all power, shall be theirs. They are to have power to resist evil, power that neither earth, nor hell can master, power that will enable them to overcome as Christ overcame.
>
> —E.G. White, *The Desire of Ages*.

Oh, how many times did I peruse those two passages! When doubts as to the leadings of God or His kindness arose in my mind I recited the first passage. Whenever I seemed to want to give up I said to myself: Christ did not fail, neither was he discouraged; courage, energy and perseverance you should possess!

You consider those words, I said to myself. They cannot be empty words. The author would not have written such powerful words unless they were borne out of her own experience. Draw inspirations from her experience.

Courage, energy and perseverance are all that you need!

Persevere—hold on to God until He brings to pass what He says He will do in your life.

As already stated, I lived on the edge of a large forest in Berlin. I made it my custom to go for a walk or a ride through the forest and speak words of encouragement to myself. On some occasions, I noticed too late that others were passing by or coming in the opposite direction. They would overhear me talking to myself.

'Is that man going crazy?' their looks seemed to betray their thoughts.

At certain times my mind was so tensed that even comforting words from the Bible seemed to lack the power to penetrate the dark wall around me.

In such a state of mind, I resorted to fasting. Soon I realised how invaluable was the help that came from fasting in situations like that.

In the course of time I was fasting at short intervals. I did not fast primarily to please God. No, I did so not to go crazy. I did it to be able to withstand the trying times. Once I engaged in a fast I was able to reach a state of mental purity and peace. With the tension on my mind gone, I seemed to be over and above all the problems around me. It was such a wonderful state of mind that I often felt reluctant to break the fast at the end of the day.

Even now my personal belief is that God does not need the fast of His children. It is His children rather who need the fast to attain the state of mind that helps them draw close to Him in their prayers. Fasting, if you like, helps to dissipate the clouds of resistance that would otherwise hamper the transmission of our prayer waves to Heaven.

I had no doubt on my mind as to the ability of God to do what He had promised. It was up to me to be patient and wait. But the waiting—the waiting and not having anything to do to occupy me!

But God did not leave me alone.

One day, when I was very down, I went to a church in Berlin which was attended mainly by the American military community there. There was a Gospel concert going on. The moment I entered the hall and took my seat, the pastor got up to introduce one of the songs about to be sung: 'Friend, when you come to the end of your rope, you just don't give up. Rather tie a knot at the end and wait for the Lord to come your way. Be assured of this—He will surely come.'

The words penetrated deep into my heart. I felt God speaking to me through His servant.

Around the middle of November 1983, when I was still battling with thoughts about how to pick up my studies in Hannover, word reached me that the Ghana Ambassador to Germany was to attend a seminar of the Ghana Students Union in Berlin in a few days' time. That evening I called the president of the Union to find out the truth.

'Yes,' he confirmed, 'the Ambassador is coming down from Bonn to meet us. He has just been posted to the country. He is coming to introduce himself to us.'

'May I bring my situation before him?'

'That's a good idea. Maybe he will be able to help you.'

I waited anxiously for the arrival of that day. Though I was uncertain about the kind of help he could offer, the idea of bringing my case to the highest representative of my country in Germany offered me some hope.

The cast on my left leg had in the meantime been removed. In its place I had been given a specially designed orthopaedic shoe that I was to wear indefinitely. I carried the pair of crutches with me.

When I got there, I could read the disappointment in the faces of those who had already arrived—unforeseen circumstances had prevented the ambassador from attending personally. He had sent a senior staff member of the consulate to deputise for him.

Not long after my arrival, the meeting got underway. The deliberations initially revolved around the political situation at home. The military was still firmly in control of the government. Reports reaching us spoke of political repression coupled with economic hardships. Comfortably gathered in a hall of the Technical University of West Berlin, far away from the national frontiers, we could freely criticise the military for what was going on at home and call for an early return to civilian rule.

After about two hours of lively discussion bearing on the political situation at home, the chairman turned finally to the last item on the agenda—general matters. Participants who wished could bring their personal grievances to the notice of the distinguished guest from Bonn, then the capital of West Germany.

I was among the first to raise his hand. The chairman, who was aware of what I was about to say, gave me the chance to speak first. Briefly but concisely I presented my case to the high ranking representative of my country.

'I am really touched by your story,' he replied after a short silence. 'Our country desperately needs doctors. There is therefore the need for us to support you. You will bear with us though that there is a limit to what the Embassy can do in a situation like this. We are guests of the German government and cannot meddle in their affairs.

'There is one thing we can do for you, however. We can issue you with a new passport to replace the one with them. How far that can help you get round the problem I cannot tell. As you are aware, in the end you will still need a resident permit to be able to take up your studies.'

I was delighted beyond measure at the offer! Although, like the officer, I did not know precisely how the new document could help me out of the situation, for the moment nevertheless joy overshadowed all other considerations.

Soon I was on my feet again. 'Words cannot describe how grateful I am to you!' I began. 'I hope the new passport enables me to take up my studies next year.'

'Well, you can see me after the meeting for us to work out the details in regard to the application procedure.'

I saw him at the end of the session as requested. Whether by chance or design, he was carrying a few passport forms with him. After I had paid the required fee, he gave me one of them and advised me to fill it in and despatch it to him without delay.

Apart from four passport photographs I was required to remit a 'guarantee deposit' of 364 DM (a fee, we were told, that was to meet part of the cost of a possible repatriation) with the completed form.

I completed the forms that very evening. The following Monday I went to a photo shop to have the required photographs taken. From there I went to the post office to despatch the forms and the guarantee money.

A few days later the new passport arrived by registered mail. I was delighted by the arrival of the document.

My joy was short-lived, though. On close examination I detected an error —my family name, a compound name, had not been written in the proper order! Instead of Peprah-Gyamfi, it read Gyamfi-Peprah.

'Poor me!' I shouted to myself. It seemed as if misfortune had decided not to leave me in peace! I began to wonder whether the officials in Bonn would be prepared to issue me with yet another passport! I decided not to bring the issue to their notice myself. Instead I begged one of the executive members of the Ghana Students Union with good contacts to the embassy to talk to them on my behalf.

They regretted the error and asked me to return it, promising to issue me a new one immediately they received the other.

I did as requested. A couple of days later I received another registered letter from Bonn. This time the passport it enclosed bore no error.

Even as I examined it various thoughts were going through my mind. The scenario that presented the best appeal at that time was to wait in Berlin until the second admission letter arrived from Hannover. Armed with it and the new passport, I would find means to travel to Hannover, leaving the old one with the authorities in Berlin.

My plan could only work on one important premise—that I would not have been deported from Germany by then.

Concerning that, there was cause for optimism, for I was yet to be invited for interview .That was very unusual, considering that all the other applicants from Ghana I had contact with who submitted their applications about the time I did had already been called for interview. Even some who submitted their applications long after I did had been heard personally in regard to their claims of running from persecution; some even faced the threat of deportation.

What was happening to my application? My friends and I began to speculate that the doctors had probably notified the authorities in Zindorf about my operation, leading them to suspend work on my file to give the doctors time to treat me! Time would tell if we were completely wrong.

30

Come down, Berlin Wall!

The Lord used several people to contribute towards making my difficult situation in Berlin bearable. Several of them have already been mentioned above.

In this chapter I wish to talk about a few who have yet to be mentioned.

Towards the middle of my stay in Hospital, Ilse picked me up one Sunday in her car to enable me attend a picnic organised by her church. I was not allowed to step on my left foot so we had to take my wheelchair along. She had some difficulty getting the device into the boot of her small car, but she persisted until she succeeded. I could only wonder at the extent to which she was prepared to go to make sure I did not miss the opportunity to break the monotonous life at the hospital for at least a few hours.

During the meeting she introduced me to Ruth and her husband Harald as well as Sabine their only daughter. Not long after the meeting, Harald died suddenly of a heart attack. As expected, his death came as a big blow to the rest of the family. Sabine, as I learnt, was close to her father and seemed for a while unable to come to terms with the new situation. In the end Ruth decided to send her to her uncle in Australia to spend some time there. That step paid off.
On her return to Germany after several weeks' absence, she was in a better position to live with the loss of her dear father.

Ruth and Sabine invited me regularly to their home to share meals with them. Not only that, but they also provided material and financial support whenever they could.

Through Ilse I also got to know Rhea, a retired neurologist. At the time of our meeting she was about 65. She had a deep love for the Lord and devoted much time in Bible reading and prayer. At the time I got to know her, she occupied a large apartment which boasted of at least six large rooms, excluding the kitchen and the toilet.

Rhea lived alone. As I later learnt, she had no children of her own. This background information might lead one to ask why she chose to rent such a large apartment. The fact is that she saw it as part of her Christian calling to invite others, particularly Christians, who for whatever reason had nowhere to live to come and stay with her until such time that their situation allowed them to leave. When Ilse told her about my situation, she asked her to bring me home. Eventually Ilse drove to the hostel to pick me up one Friday afternoon for the visit.

'Bring enough clothes to last you till Monday morning,' she told me.

'Why?' I inquired.

'Rhea wants you to spend the weekend there!'

I was surprised by the kind gesture. Ilse noticed it.

'Well, you be ready for additional surprises in the future!' she smiled. 'Rhea is a woman of the Lord who is so concerned about the suffering of others, particularly the Lord's children.'

I did as requested. Soon we were on our way.

I was heartily welcomed to the large apartment, where I met another guest, Ulrike, aged about 25, a young convert plagued with episodes of depression. Rhea had invited her there for a time of prayer.

After breakfast the next day, my host asked me to accompany her to a shopping mall not far away. She took me to a well-known departmental store.

'Select as much clothing as you will need for the summer,' she urged me.

In the end she ended up buying me goods worth about three hundred DM.

That was to be the beginning of a long association with Rhea.

One day during one of our meetings, she told me the Lord had revealed something about me to her. In her vision she saw me speaking before a large gathering. That led her to wonder whether the Lord wanted me to become a preacher rather than a doctor.

Ilse, Rhea as well as Ruth, belonged to a prayer group, whose members—about a dozen in all—happened to be all female. Eventually I became a regular male guest at their meetings. From time to time they organised a prayer breakfast, in a rotating manner, in their various homes.

Often after the indoor session, they chose to drive to an unusual spot to continue the meeting there. They intentionally selected the spot—a small hill overlooking the Berlin Wall at an area not far from Ilse's home. Gathered a few metres away from the dividing wall, we prayed intensely to the Lord to help bring the wall down.

'In the Name of Jesus, we are cursing the Berlin wall; it is the work of the Devil and not of God.' Then, addressing the wall, we cried out at the top of our voices: 'In the name of Jesus, you will one day fall!'

While supporting my sisters in their prayer for the fall of the concrete divide, I was, to be honest, at that time too much absorbed with my own problems to be diligently concerned about an issue that did not affect me directly.

Rhea did not live to see the answer to her prayer on November 9, 1989, the day the Berlin wall began to crumble. A year before that historic event she was called home after a short illness.

It is generally held by many foreigners living in Germany, that citizens of their host country are not friendly towards them. I am often questioned about my experience in this regard. To that I can only reply that even if five percent of the population happened to like foreigners, that added up to about four million people in a population of about eighty million.

My strategy was to look out for those four million residents.

In Berlin, and later in Hannover, I enjoyed enormous favours—from Ilse, Ruth, Sabine, Rhea and many more—favours I could not expect from many a fellow citizen from Ghana.

31

Facing Deportation

Not long after the meeting with the mayor of Berlin, I received a letter asking me to report for an interview on my asylum case. As I stated previously, it was overdue.

The invitation to attend the interview, coming very close on the heels of the meeting with the secretary to the mayor, led me to raise an eyebrow. Had he possibly made good his threat to prevent me from studying and written to the authorities in Zindorf to ask them to accelerate work on my case?

I had so far concentrated my energies in pursuing the academic path not only for a better future but as a means of gaining permission to stay in Germany for a while. In so doing I had all but neglected my asylum application.

Not so the majority of my acquaintances. Acting in line with the Twi saying I referred to earlier, namely, that 'when you decide to tell lies, make an effort to make your lie bear some resemblance to the truth,' these friends invested much time and energy in their efforts to substantiate the claims of the political persecution they outlined in their applications. They requested their relatives and friends back home to send them letters that alluded to the immediate threats to their lives, threats that faced them should they be obliged to return home. Some of the letters told about hordes of soldiers, police, or both, that had been despatched to the homes of the refugees back home in Ghana to look for them. Other letters spoke of homes, businesses, shops etc. of the fugitives being ransacked.

Some soldiers, according to the reports, went further. In their bid to get relatives to reveal the whereabouts of their runaway relatives, they had applied brutal force, including beating and torture. Some of the letters portrayed the soldiers and police as even more ruthless—monsters who went so far as to rape the wives of the fugitives! Rumours even had it that some managed to get some newspapers at home to publish stories which gave credence to their claims.

The applicants handed such letters and other documents to their lawyers who in turn forwarded them to the authorities. Even if these documents did not help them receive recognition as political refugees, they helped to delay their cases considerably.

Interviews were customarily conducted in the mother tongue of the applicant with the help of a translator. The authorities decided to place a Twi translator at my disposal.

'No thanks,' was my response.

While not being perfect in the German language, the level of my knowledge of the language was sufficient not only to enable me to understand the questions to be asked, but also to express myself sufficiently as to be understood. I adopted that strategy in the hope of gaining some favour with the interviewer. The future will show it was merely wishful thinking on my part.

Finally came January 6, 1984—the interview date.

When I stepped into the room, the interviewer, a man in his mid-thirties, greeted me in friendly terms. After he had introduced himself and conducted an identity check by looking at my visa, he began:

'As a matter of fact we were not sure you were still in Germany.'

'Why?' I inquired.

'Your file surfaced only by chance.'

'Really?'

'Yes. Somehow it got lost within the heaps of files in the department. We just discovered it by chance recently as we were re-arranging the files. To our surprise we realised we had not processed it since the time it got to us! We wondered whether the applicant was still in Germany. It was after we had contacted the foreign police in Berlin that we received clarification on the matter.'

There was no doubt in my mind as to who was responsible for the delay—the hand of Almighty God had been placed on my file to conceal it for a while to give me enough time to work towards my admission to medical school.

Finally the interviewer got to business.

'You arrived here about two years ago and applied for political asylum, did you?'

'That is right.'

'You claimed in your application that you were a student at the University of Legon in Accra.'

'Yes sir.'

'Do you have anything to prove you were a student, an ID-card, for example?'

'Unfortunately not; my ID-card got lost during my flight.'

'You wrote in your application that you took part in a demonstration to protest against the policies of the military regime in your country.'

'That is correct.'

'You later fled the country because you were being pursued.'

'That is right.'

'Can you please describe your escape route?'

'From Accra I travelled to Aflao. There someone helped me cross the green border. From Lome I moved on to Lagos. From Lagos I flew with the Balkan Air to East Berlin and finally to West Berlin.'

'Why West Berlin? You could as well have remained in Togo!'

'I wanted to escape to a distant land. I chose West Germany because it is a good example of a stable democracy; not only that, I learnt that the right to apply for asylum was enshrined in your constitution.'

After a brief silence the interviewer continued.

'Well, you have been here about twenty months. A lot has taken place since then. I want to know whether your life is still threatened.'

That was the question I had expected. I had decided to be honest with myself.

'Not directly,' I replied.

The interviewer seemed to be taken aback by my answer.

'I want to repeat the question,' he said. 'Will there be any immediate threat to your life should you be sent home?'

'As I told you, I don't face a direct threat. There is an indirect threat that in my opinion should not be neglected, however. As you are aware, Ghana is still under a military dictatorship. Freedom of expression as well as personal liberties are being curtailed. Therein lies the danger. I am a convinced democrat. My conviction in the principles of liberal democracy have been reinforced by my stay in West Berlin. Indeed, West Berlin has offered me a unique opportunity to learn at first hand the difference between living in a free world and living under a dictatorship. With this conviction I am certainly going to get into trouble should I return to Ghana. I will surely not be able to keep my mouth shut but instead open it to criticise the ruling government. That will certainly lead me into trouble.'

'But there is no concrete threat to your life at the moment in Ghana?'

'No.'

'I want to repeat the question: Do you fear a concrete threat to your life on your return to Ghana?'

'No, only a hypothetical one. It can become real, however, the moment I step on the soil of Ghana. I know myself very well to know that I would criticise the government at the least opportunity. That would put me in certain danger."

The interviewer paused for a while as he turned the pages of my file. At last he turned his attention to me once more:

'Is there any other reason to justify your stay in Germany?'

'Yes indeed. I am still receiving treatment on my left ankle. It was operated on about a year ago. It turned out to be a tuberculosis infection of the bone. I have been placed on medication until further notice. I will not be able to afford the cost of the medication in Ghana should I be sent home. On the basis of that I wish to appeal to the German government to permit me to stay on humanitarian grounds should my application be rejected.'

'Is there anything else you want to add?'

'No, sir!'

'Well, for the sake of procedure, I will replay the tape. You have the right to request me to delete some of the things recorded. You may also say something to clarify some points already recorded or add entirely new information.'

Soon I was listening to a re-play of the whole interview. After it was through he turned to me:

'Any objections?'

'No,' was my reply.

'Then that is it for now. You will hear from us in due course.'

Before I left the room he requested me to sign a declaration that I was satisfied with the way the interview was conducted.

I knew my application had no chance of success. My only prayer as I left for home was that the process would be prolonged till around August that year to enable me to commence my studies in Hannover.

One of my roommates at Blumeshof used to say that in the matters of asylum one's file could escape notice for a while. The moment it got on the desk of those working on it, however, it was not left to rest until that case had been brought to a conclusion. That assertion bore some element of truth—at least based on the speed at which my case proceeded once my file had surfaced.

Barely two months after the interview I received a letter from Zindorf. In it my application was rejected as utterly baseless. As was usually the case, I was given the option of appeal. For obvious reasons, I decided to make use of i t. This had to be forwarded within four weeks.

An acquaintance from Ghana, also an asylum-seeker, directed me to a lawyer who, according to him, was popular among asylum seekers for his selfless dedication to their cause.

I called on him without delay. The friendly manner in which he received me confirmed what others had said about him. After I had told him the reason for my coming, he demanded to see the rejection letter. Midway through it he began to shake his head as if to say, 'No hope trying, friend.' After he had gone through it he turned to me.

'I am afraid things don't appear favourable,' he said.

'Indeed?'

'Yes. The manner in which the letter is worded leaves us very little room to manoeuvre. The application has been rejected on grounds of being plainly baseless. From my experience such appeals have almost no chance of success. An appeal can delay deportation for only a few weeks.'

At that moment I told him about the missed opportunity to study in Hannover the previous year and the promise of a second chance in the current year. He only needed to do his best to help delay things until I could leave for Hannover, I explained.

His countenance brightened a little on hearing my account.

'Well, I will do my best. I cannot guarantee you success. though.'

Before leaving him, I requested to know how much his services would cost me.

'Nothing.'

'Really?' I inquired, surprised.

'I will apply for legal aid on your behalf. You only need to sign a pre-prepared application form. Saying that, he handed me a couple of forms to sign.

Soon I was back on the street, on my way home, and wondered whether the lawyer would be able to help.

A few days after the meeting I received a letter from him. With my hands shaking I tore it open to read the contents—but he had only sent me a copy of the appeal letter to the court. I waited anxiously for the outcome of the appeal.

The lawyer was right about the prospects of my appeal! Barely ten weeks after the letter had been despatched, I received another letter from him. It was a copy of the rejection letter from the court. They did not find any fault with the first ruling. There was no justification for my continued stay in Germany based on the laws governing asylum for there was no immediate threat to my life in Ghana. I was given four weeks to leave the country voluntarily or else face forceful repatriation.

I received the letter on June 30, 1984, a Saturday. I rushed to Emmanuel's home to show it to him.

'My friend, the tone of the letter is threatening!' he began after going through it. 'There have been talks about instances in the past when asylum seekers who had received similar letters had been forcefully seized by the police and sent home long before the time limit placed at their disposal to leave had expired.'

'What should I do then?' I inquired, almost on the point of tears.

'I have an idea,' Emmanuel began after a short silence. 'You've got to pack bag and baggage and leave the hostel immediately. It is an unsafe place for you to live. The police know where to find you should they decide to deport you.'

I knew someone who would be willing to allow me to stay—Juergen. We had got to know each other at the American Church in Berlin. Although a German national, Juergen was much more at home with foreigners, particularly English-speaking ones. His desire was to study theology and was waiting for the chance to do so—preferably in the United States. He had in the meantime become one of my close associates. He lived in an old apartment building in the northern part of the city. He had a big hall, a sleeping room as well as a large kitchen and a toilet at his disposal. Over the last several weeks I had visited him regularly. Sometimes I even spent the night there.

I called him from Mensah's place to tell him about the latest development. Without hesitation he agreed to play host to me.

Next I left Mensah's and rushed to the hostel to pack my belongings—a few old clothes, items needed for daily hygiene as well as a few books—into a small travelling bag. After I was finished, I called Emmanuel to let him know.

'Wait for me. I will come with my car to pick you up.'

He arrived after about an hour. He helped me get the items into his car. Soon we were heading towards Juergen's. After we had deposited the items there, Emmanuel invited me home to dinner.

The circumstances threatened to overwhelm me. Why, Lord, why? The thought went through my mind. The Lord provided inspiration in His own way. Shortly after I was seated in his hall, Emmanuel handed me a letter:

'This is a letter for you. It arrived a few days ago.' (I used his address for some of my correspondence.)

It was from the Oral Roberts Ministry in the US. I used to receive letters from him from time to time. I opened it and read it:

June 25, 1984

Dear Brother Peprah Gyamfi

Your needs are on my heart and in my hand now as I lift them to Jesus and pray for each one for you to receive a blessing in your spirit and know and feel God's encouragement in your life.

"In the mighty Name of Jesus, Whose I am and Whom I serve, God bless my partner Brother Peprah Gyamfi. Bring every spiritual, physical and financial blessing his way, and help him open his heart to receive everything that comes his way from God, his source. We give You all honor and praise. In Jesus' name, amen."

God called me to take His healing power to this generation, Brother Peprah Gyamfi. That includes you. Write me often. I want to help you carry your burdens. The Bible says, "Bear ye one another's burdens, and so fulfil the law of Christ" (Galatians 6:2).

I'm with you all the way. As my partner, you are a person very dear to me. I care about you and love you in the Lord.

Your partner always

(signed) Oral Roberts

I saw in his letter a message from heaven to urge me on to stand firm and not to lose hope.

The following Monday, I consulted my lawyer; he had also been served a copy. I appealed to him to do all in his power to get the authorities to extend my visa a few more months.

'It is a hopeless situation,' he began after he had gone through my file.

I sat at the opposite end of his desk staring at him, not knowing how to respond.

After a while he resumed:

'The only faint hope I have is to appeal to them to give you an extension on medical grounds. I can only forward the application if you could get your family doctor to write a medical report indicating the treatment on your leg is not over yet. In that case we are sure of getting a few months extension.'

I rushed to see my family doctor. What a person he was! His address was among the three given to me at the time of my discharge from hospital. His number was the first I called.

'Yes,' I was told by a female voice. 'We have room for a couple of patients; you may consult if you will.'

When I consulted the doctor for the first time, I wondered why he had not yet given up active duty. I estimated his age to be no less than 80 years! He had difficulty getting out of his seat. When he got going, he could hardly remain on his feet for long.

As he later told me, he had already retired from active service. Partly as a result of pressure from some of his elderly patients who seemed to want to maintain their favourite doctor to the end, he decided not entirely to give up his practice, which happened to be situated in the building where he lived, but rather to work a couple of hours daily on weekdays.

His secretary, who I later learnt was his wife, though younger than him, was also advanced in age.

Soon I dropped all my reservations towards him. In the course of time I told him about my intentions to study medicine, and also about the missed chance in Hannover. He urged me not to give up and wished me all the best in my efforts.

Much now depended on my aged family doctor. Would he be prepared to help? The moment he heard my story he burst out: 'That is irresponsible! They should give us time to complete the therapy. They should know themselves that you cannot easily come by such medication in Africa!'

He then set out to write his report, the gist of which was the need for me to continue on the anti-tuberculosis mediation for some months and his fears that this could not be guaranteed should I be sent to Ghana.

Armed with the doctor's report I returned to my lawyer. After he had gone through it, he asked me to take a seat in the waiting room whilst he tried to negotiate with the foreign police. After I had waited about fifteen minutes the secretary came to call me.

'I have some good news for you,' he smiled. 'The foreign police have promised to extent your visa a few more months. You should go there tomorrow to get it extended. Take a copy of the medical report along. They were not specific as to how long they would give you. I do however reckon it will be about three months.'

In spite of the assurance of the foreign police I was suspicious of their intentions. For once I even did not want to trust my lawyer. Why did he not talk to the authorities in my presence? Had he possibly cut a deal with them behind my back?

Thus, despite the fact that they had promised the lawyer the visa would be extended, I was reluctant to risk going there alone for it. I discussed the issue with Gary. He shared my concerns as well. He had in the meantime gained some insight into the intricacies of the asylum vetting procedure. This was due to that a considerable number of asylum seekers, the majority of them Ghanaians, were in the meantime worshipping in his church.

In the end he got a member of the church to accompany me. We developed a kind of emergency plan. Gary would stay at home to await the outcome of our journey to the foreign police. Should I be detained, my companion would inform him without delay. He would in turn consult my lawyer to fight to prevent my deportation.

My escort, a German passport holder of Indian descent aged about 35 years, drove me in his car to the foreign police. We were among the first to arrive there that morning. Not long after I had joined the queue it was my turn.

I told them what I was there for and handed them my visa as well as a copy of the medical report. I was then given a number and asked to wait.

My heart began to beat fast. I was so nervous I could hardly sit still. From time to time I got out of my seat and walked some steps down the corridors of the waiting hall.

Several verses of scripture came to mind:

> The Lord is my shepherd I shall not want (Psalm 23:1);

> God is our refuge and strength,
> a very present help in trouble (Psalm 46:1)

> Fear not, for I have redeemed you;
> I have called you by name, you are mine.
> When you pass through the waters I will be with you;
> and through the rivers, they shall not overwhelm you;
> when you walk through fire you shall not be burned,
> and the flame shall not consume you. (Isaiah 46:1b-2)

Occasionally I allowed the scene of the revelation showing the meeting between me and Grace in Europe flash through my mind. 'Don't be afraid of what human beings will do. You shall surely meet Grace face to face in Europe!' Thus I encouraged myself.

From time to time I cast my eyes over the counter separating us from the officers. The scene depicted about half a dozen of them busily at work behind their desks. Periodically one of them emerged to call out a number and attend to the person concerned.

The foreign police! The mere mention of the name was enough to cause many an asylum seeker to shiver. There was talk about instances in the past when people who went there to renew their visas were asked to wait for a while. Whilst they waited without suspecting anything, a group of officers arrived from nowhere to whisk them away into deportation cells to await their repatriation to their various countries.

Did a similar fate await me?

What would relatives and friends back home think of me should I be deported empty-handed after almost two years in Aburokyire! A complete failure? Well, I could argue that my stay had at least led to a complete cure of my left ankle. But would everybody be satisfied with that argument?

The clock hanging on the wall around the corner continued to tick loudly. The seconds turned to minutes: one, two, three, ten, fifteen; I began to wonder.

I turned to my escort sitting some few metres away. Our eyes met. I could read the anxiety in his face. Just then he also took a look at his watch. He couldn't afford to spend too much time there. He had to return to work in his laundry—the laundry he was struggling hard to keep above water financially. That he was even prepared to accompany me was a fact that had baffled me. Oh, how far Christian love can go!

Finally, after waiting about half an hour, a young lady emerged to call my number. I got up and walked to the counter supporting myself on my crutches. What was I to expect? An order to leave Berlin immediately? An extension for a few days? At last the relieving words fell from her lips:

'Your stay has been extended for eight weeks,' she said in a voice betraying no emotion. She then handed the visa sheet back to me.

'Thank you very much!' I replied, a broad smile on my face.

I took a look at the document. Yes indeed, my stay had been extended until SEPTEMBER 4 1984! A sign of relief passed my lips.

'How much did they give you?' my companion inquired when I got to him.

'Eight weeks!'

'Is that enough for you?

'Absolutely!' I replied. 'That should be enough to get me to Hannover! I expect the medical school there to send me the admission letter in the last week of August.'

In accordance with our emergency plan, I called Gary to break the good news to him. Although I could not see him, I could deduce from the tone of his voice that he was overjoyed by the turn of events.

32

Attempt at U.S. Visa

On July 12, 1984, Scott, a student of theology in an advanced stage of his study, who had arrived in Berlin from the US several months before to do his internship at our church, accompanied me to the US consulate to help me obtain a visa for the US.

Like other members of the church, he had over the months followed my encounter with the immigration authorities in Berlin. My situation moved his heart to try to help me study in the US instead.

The reader will probably ask why I was prepared to seek a US visa when in fact I was so desirous of studying in Hannover. Well, that's not an unreasonable question. One could even go on to ask why I expected to move to the US when prophesy in regard to my meeting with Grace on the streets of Europe had not yet been fulfilled?

Well, whereas I did not doubt the ability of God to fulfil His promise, I thought a visa for the US could provide a kind of double security for the future. But as things turned out, I might as well have not bothered since my application was turned down outright.

That in itself did not trouble me much. I was irritated if not angered by something else. Before my attempt at the visa, I heard some people say that it was common practice for the US visa authorities, once they rejected a visa application, to place a stamp in the passport to that effect. When I re-emerged from the consulate building I duly examined my passport—the new one I had received from Bonn. I went through it page by page and, just as I was about to breathe a sigh of relief that nothing had happened to it, I got to the last page of the document. Lo and behold, I noticed a text had been stamped into the very bottom of that page. I gave it a closer look. It read:

US Consulate General Berlin
Application Received JUL 12 1984

And this was in the new passport I would use later to try to obtain a visa in Hannover! It was my intention to remain silent on the issue of my stay in Berlin. What would happen to my application should the stamp lead the authorities in Hannover to find out about my stay in Berlin?!

I wished at that very moment I could turn the clock back! I would have told Scott politely:

'No thanks, Scott; I would very much like to visit your home country, the country Germans fondly refer to as *das Land mit den Unbegrenzten Möglichkeiten* (the country with unlimited opportunities) at a later date. For the moment, however, I will first try my luck in *das Land der Denker und Philosophen* (the country of thinkers and philosophers, which is the way some Germans refer to their country).

Too late! I could only hope that, should I ever make it to Hannover, the visa authorities there would not go to the extent of examining my passport page for page till the very last sheet of paper!

33

The Countdown Begins

The clock was ticking against me in so far as my stay in Berlin was concerned. Every day that passed brought me closer to the day when my visa for the city, the city I had in the meantime developed a great affection for, would expire.

An asylum seeker in my situation generally had three options: to go underground before the expiry of the visa, to stay on and face forceful repatriation, or to leave the country of his or her own volition before the right of stay expired.

The most important prerequisite required for someone whose visa had expired to go underground was to find someone who was prepared to offer accommodation. In order not to take chances it was advisable for one to vacate the official residence weeks before the expiry of the visa.

To contribute to a long stay underground without being detected, one had to respect some unwritten rules: one should always travel on a valid ticket when one travels on public transport. Otherwise one stood the risk of being caught by the ticket inspectors who in turn would hand one over to the police. Another important rule was to avoid going to places where trouble could erupt—parties, discos, the central train station etc—and which could lead to the police being called in to restore order. Usually the first thing the officers inspected on their arrival were passports and ID cards of those involved.

Despite all precautions, one unpredictable aspect of life—illness—could bring the person living underground in difficulty. When disease was minor, one could consult a general practitioner and pay for one's treatment.
Things became complicated, though, in cases of serious disease needing hospitalisation.

With a measure of good luck those who adhered to the precautionary rules could live for years underground. I knew people who would have agreed to allow me to stay with them had I chosen to stay on illegally. For obvious reasons, however, that option was out of the question for me.

The second alternative, to stay on and await my certain deportation, was, again for obvious reasons, a non-starter.

Leaving the country on my own volition—or at least feigning to do so—was the only option left to me. That would allow me to get my original confiscated passport back. Then, with my new passport, I could begin a new life in Hannover.

I had two options—to leave for the native country or for a third and neutral destination. In either case the procedure was the same. The refugee had to approach the authorities with a plane ticket indicating the destination of one's choice. In case one wanted to leave for a third country, the authorities had to satisfy themselves that the refugee would be allowed to disembark in that country.

Generally out of the question was a destination involving a member of the European Union or other parts of the western industrialised countries, in particular the US, Canada, Japan etc—unless one could produce an entry visa issued by the country involved (a condition hardly any asylum seeker could fulfil).

There were two possible points of departure from Berlin—by way of the Tegel International Airport on the western side, or the Schoenefeld International Airport in the east. Based on the airport from which one chose to fly, the authorities arranged to hand over one's passport at the appropriate point shortly before departure.

Eventually I came up with a plan. I would purchase a one-way ticket from East Berlin to Cairo. With that I would approach the authorities and pretend to be leaving for Egypt. I would then withdraw my application. The moment I got to East Berlin I would make a U-turn and return to West Berlin. From there I would move on to Hannover, probably with the help of a 'connection passport'.

'Why Egypt?' one might ask.

First, because of its proximity to Europe.

Secondly, Egypt had a special relationship with Ghana. The wife of Ghana's first president, Dr. Kwame Nkrumah, was an Egyptian. Although Dr. Nkrumah has since died, I was told by some of my friends that the special relationship between the two countries still existed. Among other things, citizens from either country could visit each other's country without a visa.

The grey area of the plan lay in the problem as to how I was to travel from Berlin to Hannover.

In the meantime I was growing increasingly nervous with each passing day. All my hopes centred on Hannover—would they keep their promise? The tension would soon become almost unbearable.

More out of the need to assure myself, and less because I doubted they would keep their promise, I decided to contact Hannover at the beginning of August. I asked a close associate of mine, a medical student from Ghana at the Free University in Berlin, to do so on my behalf.

No, they had not forgotten their promise to me, they let him know. The meeting for the official selection was a few days away. I should expect to hear from them around the last week of the month.

◆   ◆   ◆

Just as I was pondering over how I could travel from Berlin to Hannover, I ran into a countryman in the train one evening. At the time of our meeting I had barely fourteen days to leave the city. That was not our first meeting. Because we happened to take the underground at the same station our ways crossed sporadically. Whenever we met we exchanged only casual greetings. At times when we were not in a hurry we spent some minutes chatting on the street—about issues of general interest, especially about the political situation at home.

On this particular meeting, my acquaintance read from the look in my eyes that all was not well with me.

'Come on, what's the matter with you, boy?' he inquired.

'My asylum case has been rejected.'

'Really?'

'Yes.'

'Go and see a lawyer!'

'I have.'

'And?'

'He made an appeal on my behalf. That also has been rejected. I have about two weeks to leave the country.'

'You are not leaving, are you?'

'What else can I do?'

'Go underground! You cannot survive in Ogyakrom, friend! I received a letter from one of my relatives recently—Rawlings and Co have messed up things.' He shook his head. 'Life is unbearable there—it's like hell.'

At that juncture I decided to tell him briefly about my missed chance the previous year and the prospect of being admitted for the second time that year. The problem that remained to be resolved was how I could make it to Hannover.

He listened attentively to my narration.

'I have a solution for you,' he began after he had heard my story.

'Really?'

'Yes, indeed. I have good contacts with a Ghanaian resident; he can definitely help you. There is some money and some risk involved, though.'

'Give me some details, please.'

Well, he has taken advantage of the special situation prevailing in Berlin to make money.'

'How?'

'By helping people like you wishing to travel to West Germany to do so on other peoples' passports.'

'Are they genuine passports?'

'Of course they are. As far as I know such passports belong to people who have legal resident permits in Germany and other EU countries.'

'But one could be caught!'

'That rarely happens! My friend knows his job. Indeed, he has a suitable passport for any type of person. He has another advantage. Indeed, it is no secret that the Europeans generally have difficulties differentiating one African from the other. I have even heard people make claims about instances in the past when some Africans have succeeded in entering Europe on the passports of people of the opposite sex! Only a European first name could serve as a hindrance!'

'I have my reservations!'

'What reservations?'

'The idea of travelling on someone else's passport; besides, I could be caught.'

'You tell me, friend—what other options do you have? The police will definitely place a stamp in your passport to indicate you were deported from here. In a situation like that, which German Embassy will grant you a visa?'

'How much do I have to pay for the passport should I agree to the deal?'

'600 DM.'

'600 DM?! That's a great deal of money!'

'Well, he won't accept anything less!'

'What about 400 DM?'

'Friend, we are not on the African market; there can be no bargaining here. The connection man is a shrewd individual—he won't be satisfied with even 10 DM less than what I have quoted.'

'Well, give me a day to consider the whole issue.'

And so we parted.

The whole of that evening and also as I lay in bed that night waiting for sleep to descend, I pondered over our meeting. I wrestled with myself. Should I give it a try or should I not?

My acquaintance's question—what other options did I have?—rang through my mind.

He was indeed right. Even if I succeeded in re-entering Berlin with the new passport, what next? There was no way I could travel to Hannover with it without a West German visa in it.

Go back to Accra to apply for a German visa there? The most optimistic outcome of my attempt would lead to the acquisition of a student's visa. At best, the process could take a minimum of six weeks. In that case I wouldn't be able to sit for the German test. Without that I could not matriculate again that year—and what was the guarantee that Hannover would be prepared to offer me a third chance?

To believe that any German consulate would be prepared to issue me a visa was, in view of what I said earlier, tantamount to mere wishful thinking.

It began to dawn on me that the 'connection path' offered a more realistic chance of success under the prevailing circumstances. Why was I reluctant to give it a try? After all, that was exactly the means I would have used to move to Hamburg on my arrival had I had the financial means at my disposal. Extraordinary situations call for extraordinarily deeds, I said to myself. Why should I allow my future to be jeopardized by a strict adherence to formality? And so for the sake of my poor parents at Mpintimpi, for the sake of the poor residents of Mpintimpi in particular and that of my countrymen in general who could benefit from my knowledge as a doctor, I was prepared to take the risk.

I ventured even to rationalise the strategy based on my understanding of the teachings of the Lord. What sin, after all, does one commit at the end of the day, beating the immigration to move from one place in Germany to the other simply for the purpose to study—a chance that had been placed at my disposal in any case by a German university? My conscience was clear on that matter. I assured myself that when, one day, I stood before my Creator, I would be in a position to explain why I did what I did. It was simply a matter of being as wise as a serpent and as harmless as a dove. Resolved, I thought, 'Come what may, I will at least give the idea of the connection-passport a try!' So from that moment my mind was fixed.

One thing made me sure of victory as I struggled to reach a decision on this issue was this: He who knew the end from the beginning had revealed to me that I would meet Grace personally in Europe—and that had not yet happened!

Accordingly, I met my acquaintance as promised the next day.

'Tell your friend to reserve me a passport. I cannot make any payment, though, until I receive the second admission letter from Hannover. I am expecting it any time from now.'

'Okay; I will give you my number. Give me a call whenever you are ready.'

'You should also give me your address; in case I don't get you on the phone, I will come round and leave a note.'

He took a pen from his pocket and wrote down his address and telephone number. Shortly after that our ways parted.

Beginning from the middle of August I called Nina every day to find out whether a letter had arrived. (At the time I filled the forms the second time, our friendship was still on the best of terms. On Margarethe's suggestion, I had given their address instead of Tony's.)

Finally on August 22 the much awaited letter from Hannover arrived. I gave the Lord thanks for moving the hearts of the authorities in Hannover to remain true to their word.

That evening I called my contact man to break the good news to him and requested a meeting at the shortest possible time. Eventually we agreed to meet at the Underground Station familiar to both of us. After he had congratulated me, he went straight to business.

'In order to convince the connection man to hand out the document to me, you have to make a part-payment of 400 DM. You'll pay the rest on collection.'

'Give me three days,' I said. 'I have to collect it from someone I keep my money with.'

'You have to hurry, friend—the passports are in high demand. We have to make the reservation early or it will be too late.'

'I will do my best.'

We bade each other goodbye and headed for our respective homes. I had gone just a few metres when I heard him shout my name. I turned. He ran towards me.'

'I forgot one important thing!' he began.

'What then?'

'He will need a recent picture of you, preferably a passport-sized one to assist him select a suitable passport for you.'

Fortunately I had a couple of such pictures at home. I asked him to wait whilst I rushed to the hostel to fetch them. When I returned with them, we agreed to meet about the same time in three days.

I called on Mensah the next day to collect the money I had saved with him. It amounted to about 1500DM. I had earned it mostly by doing cleaning jobs in the homes of American military personnel stationed in the divided city. Gary had served as go between to help find myself and other refugees those jobs.

At the appointed time I met with my countryman and handed him the 400 DM. We agreed to meet two days later to seal the transaction.

He kept his word. He asked me to follow him to an isolated area in the vicinity of the Underground station. When we were alone, he unzipped a bag hanging on his shoulders. Next he removed a passport coloured green and handed it to me.

'You have a look at it. It's a refugee passport issued to the bearer by the French authorities. It is a genuine document, I can assure you. With it one can travel to several countries, including Western Europe without the need for a visa.'

I began to go through it. Most importantly, I took a look at the picture in it to see if it bore any resemblance to me. Yes indeed, my companion was right in describing the 'connection man' as someone who was no novice in his trade! Only a person who had a tip-off or one who took minutes to scrutinize the picture could make out the difference between my face and the face in the passport.

'How does your friend come about such documents?' I inquired after I had finished examining the pages.

'Why should you be bothered by someone else's business secret? Surely your main concern now is to be able to make it to your destination, not so?'

'I was just curious.'

'Well, I'm afraid I cannot tell you, because he hasn't revealed anything to me.'

I then made an attempt to place the document in my pocket.

'No!' he protested, yanking the document from my hands.

'Why?' I looked at him, startled.

'First give me the remaining fee!'

'That's precisely what I was about to do!'

'Payment first!' he insisted.

I removed 200 DM from my wallet and handed it to him.

'Here you are!' he said, placing the document in my hands. 'Please promise me one thing—please register the passport back to the 'connection man' immediately you get to your destination. Here is the address to use.' He handed me a paper folded in the middle.

Moments later we parted. I never met him again and wondered what happened to him. How did he fare in Berlin? Was he granted asylum? Did his dreams of one day returning home to set up a business to help his relatives ever materialise?

◆ ◆ ◆

On August 30, just four days before my visa was due to expire, I bought a one-way ticket for a flight from East Berlin to Cairo. Armed with it I made my way to the foreign police.

'What can I do for you?' the officer, a good looking lady in her mid-twenties, inquired.

'I have come for my passport.'

'What for?'

'Well, I arrived here about two years ago to seek the protection of the German government from the aggressive military dictatorship back home in Ghana. Unfortunately my application has been rejected. I have been given two options—to leave voluntarily or face forceful deportation. Well, I have opted for the former.'

'Let me see your ticket.'

I gave her the ticket and my visa for West Berlin.

After examining them she left to pick out my file. She returned a few minutes later, a brown file in her hands. She began to go through it once she had resumed her seat.

'You are from Ghana; is that right?' she inquired after a while.

Yes, gracious lady;' I replied in a relaxed voice. 'I am a citizen of Ghana, formerly the Gold Coast.'

I could not remember the last time I appeared so relaxed and confident before the law enforcing agents of the state. Why shouldn't I? I pictured myself as a boxer who had met in the ring in a contest with the law-enforcing agents of the state. Having been battered to the extent of no longer being able to pursue the fight I had decided to throw in the towel. At that stage the rules forbade my opponents from inflicting any further injury on me. I could even afford to crack a joke.

'Gold Coast?' she seemed surprised.

'Yes, indeed. At your request I can even send you some jewels the moment the situation there permits me to return!'

'That's very nice of you! It has always been my desire to impress my husband with beautiful golden jewellery!'

There was a short silence. After a while she continued: 'If there is that much gold in your country, why are people from your country in particular fleeing to us? Asylum seekers from Ghana are all over the place!'

'The military government there is chasing us all over! That's the reason why I have bought a ticket for Cairo. No, I cannot return to Ghana, not for now.'

'Well, you must know what is best for you.'

She then gave me a sheet of paper to sign—to confirm that I had decided to leave the country voluntarily.

'You will receive the passport at the border between East and West Berlin on the day of departure!'

'Sure?'

'Of course! That is our job. You will be travelling with the special bus which commutes between West Berlin and the East Berlin airport, won't you?'

'That's what I was told by the Travel Agency when I bought the ticket.'

'At the border, the officer who will carry out immigration check on the bus will hand your passport back to you. . This is a precautionary measure to prevent rejected asylum seekers going underground with their passports.'

◆   ◆   ◆

I spent my remaining days in Berlin bidding farewell to my numerous friends. Emmanuel and Anna as well as Tony knew about my exact plans. As far as the rest were concerned I only mentioned I wanted to avoid forceful deportation and so had decided to leave on my own. I would attempt to obtain a visa from a German consulate abroad, I said. Should that succeed, I promised to visit Berlin in due course. To assist me in my effort, Gary, on behalf of the American Church, donated an amount of 500 DM.

On Monday September 3, 1984, I used the refugee passport to buy a one-way ticket for a flight from West Berlin to Hamburg on the now defunct PANAM Air. I decided to book for the last flight of the day, scheduled for 8:45 p.m. I deposited the passport and the ticket with Tony. Should things work in my favour, my plan was to leave Berlin that very day for West Germany proper.

In the course of the day, Erika, a middle-aged woman, a member of the American Church, drove to the hostel to pick up the few items I still had there for safekeeping in her house. Originally Margarethe had offered to keep them. Apparently, because her husband Seidu had done something to annoy her that day, she changed her mind. Not only that—she also refused to allow Nina to come round to bid goodbye.

Sarfo and his wife Aggie kept vigil with me. Both citizens of Ghana, they had arrived in West Berlin from Nigeria. I considered them a lucky couple. They had arrived just in time to take up all the cleaning jobs which, in the course of my stay there, I had accumulated and which now constituted a reasonable income.

I spent the whole of day in fasting and prayer. The exercise helped to boost my faith in the Lord. I felt like a swimmer on a wave of a spiritual tide, ready to plunge through any cross currents that might threaten to divert me from my chosen course.

A few minutes before midnight I invited Sarfo and Aggie to join me in prayer. When we had finished praying I took my bag and got ready to leave.

'Wait, a moment! I want to take a picture of you before you leave!' Aggie suggested and made for their room nearby.

Soon she was back. I held my Bible up as a sign of victory. Aggie released her finger from the knob she was pressing. Splash—the light from the device illuminated my face!

All was now set for me to leave the divided city.

Although I had lived in West Berlin only two years and about four months, the city had, in spite of my difficult relations with the authorities, become endeared to my heart. My stay there had among other things led me to come to know lovely people such as Anna and Emmanuel, Ilse, Gary, Kurt and Karen his wife as well as Tony and Joyce. It was not without exaggeration that I referred to the city at that time as my second hometown.

I looked forward to a time in the future when I could visit there or even re-settle there. In the short term, though, I had no choice, for now, than to depart from it.

34

D-Day

Each one of us has personal landmarks, days one will not forget.

September 4, 1984, is my personal landmark. So long as I have breath, the events of that day will never be forgotten.

On Sept 4, 1984, almost six years to the day the Lord sent Grace to call me to follow Him, I stood at the crossroads of my life. I had no illusions as to the dangers involved in the adventure on which I was about to embark. But as I stated earlier, what other option did I have?

I could either fail or succeed in my scheme. Furthermore, failure was guaranteed if I did nothing. There is a saying that life is full of risks. Six years had elapsed since I left Mfantsipim. Some of my earlier classmates would be graduating, if they had not already done so—as doctors, economists, engineers, lawyers. What could I show in comparison should I meet any of them on the streets of Accra after a possible deportation?

I was still clearly convinced about the prophetic nature of the dream of December 1978. It was true that Grace and I had both made it to Europe. Prophecy in its entirety was yet to be fulfilled, however. Grace and I would have to see each other face to face. I trusted the Lord to completely fulfil what He had promised to do.

Shortly after midnight I left the hostel on my way to the underground station, Krumme Lanke on Line 2, about five hundred metres away. Sarfo and Aggie accompanied me there.

Packed into my small traveller's bag were all the very essentials—the new passport, the admission letter for Hannover, my plane ticket as well as a few clothes and items of hygiene. I decided to take the admission letter as a precautionary measure, should things go contrary to expectations and I had to fly to Egypt. In that case I would, despite the poor prospects of success, produce it at the German embassy and apply for a student's visa.

My destination was a district in Berlin known as Wilmersdorf. There, near a place known as the Funkturm, was a Central Omnibus Station. That was where I would take the Bus bound for the Airport in East Berlin.

Shortly after our arrival a bright yellow train emerged from the dark tunnel heading towards the city. Only a few commuters were on it at that time of day. Waving a final goodbye to the couple from Ghana, I boarded it. Soon I was on our way. After I had changed trains I finally arrived at my destination.

The special bus was waiting. It was about half full, about a dozen more passengers arriving after me. Finally, at about 2:30 in the morning, it was set in motion.

Soon I was saying goodbye to my favourite city. Partly as a result of my bike, partly because I had considerable leisure time at my disposal, I had managed to explore it quite well. Was this going to be a permanent goodbye to Germany, or was it, as was my prayer, going to be a momentarily absence?

My seat was not far from the driver. I took a look around me. Some of the passengers seemed half asleep; others were reading their newspapers. Everybody, as usual, seemed to be occupied with their own business.

After we had travelled a few minutes the large vehicle pulled to a halt. Because it was quite dark I couldn't make out what was ahead of us.

'Please take out your travel documents,' the driver announced.

Shortly afterwards a middle-aged man in uniform stepped into the bus. He introduced himself as a boarder guard. He asked everyone to produce their travel documents. Beginning from the front row, he set out to inspect them.

Soon it was my turn.

'Your passport please?' he inquired in German.

'You are supposed to hand it back to me,' was my reply.

'Are you the asylum seeker leaving voluntarily?'

'Yes indeed.'

'Wait a moment.'

He then opened a little bag hanging on his shoulders and pulled out a passport. After he had taken a close look both at me and the picture it bore he handed the document to me. I recognised it instantly as the document that had enabled me to embark on my adventure to Nigeria and later to Europe. For the first time in a little over two years I was re-united with it. Not for long though, I thought to myself.

I took a quick glance through the pages. What I had feared all along would soon become reality before my eyes. Stamped boldly on one of the pages towards the centre of the document was a statement in German to the effect that I had sought Asylum in West Berlin and was leaving the country only after my application had been rejected!

My doom was sealed as far as that document was concerned, for it was highly improbable that any German visa authority would be willing to issue me a visa after reading the statement stamped in it.

In all, the immigration checks lasted about twenty minutes. Soon we put the territory of West Berlin behind us. Just as we entered East Berlin the bus pulled to a stop for the second time. This time it was the turn of the East Berlin officials to conduct their immigration check. It took about half an hour for them to complete their formalities. An arrival stamp as well as a transit visa were placed in my passport. At long last the bus set out on the last stage of the journey. A look at my watch told me it was around 3:30 a.m.

The contrast between East and West Berlin dawned on me more powerfully this time. The streets we were now driving through were not only narrower compared to what I was used to in the West, but their surfaces were rugged in several places. Potholes in the middle of the streets, something I had thought was only a feature of a developing country such as Ghana, confronted my eyes on several occasions along the ride. The communists seemed to be saving energy, for the streets of the city were poorly illuminated in several places.

A contrast that was more remarkable was the state of the buildings in the East vis-à-vis those of the West. The typical building I was seeing appeared very old, looked grey and yearned for renovation. For most of them the clock of time appeared to have come to a standstill after the last battle shots had been fired and World War II had ended.

We arrived at the East Berlin International Airport around 4 a.m. The flight for Cairo was scheduled to take off in about an hour.

The first thing I did when I stepped into the Airport complex was to look out for the toilet. About ten metres ahead of me was a middle-aged woman who was dutifully going about cleaning the floors of the corridors.

'Could you please direct me to the next toilet?' I asked her in German.

'You go straight; before the glass door turn left.'

'Thank you so much!'

'It's a pleasure!'

I hurried on.

Soon I was alone in the small cubicle enclosing the water closet.

The first thing I did was to lock the door. With the door safely locked and the three concrete walls helping to shield me completely from all intruders, I nervously unzipped the small traveller's bag and pulled out the new passport. With it safely in my grip, I took a deep breath and placed it in the pocket of my coat.

Next, I removed the old passport. A look at my watch read exactly 4:15 a.m. Solemnly, I began, page for page, to tear the sheets into pieces, throwing the fragments into the water-closet in the process. Tearing up the hardcover provided some difficulty; eventually, however, this was reduced to only small fragments of their original size.

Finally I pulled the chain of the water closet. R-u-u-u-u-u-r-r!—the sound of flowing water filled the small room. The first attempt was not enough; a considerable amount of paper, probably reluctant to part with their owner, remained in the closet. I waited for a while for the water to refill; then, a second pull at the handle; then a third; finally, a fourth. At last no more traces of my first ever passport was left.

The dice was cast. I had crossed the Rubicon—there was no turning back.

I got ready to go out and face the consequences. Zipping shut my small bag, I opened the door and stepped back into the hall of the airport.

I headed straight for the Taxi stand near the entrance to the building complex. As I moved on I heard the announcement emanating from the speakers of the hall: 'This is the last call for passengers on the flight bound for Cairo to check in.'

'I wish you a safe flight to North Africa,' I murmured to myself and hurried away. Moments later I stepped out of the building.

I made for the Taxi stand. A few of the cars had already lined up.

'Good morning,' I greeted the driver as I boarded the first vehicle in the queue.

'Good morning,' he returned my greetings in a friendly tone. 'Where is mister heading for?'

'Friedrichstrasse please!'

Soon we were on our way.

'How much does it cost?' I inquired after we had gone a little distance.

'Twenty marks. I mean West German marks.'

'Why not East German marks, sir?'

'This is not the time for discussions, sir!'

I shifted the conversation to the weather.

It was around 5 a.m. when the Taxi turned into Friedrichstrasse. I was delighted and relieved by the smooth turn of events so far.

◆   ◆   ◆

My encounter with the STASI, the East German Secret Police.

I joined the queue in which there was about half a dozen others before me. I expected the officer to question me about the passport, about the fact that it didn't bear any transit visa or have an arrival stamp in it. As I waited for my turn I thought about what to give as an excuse. I had entered East Berlin early in the morning with the special bus to catch the flight to Cairo. Just before I was about to check in for the flight it occurred to me that I had left the bulk of the money I was travelling with back in my apartment. Consequently I decided to postpone the journey. I had dutifully presented my documents at the point of entry and it wasn't my fault that the immigration official had overlooked placing a stamp in the passport.

I knew the story would probably be taken with a pinch of salt and that it would bring me some difficulty. Why they might make a big issue out of something I regarded as a minor matter was beyond my imagination.

At last, after a few minutes of standing in the queue, it was my turn.

'Good morning!' I greeted the officer heartily.

'Good morning,' he replied in an icy tone.

Next I handed him my passport. He began to examine it. He took a critical look at the picture in it, then back to me, then back again to the picture and finally to me. Next he began to examine the document, page by page. As he progressed through the pages I noticed an increasingly astonished look on his face. His stern countenance turned even sterner after he had gone through all the pages.

Was it anger, or surprise, or dismay that was written on his face? In any case after he had gone through it, he gazed at me and asked: 'How did you enter this country?'

I pretended not to understand him.

'How did you enter our country? Where is the stamp; the arrival stamp? Where is the stamp to indicate the time of your arrival in our country?'

One question followed another.

'It should be inside,' I began at last. 'I gave it to the border guard. Maybe he forgot to place his stamp in it.'

'You are the chief of all liars! What you are alleging can never happen here, never! I assure you I know how my people go about their duties. So one more time—where is the arrival stamp?'

I fumbled for words. The queue began to swell behind me. The man began to lose patience. 'If you won't tell me the truth, then stand aside.'

Saying that, he placed my passport aside. Next, he took the phone and dialled a number. Soon he was engaged in a conversation with someone else. Though I could not follow the conversation from where I stood, I had little doubt that it was about my passport.

Not long after that conversation, a second officer arrived. I got the signal to follow him. He led me into a small room. After he had shut the door behind us he began:

'Tell me the whole truth—nothing but the truth. That is the only way I can help you. Once again: how did you manage to enter the GDR without anyone noticing it?'

Once again I recited the story I had concocted, something that seemed to infuriate him.

'You are going to remain here for as long as you refuse to tell the truth! That could be months, I assure you!'

He then headed for the door. Soon he stepped out of it, banging the door behind him as he left.

For about an hour nothing happened to me. I began to reflect on what had happened and what was to be done. Was I going to miss the chance this year as well? A look at my watch told me it was around 7 a.m. In about thirteen hours from then I should be on my way to Hamburg. Would I be free by then? About seventy minutes after the departure of my interrogator I heard the door lock being turned.

The officer stepped in again. This time he was not alone—two colleagues accompanied him. The interrogation began all over again.

'Tell us: what brought you to East Berlin this morning? Tell us the truth, the whole truth and nothing else.'

'I was here on my way to Cairo. Will you please have a look at my ticket?'

I showed it to them.

'Go on! What happened next?' one of them asked.

Once again I repeated the version of my concocted story about the money left in West Berlin. Just before my turn to go through the immigration procedure, I explained, it occurred to me that I had forgotten something important at home, so I decided to abort my journey.

'What did you forget?'

'Money, a few hundred DM, the money I needed for my journey.'

'Are you sure of what you are telling us?'

'Oh yes. Indeed, I withdrew the money from the bank a day prior to my departure.'

'You sit down and think about it. Among all things you do, you forget the money you need for your journey!'

'Unfortunately that is what happened. Part of it was in my wallet; the bulk of it, however, I placed in the drawer of my writing table. In my rush I forgot to take it along. I travelled on the special bus. We left West Berlin around three in the morning. I went through the routine checks at the west and east part of the city respectively. I didn't bother to examine the passport after the checks. I trusted the officers to have dutifully carried out their duty.'

Then came a question I hadn't expected: 'You are spying for the Americans, aren't you?'

'What?'

'I spoke audibly enough, friend. I assure you, we are not joking with you—we are very serious. You heard the question alright; in case you didn't, however, I will repeat it. Are you an American spy? Are you an agent of the American Secret Service?'

'No, sir!'

'Tell us—are you associated with the Americans in any way?'

'Well, to be honest with you; I have contacts with some Americans in Berlin.'

'How did you get to know them?'

'Through the church. I attend the American Lutheran Church in Berlin.'

'Why don't you attend a German church?'

'Well, at the time I arrived in West Berlin, I had little knowledge of the German language. I was looking for an English speaking church in which to worship. Eventually I joined the American Church.'

'Still, you have not told us the truth. Either you tell us the truth and go free or you stand by your lies and remain here indefinitely.'

At that juncture he began to search me—first my bag, then myself, from head to toe.

'Where is the second passport?'

'Which second passport?'

My question in answer to his question nearly drove him mad! For the first time, physical force was applied as he hit my body with one of his feet. He began to threaten and curse me.

'We are serious with you; either you co-operate with us and hand over the second passport with which you entered this territory or we hand you over to the police in West Berlin!'

That threat sent cold chills running all over my body. To hand me over to the West Berlin police—oh, what a terrible prospect! That would mean an end to all my hopes of making it to Hannover.

I took the threat seriously. What I didn't realise at the time is that there was hardly any co-operation between the two bitterly antagonist states. Indeed, I thought that despite the enmity between them, there existed a kind of communication when it came to matters of common interest. I assumed that getting rid of a poor African male with highly suspicious intentions would be something both sides would agree on.

On realising I was not prepared to give in, the three officers left the room. As in the previous instance, they locked the door.

Once again I found myself alone. I pondered on my next move. Should I let the cat out of the bag? What would happen next if I did? Would they refuse to allow me to return to West Berlin? Would they themselves organise my deportation to Ghana? Or would they make good their threats to hand me over to the West Berlin police? I was perplexed beyond measure.

After I had been alone for about forty five minutes, I heard steps in front of the door. Soon it was unlocked. Several officers entered. One of them, a new face, introduced himself as a high-ranking officer on duty that day. His subordinates had informed him about my unusual story. He was the highest authority to decide on the issue and had decided to interview me personally to inform himself first-hand of the issue. He could decide to release me or else recommend further detention. What counted at that particular moment was the truth. Under no circumstance could I escape without telling the truth, he stressed.

The clock meanwhile read 9:30 a.m. I had not been served any meals. Even if they had, I doubt whether I could have eaten anything. Appetite, thirst, hunger—what were those feelings or sensations to me! I grew increasingly nervous. Would I ever make it to Hamburg that day? Just then the dream flashed through my mind. I had not yet met Grace on the streets of Europe! So long as that had not yet happened, I would continue to trust the Lord for a miracle. Under what I regarded as a dead-end situation, however, I could not figure out how prophesy was going to be fulfilled.

The high-ranking officer continued: 'No one within the forces can ever believe the claim you are making to explain why your passport was not stamped. Indeed, never during my long years of service has something of that nature ever happened. I can assure you my boys are professionally trained! Professionalism is essential if we are to be able to defend our Fatherland against the evil machinations of the imperialists, spearheaded by the Americans.'

He paused for a while, probably to give me time to think about my response. He went on after a brief pause.

'Now I want to hear the absolute truth from your lips! Where is the passport you presented at the point of entry?'

'I have told the truth to you…'

With two strong blows to my body the officer interrupted my sentence. Coming unexpectedly and being ferocious, they nearly caused me to lose my balance!

'I do not want to hear any more of those lies from your lips!' he yelled at me. 'Otherwise you'll suffer even more serious harm.'

At that moment all my fears about what would happen to me if I told them the truth evaporated into thin air! A still small voice within me urged: Boy, tell the truth, whatever the consequences, rather than allow these communist to beat you to death!

'Well, you are right,' I capitulated. 'I entered on a different passport!'

'What has happened to it?'

'I have destroyed it.'

'Why?'

'To prevent the West Berlin police, in case they arrest me, from knowing that I had just been deported.'

'What were you doing there?'

'I sought asylum.'

'What happened?'

I decided to tell the whole story. Starting from my arrival in Berlin two years earlier, I told him everything—the application for asylum, the surgery on my left ankle, my first admission to the MHH, my meeting with Herr Weizacker, how I got my second passport, the threat of deportation, my second admission to Hannover and my desperate attempt to get there this time.

To support my case, I produced the admission letter from Hannover.

All present listened attentively to my story. As my story progressed, I detected a change of countenance in their faces. After I was done I waited anxiously for their response.

The dramatic turn of events baffles me even to this day!

'Congratulations, friend, for this show of courage and resilience!' the high-ranking officer began. 'If you had told us this earlier, you would be gone by now. We seriously thought you were spying for our enemies, the Americans!'

I was totally baffled by the 180 degree turn of events. Instead of the enemy, I became a friend. Instead of consternation, I now received their sympathy.

'We share one thing in common—we are both victims of the inhuman capitalist system! Indeed, we are not unaware of the inhumane treatment meted out by the Federal Republic to asylum seekers. Your case is a good example. Pity! Why should they place so many impediments in the way of such a poor person! What do they stand to lose by giving a person like you the chance to study?!'

The officer seemed to be genuinely touched by my story! His tirade against the West continued.

'The imperialists! Very cold-hearted people, they are! They have exploited and continue to exploit the poor! They are mostly responsible for the political instability, poverty and human suffering prevailing in many parts of the developing world. The world-wide refugee problem is mainly a direct result of their policies. Let me assure you of one thing: the victims of the inhumane policies of the imperialist can always count on us in their fight against exploitation, oppression, and injustice!'

'Thank you very much for your kindness,' I replied, hardly able to believe what I was experiencing. For the moment I thought I was day-dreaming.

I was then asked to pack my items and get ready to leave. I could barely express my joy at the dramatic turn of events in my favour.

Just as I was about to leave, one of the officers turned to me:

'Do you want anything to drink?'

'A cup of tea or coffee, if possible!'

He left the room. He returned after a while with a small container filled with coffee together with a cup.

Their superior accompanied me personally. I didn't have to line up. Instead he led me through a special exit. Wishing me all the best for the future, the high ranking officer parted from me.

The encounter with the security officers gave me food for thought. I wondered how people who spoke the same language, shared the same cultural background, who were brothers and sisters in the broader sense until World War II divided a single nation, could develop such aversion towards each other!

A little over five years after that meeting, the dividing wall of Berlin was torn apart, leading eventually to the re-unification of the two German states. I wonder how those officers I met, people who left no doubt in my mind as to their determination to go to any end to defend their nation, reacted and adjusted to the changed situation? How did they cope with life under a system which, judging from what they told me during our encounter, they genuinely despised?

For once I found myself in a situation similar to that when I first arrived in Berlin. This time, though, I was no stranger to the environment. My wish was to get back to West Berlin as soon as possible. I didn't want to take any chances, however.

I had been in West Berlin long enough to know some of the tactics the police adopted to track down illegal immigrants to the city. They carried regular checks on the trains arriving from the eastern part of the city. To avoid arousing any suspicion, I decided not to carry any bag on me. For a token fee I obtained a key to one of the lockers in the station where travellers could securely leave their belongings for a while. I deposited my bag there. The plan was to request Emmanuel to collect it the moment I got to West Berlin.

Moments later a train arrived. I got down at the first stop. Hurray! I was back in West Berlin! I breathed a sigh of relief as I mingled with the pedestrians on the streets of my beloved city.

A look at the watch told me that it was a few minutes to eleven.

It just dawned on me that Fredua, a close associate of both Emmanuel and myself, a student from Ghana in his final year, lived in a students' hostel not far from where I was. I would call on him and relax for a while before going on to Emmanuel's, I resolved.

Luckily he was at home. I told him what I had just been through. He could only congratulate me and wish me the best in regard to what was still ahead of me. I left my new passport with him. He promised to despatch it to me the moment I arrived safely in Hamburg.

From there I hurried to Emmanuel and Anna. As expected, Emmanuel was delighted to see me back in Berlin. Anna was yet to return home from work. I told Mensah all that had happened including my detention in East Berlin. He was also surprised at the reaction of the STASI.

There was little time for celebrating. It was around 3 p.m. In about five hours' time I would have to embark on the next stage—the flight to Hamburg.

Two important things had to be done. First, I needed to collect my connection passport as well as the ticket from Tony. I would need about two hours to travel there and back.

Equally important—the bag in the safe at the Friedrichstr had to be collected. Emmanuel was his usual kind self and did not hesitate to carry out that assignment on my behalf.

Though the whole operation was not over yet, Tony and family accorded me a hero's welcome on my arrival. For the sake of time, I could only give them a brief summary of what I had gone through so far.

'Don't be scared, friend, the Lord who has brought you this far will not desert you midway in the journey. So rest assured, you will make it!'

With those words of encouragement still ringing in my ears, I left Tony's apartment to walk the approximately six hundred metres to the Schleisches Tor Station to join the Underground Line 1 on my way to the district in Berlin called Tegel, where Anna and Emmanuel lived. On my arrival at Emmanuel and Anna's I found my bag resting comfortably in one corner of the room!

Anna, who had just arrived, hugged and congratulated me.

Anna! Was is it because of her long association with Emmanuel? Was it because of her Christian upbringing? Whatever the reason she had grown to become so sympathetic for the poor and needy, particularly if they happened to be Africans! She was a wonder of Christian love and charity!

'Dinner is ready!' she proclaimed shortly after I had taken my seat.

It then occurred to me that I had barely eaten anything that day. Was it because of excitement or a result of the tension building up in me ahead of the impending flight to Hamburg? Whatever the reason, I had no appetite and I seemed to have lost the desire for food entirely! I forced myself nevertheless and ate a piece of bread.

Just about half past six in the evening Emmanuel, accompanied by Anna, drove me to the Airport. We needed only a few minutes to get there, for their apartment happened to be close to the airport. As we drove on I pondered over the next stage.

The battle ahead was not without risk. In the worst possible scenario the officer could detect the picture was not mine. That could lead to my arrest. I could re-apply for political asylum, I supposed. Very soon, however, it would certainly come to light that my application had already been rejected. Deportation would unquestionably follow.

But a wave of optimism was blowing all over me and all thoughts off ailure were quickly dispersed. Oh indeed, I was optimistic of victory! If the Lord had helped me to overcome the East German secret police, He would certainly help me through at the Tegel International Airport.

We got to the airport several minutes before check in. Together with my two good friends, I hung around the departure hall. Finally, the check in began. Reciting a silent prayer, I took a stand in the queue. Before me were about half a dozen others.

Just before it reached my turn, I turned to the place where Mensa and Anna had been seated. Was it out of excitement? They were no longer there! Instead, they had taken their stand in a corner from where they had a better view of proceedings.

At long last, it was my turn. I handed the officer my passport—the green refugee passport—as well as the ticket. My heart began to accelerate. He began to inspect the passport; first a look at the picture and then back to me. He seemed satisfied with a single glance, for he turned his attention to the ticket.

Finally he pronounced the words which even to this day continue to resound in my mind: ALLES KLAR! (German for everything is okay!) He then handed my documents back to me.

'Ich wünsche Ihnen einen schönen Flug('I wish you a nice flight'), he added.

'Vielen Dank! Ihnen auch einen schönen Feierabend! I replied. ('Thanks so much. I also wish you a nice evening after work.')

'Der Dienst hat gerade begonnenhe smiled. ('I have just begun my shift.')

'Auf jeden Fall alles güte!('Whatever the case, I wish you all the best!')

From there I went through a couple of security checks before I finally got to a hall where we were to wait until we got the call to board the plane.

The room was separated from the departure hall by glass panel. From there I spotted Anna and Emmanuel about twenty metres away. I waved a strong goodbye; they waved back in excitement. For a while neither side seemed to want to end the wave of goodbye. My dear friends waited a while. At last the order came for us to move on to board the plane. I gave them a signal to that effect and waved them a final farewell. They did likewise and left.

As I later learnt from them, after they had driven a few metres away from the Airport, their car was stopped by the police! What was the matter? they wondered. Had the immigration perhaps arrested me? Were they being arrested as accomplices? But no, the police had stopped them for a different reason. Although it had turned dark, they had forgotten to switch on their lights, no doubt due to the excitement surrounding my journey. The police drew their attention to their oversight and allowed them to continue on their way.

It was around 9 p.m. when the Pan-Am flight took offon the approximately forty-five minutes' flight to Hamburg. Although I had been awake over thirty six hours, there was no sign of tiredness in my eyes.

And so finally I was moving to West Germany proper. My thoughts went back to my struggle with the authorities. The realisation of my dream of studying medicine seemed to be drawing nearer.

After about forty-five minutes' flight we landed at the Hamburg International Airport. Flights from West Berlin to Hamburg were regarded as internal flights so I was spared the ordeal of an additional immigration check.

The first thing I did when I came out of the airport building was to call Mensah and Anna as well as Tony to inform them of my safe arrival in Germany's largest harbour city. Next I called Grace and Dan to break the news of my arrival. They could not believe their ears when I told them where I was. Because of the uncertainties surrounding the whole undertaking, I had not forewarned them about the prospect of my imminent arrival!

They directed me to their home. After some difficulty, I finally located it around 10:30 p.m. For the first time since her departure from Ghana in February 1980, *we were meeting again face to face in Europe—just as the Lord had told me in the dream!*

My eyes went back to our days in Accra, to our struggles.

For the first time I had the opportunity to meet her husband face to face. I took the opportunity of the meeting to offer them my personal condolences—for a few days prior to my arrival they had lost their second child through tragic circumstances.

That night I just couldn't cease thanking God for what He had done for me. I felt humbled by my experience. Having been brought to the very urge of complete failure, the Lord had held my hands and held me upright. He seemed to say to me: 'Trust only in Me, and not in the arm of man. Man can fail you, I cannot. I alone have the power to destroy everything and remould it again. The fight indeed is not yours, but Mine.'

I spent the night with Dan and Grace. It became evident to me that I could not stay there for long, for they hardly had enough room for themselves. The two-room apartment in which they lived had an area of barely forty square metres. Apart from the two of them and their two year-old daughter, Dan's sister was also living there.

The next day I moved to be with Samson, Kwasi's brother. Kwasi had told me much about him, though I was yet to meet him personally. He had also arrived in Germany about the time Emmanuel did. He was doing his doctorate in the social sciences at that time and lived in a student's residence of Hamburg University. He welcomed me with open arms.

35

Hannover Medical School

Many battles had been won along the way to medical school—but the war was not over. Two major hurdles remained to be surmounted.

First I had to pass a German language test before I could be permitted to register to become a student. This fact was emphasised in the admission letter. The test was about two weeks away.

Also, of equal importance, I needed to obtain a residence permit to enable me to stay on for my studies. I didn't have any illusions as to the difficulties I was going to encounter about that! A difficult official could be legalistic and quote existing rules and regulations the foreign student was required to abide by. For example, a foreign student had to enter the country with a student's visa issued by a German consulate in charge of the home country. A retrospective application could therefore lead to a refusal of a visa.

I was confident of one thing, though. Once I managed to pass the test and became an officially registered student, the university authorities could persuade the authorities to grant me a residence permit.

Where could I stay in Hannover initially? The Lord had made provision for that in the form of Gyasi who used to be my roommate in Blumeshof. From Berlin he was transferred to Lower Saxony—first to a small town, Wunstorf, a few kilometres away from Hannover, and later to Langenhagen, a town bordering directly on the state capital. Shortly before my departure for Hamburg, someone gave me his number.

A day after my arrival in Hamburg I called him to inform him about the latest developments in my life and to request him to offer me temporary accommodation, to which he agreed. So on September 11, 1984, exactly a week after my arrival there, I left Hamburg for Hannover.

I was eager to get to know the city which would forever play an important role in my life. After about seventy minutes' ride on a fast train I arrived at the central railway station of the northern German city with a population of about half a million people. I was impressed not only by the city's beautiful and modern buildings (a large part of the city is said to have been destroyed by World War II) but also by its tidy lanes.

I had little difficulty in locating Gyasi. He lived in a tall apartment building on a street known as the Soeseweg.

The barely two-year-old building was one of several newly constructed apartment houses in the area. Many middle income Germans lived there.

One thought came to my mind when I saw the quite comfortable conditions in which my companion had been housed - in providing accommodation for asylum seekers the state of Lower Saxony appeared to be more liberal than Berlin.

With the help of my host, I set out to legalise my stay. In line with German laws, I could only approach the authorities for a visa when I provided proof of official residence within the jurisdiction of the authority where I was applying for the visa.

How could one obtain such proof of official residence? A regular tenant could normally get the landlord/landlady to issue such a declaration without difficulty.

In my case it was up to Gyasi to persuade his house owner to issue me with such a paper. To that end we approached him with my admission letter and explained my situation. I intended to stay with my companion for a few weeks if not days after which I hoped to find accommodation in one of the several students' hostels in the city. Fortunately, Gyasi's landlord was sympathetic and provided the needed letter. After producing the letter at the state agency charged with the registration I was officially registered as co-resident of Gyasi's apartment.

Next my host took me to see his lawyer. He spoke well of him, for it was mainly through him that his asylum case had so far been prolonged, he told me. Before we left home we agreed to maintain silence on the issue of my stay in Berlin. By dint of the address on the admission letter, however, we could not entirely avoid the name Berlin. We decided to mention only that owing to the long time letters took to travel from Germany to Ghana, I had applied using the address of a good acquaintance of mine living there. The story went that the moment the contact person in Berlin informed me about my admission, I left for Germany. I didn't attempt to apply for a visa in Ghana because from my information such applications could take about eight weeks to process, too long for me to reach Hannover in time for the language test. I travelled through Romania on my way to Germany.

I had indeed a 30 day tourist visa for Romania in my passport. This I had applied for a few days prior to my departure from Berlin.

The Romanian Consulate happened to be situated not far from where I lived. I just decided to walk there to find out whether they would be prepared to give me a tourist visa. To my surprise I was issued with the visa without difficulty—I was only required to pay some hard currency.

The solicitor, on hearing what I had to say, asked me to return home and put everything in writing, something I did overnight.

I approached him early the next morning with my statement.

Together with the letter of admission he filed an application for a student's visa on my behalf. Owning to the urgency of the situation he handed me the documents and asked me to present them personally at the visa office.

A pleasant surprise awaited me there. Without asking many questions, the officer I met issued me with a ten week visa! It was provisionary, though, the officer stressed, and pending further investigations into my person.

I left for home with mixed feelings. On the one hand I was delighted that I had been issued with a visa at all; on the other hand I was frightened about the investigations they wanted to conduct concerning me. What would happen should they find out I had been in Berlin previously?

Those anxious thoughts would not occupy my mind for long, however, for soon a problem that needed more urgent attention surfaced.

From the visa office I contacted the main university in the city which was conducting the language test on behalf of all the other institutions of higher learning in the city and requested for past questions of the impending language test.

I began to shiver on seeing the questions. It immediately dawned on me that the test was not going to be a pushover! I decided therefore to dedicate the greater part of the time remaining to prepare seriously towards it.

The atmosphere in the apartment was not conducive to serious academic work, for Gyasi shared the room with another asylum seeker from Ghana who happened to possess a never-ending number off riends who seemed never to tire from calling on their friend for endless chats.

For the next few days, the central library of the city would become like a second home to me. I needed to pass the test at all costs; indeed, I suppressed the possibility of not being able to do so from my mind.

Finally September 20, 1984, arrived! The test consisted of three parts. The first was written grammar, the second what is known in German as Textwiedergab (one could define it in English as text reproduction). The final part involved oral conversation. We were informed at the outset that the main weight of the test lay in part two. A pass in it was a precondition for success in the test as a whole.

I doubt whether I have ever in my life paid so much attention to the reading of a text than I did that day! Several years have passed since then, yet the gist of the text still remains in my memory.

It was the story involving the discovery of the X-ray. The discoverer, a German named Röntgen, sought to present his discovery at a conference of renowned scientists, the majority of whom were sceptical of his assertion. Indeed, prior to the meeting, some of them had openly challenged his claim. In the end, however, he proved his case to the astonishment of his critics.

I was aware of my weakness in the language. I was not at home when it came to the fine details of German grammar. Still, I was determined to give a good reproduction, albeit not in the finest grammar.

The second part was followed by a break for lunch. Before the recess each candidate was told when to report for the last part.

As it turned out the time allocated was based on how fast one had submitted his or papers for the second part. Because I was among the last to do so I was asked to report late in the afternoon, towards the end of the whole session.

I waited impatiently for the all decisive battle. I did not want to take any risks and returned to the venue about an hour earlier than scheduled.

One after the other, candidates were called in for the last part of the test. Some emerged about ten minutes later showing no emotion; others smiled their joys while a few openly talked about their disappointment for not having made it.

Just before it came to my turn, a young and attractive young lady with European features was called in. I built up confidence by allowing various encouraging portions of scripture to run through my mind. Just as I was mentally getting ready for the fight, something happened that almost caused me to lose my composure—the young lady I just referred to burst out of the room, weeping uncontrollably.

'Please, help me!' she pleaded. 'I cannot return to Poland, please! I hate the communists! Please have mercy on me!' (Readers may recall that in 1984 Poland was in turmoil with the Solidarity Movement battling it out with the Communist regime.)

It was a pitiful scene to behold. She cried so loud, one of the examiners was prompted to come out of the room to try and calm her down.

'Young woman, don't be afraid. This is not the end of the world!'

'Please help me!'

'Let me finish what I want to say,' the examiner continued. 'Failing the test does not mean you will immediately be deported to Poland. You can register with the University to do a language course and repeat the test in six months. That will qualify you for an extension of your visa.'

Those words only helped to calm her down momentarily. After a while she left, sobbing as she left.

Finally it was my turn. An attentive listener could probably hear my heart beating wildly within me. Would I make it? Or would I end up like my Polish counterpart?

Soon I was seated before the panel.

'How and where did you learn the German language?' one of the members inquired.

'I did most of the learning myself back home in Ghana. A friend of mine, resident in Germany, sent me the necessary material." (I had in the meantime made up my mind not to mention my stay in Berlin at any official level.)

'German is a difficult language, isn't it?

'I won't say no to that. In my opinion, though, Russia is more difficult than German!'

'Do you speak Russian also?'

'Not very much. I tried to learn it back home in Ghana but stopped at the initial stages for personal reasons.'

Two or three additional questions followed which centred on the reason why I wanted to study medicine and also how I was coping with the new environment.

Finally I was asked to wait outside to give the panel time to deliberate on my performance. A few minutes later, one of them stepped out and requested me to re-enter the room.

Shortly after I was seated, the chairman smiled at me and began:

'The panel has reached the conclusion that you deserve the chance to take up your studies. We would advise you, however, to use your spare time to further improve upon your skills. In this regard you could attend the free German classes offered by the University.'

I was so delighted I was almost speechless. Finally I found my tongue. 'Thank you very much! I promise to make the best of the chance you have given me.'

The chairman then handed me my certificate.

As I left the room I struggled to keep my emotions under control. The moment I got outside I burst out into shouts of joy. 'Thank you Jesus! Thank you Jesus!' I cried aloud as I hurried along the corridors of the university and headed home.

Armed with the language certificate I registered on September 24, 1984, to become a first-year student of the Hannover Medical School. What a tumultuous month September 1984 had been for me!

On October 4 lectures began for first year students. Thus, six years after I obtained my 'A'-Levels, at the time when my classmates from Mfantsipim were passing out as doctors, I was given the chance to begin my studies. I didn't consider the time lost, however. I had gone through the training school of the Lord of Hosts. He had prepared me for service. I had been broken, broken, broken into pieces. I felt all the pride in me broken down.

Never could I ever trust in my own ability to attain anything in life.

What would have become of me had the Lord in His Grace not decided to piece all the broken pieces together?

One thing also became clear to me—medicine would not be an end in itself but a means to an end. My goal was to use all the means at my disposal to fulfil, in my own way, the Lord's command: 'Go ye into all the world, and preach the gospel to every creature.'—Mark 16:15 (KJV).

36

The Lord providing for my needs

It is one thing gaining admission to the University; it is another being able to finance oneself.

As I mentioned earlier, I was not expected to pay for tuition. I needed to pay for accommodation, food, books as well as for the other necessities of ife. It was calculated that the average student needed, at that time, around six hundred German marks to meet monthly expenses.

God in His mercy had already made provision for the means I could live on through the early months. I myself could boast of about 2000 German Marks in my savings account. It was, in the main, money I earned from doing odd jobs such as cleaning the homes of some American army personnel. I also paid part of the 500 DM I received on behalf of the American Church from Gary into the account. (I was so confident I would succeed in returning to Germany after my 'trip' to Cairo I decided not to close the account prior to my departure.)

Shortly after I was granted my first visa I travelled to Berlin to thank friends and well-wishers for their financial and moral support. This time I travelled by road, through the territory of the then East Germany.

My first experience with the   Transitstrecke

The immigration check on the West German side of the border was smooth; not so that on the East German side. The immigration officer after spending minutes comparing the picture in my passport with my face was not fully convinced. He asked me to get down from the vehicle whilst he invited his superior officer to check me as well.

My mind went back to my experience in East Berlin and I prayed the Lord to spare me the ordeal. Meanwhile the others travelling with me were beginning to lose their patience. My prayer was heard for shortly after the 'boss' had seen things for himself I was allowed to go.

The two remaining checks—at the exit from East Germany and at the entry to West Berlin—were devoid of incident.

Whilst in Berlin I called on friends to thank them. As expected, they all expressed their delight at the favourable turn of events in my life. Kurt promised to provide assistance to enable me go through my studies. Although he had given me the sponsorship letter I had not expected to receive anything from him. It was a delightful surprise therefore when shortly after my return to Hannover I received a letter from him in which he had enclosed a cheque for 400 DM. That was only the beginning, he wrote. From then on, he went on, he would contribute 200 DM every month towards my education. At that time my assumption was that it was his church that was assisting me. As I found out later it was money he and Karen had decided to donate from their own resources.

Kurt went on in his letter to say he had written to a friend of his, also a pastor, in Hannover, to inform him about my situation and requested him to do what he could to help.

A few days after the arrival of Kurt's letter, Gary called from Berlin. He had some good news for me. His church had decided to remit me 300 DM every three months! Next in the line of my sponsors was Rhea. For a long period of time she sent me 100 DM every month.

Ilse, despite the fact that she had three children to care for, also provided me substantial assistance in the initial stages of my education.

The assistance from Berlin, as well as the assistance I received from various individuals and churches in Hannover, continued for over three years. It was stopped at my own request shortly after a semi-government organisation had awarded me a scholarship.

A few days after the arrival of Kurt's letter, Friedo, his friend in Hannover, contacted me. At his invitation I travelled one evening to meet him at his office. Friedo made a kind impression on me. Like his friend in Berlin, he was also in charge of a Lutheran Church. The Messiahs Gemeinde, which he pastored, happened to be located in an eastern district of the city, not far from where I lived. A man with a great passion for talking, he promised to do whatever he could to assist me. He made it clear, however, that because his congregation was small in number, they could only provide a token help.

Later he invited me to become an active worker for the church, an offer I readily accepted. My duty was to read one of the two scripture passages that preceded the sermon. On the average my turn to do so came once every month.

I had since joined a Pentecostal church in Hannover whose members were mainly Africans. I only worshipped at the Messiahs when my turn came to read a lesson.

Just before such a worship service, Friedo invited me to his office and gave me an envelope enclosing 100 DM. In return I was asked to sign a piece of paper to acknowledge receipt of the offer. That procedure would continue month after month for several months.

When I first met Friedo, I was still resident with Gyasi in Langenhagen. When he got to know that, he suggested that I contacted his colleague responsible for the Lutheran church there. He advised me to make that a priority. Not only was he in charge of a much larger congregation than himself, he happened also to be the superintendent of all the Lutheran churches in the northern district of the city. By virtue of his sphere of influence he was in a better position to help me financially, he reasoned. Before we departed, he provided me with the address and telephone number of his colleague.

The Elisabeth Lutheran Church which Gottfried pastored was situated about one kilometre away from our home on the Soeseweg. Following Friedo's advice, I called the number he had given me the next day. The secretary directed the call to her boss.

The first impression I got talking to him on the phone was that he seemed to be very much in love with Africa. All the better for me, I thought to myself. We agreed on a meeting around midday on October 19.

I was heartily received not only by Gottfried but also Sabine, his wife. I began to wonder how they could spontaneously open up to a stranger, for that matter an African, whom they were meeting for the first time.

The reason would soon become clear to me. The family had a special relationship with an African doctor and his family. Shortly before our meeting they had returned from a trip to Cameroon that took them several weeks. They were there to visit their friend, a doctor, and his family. As they went on to say, that doctor friend had also trained in Germany. After working a while in Germany, their friend had decided to return to his native land. His wife, a citizen of Austria, had accompanied him.

'You rest assured,' Gottfried told me. 'You have come home. Had you told us you were stranded, we would have asked you to pack your things and move here!'

'That is very kind of you!' I replied, taken aback by the kind gesture.

'Africa fascinates me,' he continued.

'Yes, indeed?'

'To be honest with you, I was baffled by the warmth that emanated from the hearts of the majority of the people I met during my stay. Those people, some of whom were clearly deprived of the basic necessities of life, could still display so much happiness—a kind of happiness I am convinced was not feigned but genuine! My goodness, take it from me—Europe has a lot to learn from Africa!'

Gottfried would have continued his praises for Africa for a while, but for Sabine. By accident or design our meeting happened to be on my birthday. As I mentioned before, I am not used to celebrating such occasions. Added to that was the rapid turn of events taking place in my life. I had consequently forgotten all about that special day of the year. Not so Sabine! By virtue of going through some of the documents I took along, she had noticed the uniqueness of that day to me. While I was going through some details with her husband in his office she left for the part of the parsonage that served as home to them. Just as her husband was singing his praises for the continent with the many faces, she burst into the room, a big parcel in her hands. As soon as she entered the room she began to sing:

'Happy birthday to you, happy birthday to you, happy birthday, dear Robert—happy birthday to you!'

Her husband joined her. After they had gone through the lines a couple of times, she presented me my birthday surprise!

In the end Gottfried drew up a plan. He opened an account and launched an appeal for help from members of his congregation as well as his numerous acquaintances and associates. From that account he transferred a minimum of 200 DM every month into my account.

For a long time I also received a substantial amount of money every month from an anonymous source. Later the person revealed his identity. He was a young man in his mid-thirties, a member of the Elisabeth Church in Langenhagen.

I do not know how to thank the Lord for leading me to Gottfried. From the day we first met, I became like a member of the family. Indeed, it will require pages, if not an entire book to talk about the kindness that Gottfried and Sabine, together with their two teenage sons, Goetz und Axel, showed me.

Through the works of the Mysterious Hands of the Almighty, the poor African student became one of the wealthiest, at least among the non-Europeans at the Medical School. A close associates in my year group, an Iranian, could only wonder. 'Robert,' he said, 'your Jesus seems to want to give you everything!'

I invited him to come and try Him, but like my roommate at Legon, he was stuck in the tradition of his environment and seemed unwilling to try anything new.

37

All's well that ends well

Those who have taken the trouble upon themselves to study medicine will tell you how intensive the course is. It didn't take long for me to begin to feel the pressure. Right from the word go our professors began to bombard us with material of every kind. Particularly in the field of Anatomy the stuff we had to absorb was literally threatening to blow our brains apart! Every week there was quite a tough test in that field that needed to be passed before one could be allowed to move to the next stage of the test series.

It was during a period like that, that an event nearly came to unsettle me. As I mentioned earlier, I was granted a ten week visa pending the outcome of investigations to be conducted. On the expiry of the visa, on November 9, 1984, I approached the authorities to get it renewed.

I met a young lady in her twenties.

'What can I do for you?' she inquired after I had taken my seat.

I told her the reason for my coming. She then asked to see my passport. After taking a careful look through it she got up to collect my file.

A short silence followed as she examined the sheets in the file. Finally she turned to me. 'Please take a seat outside,' she said, 'I need to consult my superior.'

I obliged. Soon she emerged from the room, locked it behind her and headed for another room about ten metres away from her own, my file in her hand.

I waited nervously for her to return. Finally, after about ten minutes, she reappeared.

'Please follow me to my room,' she said when she reached me.

I did as requested and soon both of us were back in her office, seated facing each other. At last she began:

'I am afraid we do not have any good news for you. We contacted our Embassy in Accra. According to them, you didn't make any attempt to apply for a visa there. That is what you should have done. Consequently we have decided to reject your application.' She told me this without any display of emotion.

I was so stunned by her reply that for a moment I was speechless. Finally I regained my composure.

'No, please!' I pleaded. 'Have mercy on me! I need the visa to be able to continue with my studies!'

'I am afraid there is nothing I can do. It is the decision of my superior. I cannot act contrary to his directives.'

'Please!'

'No, I can't help you—it is final.'

'What should I do then?' I asked, on the point of tears.

'Well, you may contact any German embassy: in London, Amsterdam, Paris or elsewhere for a student's visa. When you return with such a visa we will extend it for you.' Saying that, she handed my passport back to me. Next, she pressed a knob on a device on her table to invite the next person in.

Reluctantly I got up, said goodbye to her and left the room.

Words can hardly describe what went through my body as I stepped out of the room. To put it mildly, I was baffled beyond measure. My goodness, why should the officers choose to be so formalistic! I could only wonder.

As I cycled back to the Medical School, a thousand and one thoughts went through my mind as to what to do next!

One more time I turned to the Hills for my Help. Even in the confusion I was sure of one thing—the Lord would not lead me that far only to desert me at the very moment when the war was almost won and the victory celebrations already begun! I regarded the hitch as one of those mopping up battles or operations that victorious armies had to fight even after the main battle was over

Just then my favourite passage from E.G. White's book *The Desire of Ages* flashed through my mind:

> Christ did not fail, neither was He discouraged, and His followers are to manifest a faith of the same enduring nature; the courage, energy and perseverance they should possess. Though absolute impossibilities obstruct their way, by His grace they are to go forward. Instead of deploring conditions they are called upon to surmount them.

Instead of deploring the present situation, I pondered over how best I could overcome it. My thoughts went to Ms Diel, a middle-aged woman in charge of the *Akademisches Auslandsamt* or, translated in English, the Foreign Students' Secretariat.

What a person she was! She performed her work not out of duty but out of a deep love for it. It was not without exaggeration that many of us had come to call her the mother off oreign students. Although I had not been a student for long, I had already learnt to cherish her love and kindness.

If there was any human being the Lord could use to help me, it was she, I said to myself.

I called on her at her office on my way from the immigration authorities to inform her about the latest developments.

'Incredible!' she exclaimed angrily on hearing my story.

She immediately reached for the phone and dialled a number.
It followed a long conversation between her and the person at the other end.

From what I was hearing, she was trying to find out whoever it was who could help me out of the situation. When it was over she turned to me, a broad smile on her face.

'Don't worry, we shall find a way out!' she said assuredly. She then gave me the details. 'You have not been long enough in this city to become aware of one fact—that there are two visa offices in the city, each working independently of the other. One of them is responsible for foreigners resident within the boundaries of Hannover City; the other is responsible for foreigners living in the towns and villages surrounding it. Because you happen presently to reside in Langenhagen, your application was rejected by the latter. I have almost no working relation with that authority. The situation is different in regard to the immigration authorities responsible for Hannover, however, where the majority of our foreign students normally reside. In the same way that you decided to approach me, several of our foreign students also come to me for assistance when they experience difficulty getting their visas extended. By virtue of years off ollowing up such cases with the authorities, a good working relationship has developed between me and several of the clerks there. I just spoke to one of them. She has promised to help you.' She smiled. 'There is one thing we need to do quickly, however. You have to rush to Langenhagen, to the office where you registered your place of residence. Tell them you are moving from there to Hannover proper so they can register you off.'

'But,' I pointed out, 'I don't have any accommodation in Hannover!'

'Don't worry about that. I have already thought of a plan. The medical school has a hostel that serves guest students from home and abroad who come to do their electives here. Normally our regular students are not allowed to stay there. As it happens I have a big say in the running of the hostel. I have decided to make an exception for you, to enable you to live there temporarily, until such a time that we can find a permanent solution.' At that moment she reached for the phone the second time. 'I want to instruct the guardian of the hostel to reserve one room for you,' she said as she dialled a number.

She then engaged in a short conversation with the person on the other end, directing him to reserve a room on the ground floor for a first-year student who would arrive shortly to pick up the key. After she had placed the receiver she took a quick look at her watch.

'It is about 10:00 a.m. You have to hurry. Most government offices in Germany close around midday on Friday. The hostel is located on the way to Langenhagen. You have to collect the key from the guardian on your way back from the registration office before he leaves for the weekend.'

I thanked her for her kindness and made for the door.

'Wait a second,' she urged me. 'We need to prepare the tenancy agreement. You need to present it together with the paper indicating you have moved from Lagenhagen at the visa office in Hannover.'

She pulled her drawer open and removed two copies of a pre-prepared tenancy agreement. Quickly she filled in the necessary details—my particulars as well as the monthly rent; she signed the portion reserved for the landlady and gave it to me to sign as tenant.

Soon I mounted my bike and headed for Langenhagen, about five kilometres away. I got there in good time to get things done.

On my way back to the medical school I passed by the Guest Hostel as planned to collect the keys. The guardian was expecting me. He handed me two keys—one for the main door, and the other for my room.

That evening Gyasi got one of his close associates who lived nearby to drive to the Soeseweg to take me to my new accommodation. For the next several months the Guest Hostel would be home to me.

I spent Saturday and Sunday as an illegal immigrant, for my visa expired on the very day that I was denied the extension. I decided to remain indoors for most of the time to avoid any confrontation with the law-enforcement agents.

I left home early Monday morning for the immigration authorities. For the first time since my arrival in Germany I met a clerk at the visa office who was committed to help me. After handing her my papers, the lady, aged about 35, quickly went to work to open a file for me. After waiting only a few minutes, it was all over.

'I have granted you a three months visa,' she said as she handed me back my passport. 'That is only a formality. We need to request your file from our colleagues at the other office. I can assure you though—next time you come you will receive a proper resident visa to enable you carry on with your studies.'

I expressed my sincere thanks for her kindness. Soon I was heading back to the medical school. As I went I began to reflect on the saying, where there is a will there is a way! Yes indeed, the will to help was all that made the difference between the disappointment of Friday and the joy of Monday, I said to myself.

True to her word, I was granted a proper stay permit after the expiration of the three months. As was usual for students in that federation, the stay was granted for one year subject to renewal. So long as one was officially registered as a student, one had no difficulty getting the authorities to renew it. With my stay permit granted and the issue of finance settled, I could finally concentrate on my studies.

This is not to imply that the battle of the Christian soldier was over. It would be apt here to quote another believer's admonition to fellow Christians based on Psalm 11: 5: :

> The Lord trieth the righteous.
>
> Since we are not in paradise, but in the wilderness, we must look for one trouble after another. As a bear came to David after a lion, and a giant after a bear, and a king after a giant, and Philistines after a king, so, when believers have fought with poverty, they shall fight with envy; when they have fought with envy, they shall fight with infamy; when they have fought with infamy, they shall fight with sickness; they shall be like a labourer who is never out of work.
>
> —*Harry Smith*

Indeed, that experience can be said aptly to describe my own. The account of how I have fared on the battlefield since I entered Medical School could fill at least one additional book, if not more. In particular I consider it a duty to inform readers about the way the Evil one has chosen to inflict one of my three children with a mysterious disease that baffles even the experts in the field of medicine. Of course I know the Great Physician has the answer. What I regard now as His delay in acting, is to Him no delay at all. Come what may, I believe He will surely deliver that innocent seven-year-old from the disease that has afflicted him since childhood, not to anyone's Glory but to His Own Glory.

For the moment, however, readers may content themselves in knowing that I obtained my first medical degree in December 1992. In September 2001, I qualified as a Specialist General Practitioner (*Fachaerzt für Allgemein Medizin*).

At the moment I have my practice in Duesseldorf, a city about three hundred Kilometres to the south-west of Hannover. Naturally this does not conclude my medical career and calling, for I have plans to set up what I have decided to call the Christ The King Hospital in Ghana to cater for the poor and needy in particular and the general population at large. But that, again, will be a story for another book!

End

0-595-32298-0

Lightning Source UK Ltd.
Milton Keynes UK
UKOW051954060312

188482UK00001B/239/P

9 780956 473417